Princeton Theological Monograph Series

Dikran Y. Hadidian

General Editor

24

GOD WITH US

A THEOLOGY OF TRANSPERSONAL LIFE

GOD
WITH
US

A Theology
Of
Transpersonal Life

Second Edition, Enlarged

JOSEPH HAROUTUNIAN

PICKWICK PUBLICATIONS
Allison Park, Pennsylvania

Second Edition Enlarged
With new prefaces and two new chapters added:
"The Worship of God"
'Education and Humanity"

Published by Pickwick Publications
4137 Timberlane Drive
Allison Park, PA 15101-2932

Printed in the United States of America

Library of Congress Cataloging-in-Publication Data

Haroutunian, Joseph, 1904-1968
    God with us : a theology of transpersonal life / Joseph
Haroutunian. -- 2nd ed., enl.
        p.   cm. -- (Princeton theological monograph series ; 24)
    Includes bibliographical references and index.
    ISBN 1-55635-008-2
    1. Theology, Doctrinal. 2. Fellowship--Religious aspects-
-Christianity. 3. Man (Christian theology) I. Title. II. Series.
BT78.H29   1991
230'.044--dc20
                                                    91-12038
                                                        CIP

CONTENTS

Introduction - Stephen D. Crocco   vii
Preface - Helen H. Haroutunian   xi

Foreword   1

Introduction: Toward a New "Image" of Man   5

PART ONE - GOD IN THE CHURCH
     1. Reflections on the Doctrine of the Church   27
     2. The Spirit of the Living God   43
     3. The Knowledge of God in the Church   59

PART TWO - HOW GOD ACTS
     4. Three Dimensions of Will and Willing   81
     5. Grace and Freedom Reconsidered   97
     6. On Hearing the Gospel   125

PART THREE - LOVE IN THE COMMON LIFE
     7. The Problem of Love   143
     8. The Prospect of Love   165
     9. Freedom and Liberty   185

CONCLUSION. THEOLOGY OF COMMUNION:
PROPOSALS FOR INQUIRY   203

NOTES   223

INDEX   233

APPENDIX ONE
    THE WORSHIP OF GOD   239

APPENDIX TWO
    EDUCATION AND HUMANITY   253

INTRODUCTION

"I have been trying, mainly in articles (a volume of which appeared under the title *God With Us: A Theology of Transpersonal Life*), to feel my way toward a theology which shall explore fellowmanhood as a correlative of a doctrine of God. If God has a peculiar business with man, as suggested by the places of Jesus the Christ and the Church as God's people in the Christian faith, I think it will be helpful to learn what this business is and *how* God does it."[1] Published a few years before his death in 1968, *God With Us* was Joseph Haroutunian's last major attempt to consider these issues.[2] The essays reflect Haroutunian's lifelong effort to craft a theology faithful to the essentials of Protestantism and the cultural experiences of North American Christians. The result was a substantial theology of communion by a "major Reformed theologian."[3]

Haroutunian set the stage for this work in the 1930s. In "Modern Protestantism: Neither Modern nor Protestant," he rejected liberalism and Neo-orthodoxy as viable theological options for Americans in Reformation traditions.[4] He recognized in liberalism a kinship with the service-oriented bent of American Christianity, but its theological anthropocentrism made it irrelevant to moderns who were unable to believe in a "man writ large" Deity. Although Neo-orthodoxy gave notions of God's sovereignty and "otherness" a fresh hearing in the twentieth century, its theological roots and political context made it largely untranslatable into the North American situation. What Haroutunian strove for was a theology true to the Biblical and Reformed traditions which could plumb, probe, and shape a North American ethos.

God With Us: A Theology of Transpersonal Life is a programmatic essay for that theology. It is a theology of the "'communion of saints,' or life together in Christ's company, by the interdwelling of the Spirit of the living God."[5] Haroutunian argued against individualistic theologies by arguing for communion as the precondition of personhood. He invented the word "transpersonal" to stress that an individual becomes a person in community only by the power of the Holy Spirit who works communion in the church. Christians have a new self-awareness as "a koinonia, a communion, who severally exist as a covenanted people, to be and behave as fellowmen, as Christ's fellowmen and therefore fellowmen with all people."[6]

Haroutunian could still assert *extra ecclesiam non sit salus*, but only with a twist. Instead of the church as the place where God is known by an exercise of the traditional means of grace, God is known in and by communion. The church is a means of grace because persons in the church love and forgive one another. They are so enabled because Jesus Christ "was the Son of God and Savior as a fellowman".[7] When Christ is "God with us" Christians partake of his communicating nature, and externalize inter-Trinitarian love. There is no salvation outside the church for Haroutunian "because salvation is communion and communion is the church."[8]

Any novelty in *God With Us* lies in the author's rigorous prosecution of communion as an organizing principle for theological reflection. Haroutunian readily conceded that the communion model would have an impact upon the loci communes and envisioned a rethinking and restating of them in this light. His book, however, is a restatement of the tradition in terms compatible to that tradition, not a replacement of it. To this end, he took special care to place his argument in a broad ecumenical context. In so doing, he engaged in conversations with Augustine, Calvin, Barth, and a host of other theologians, philosophers, and social scientists. Haroutunian's life-long fascination with Jonathan Edwards, his interest in George Herbert Mead, and his sense that American Christianity has a pragmatic bent to it, have an impact on the book and illustrate his use of distinctly American sources for constructive theological work. Given the present concern for contextual theology, Haroutunian's conscious debts to the American philosophical and theological traditions make his work worthy of particular attention.

The appearance of this volume marks the first in Pickwick Publications' reprint of the works of Joseph Haroutunian. Volumes to follow include *Piety Versus Moralism: The Passing of the New England Theology* (1932), *Wisdom and Folly in Religion: A Study in Chastened Protestantism* (1940), and *Lust for Power* (1949). A volume of previously unpublished materials, together with a substantial introduc-

viii

tion and bibliography, will complete the series. *God With Us* is being reprinted first to meet the need for a theology text that is grounded in the Reformed tradition, sensitive to the American situation, and germane to the church's quest for identity as a community in a post-Christian world.

The Pickwick edition of *God With Us* contains two chapters not in the Westminster edition. "The Worship of God" and "Education and Humanity" were deleted from Haroutunian's manuscript, presumably the result of an editorial decision. They are included here as an appendix because there is insufficient evidence to determine where Haroutunian envisioned them in relation to the book's other chapters.[9]

Haroutunian wrote in a time when inclusive language was not an issue. The text of *God With Us* is being reprinted as it appeared in 1965 as a reminder that forward-thinking men and women do not see all things even in the most enlightened of ages, including our own. The index has been expanded to give readers better access to Haroutunian's rich background of reading. Proper names from the notes are indexed only when there is no referent in the text. Subject entries were left intact except for several minor changes.

For years I knew of Joseph Haroutunian only as the author of *Piety Versus Moralism* and *God With Us*. When dissertation research led me to investigate how and why Jonathan Edwards was recovered by American "Neo-orthodox" theologians in the 1930s, I discovered Joseph Haroutunian, the man. At first I viewed this Armenian immigrant who taught at Wellesley, McCormick Theological Seminary, and the University of Chicago, as a minor American theologian standing in the shadows of H. Richard Niebuhr. Ten years of reflection have convinced me that he may well be the most significant American *Reformed* theologian of this century. That his thought may no longer be neglected, I am delighted to cooperate with Pickwick Publications to make his works available once again.[10]

Stephen D. Crocco
Pittsburgh Theological Seminary

NOTES

1. Joseph Haroutunian. Untitled essay. *Criterion* no. 6. Spring 1967, 18.

2. Joseph Haroutunian. *God with us: A Theology of Transpersonal Life* Philadelphia: The Westminster Press, 1965.

3. In his review of *God With Us* Terrence N. Tice portrayed Haroutunian in this way. *Scottish Journal of Theology* vol. 20, 1967, 353.

4. Joseph Haroutunian. "Modern Protestantism: Neither Modern nor Protestant" *American Scholar* vol. 8, no. 4, October, 1939, 479-93.

5. Haroutunian. *God With Us*, 303f.

6. Ibid., 37.

7. Ibid., 288.

8. Ibid., 96.

9. "The Worship of God" was a 1963 convocation address at McCormick Theological Seminary and was published in *McCormick Quarterly* (vol. 17, no. 1, 1963, 3-15). A typescript of this essay in the Haroutunian Papers at the University of Chicago Library has "Chapter V" at the top of the first page which may indicate its place in *God With Us*. "Education and Humanity" was a lecture at Teacher's College, Columbia University in May 1959 and was published in *Teacher's College Record* (vol. 60, no. 8, May 1959, 415-425).

10. Stephen D. Crocco. "Joseph Haroutunian: Neglected Theocentrist" The Journal Of Religion vol. 68 no. 3, July 1988, 411-425.

Preface to the 1991 edition of
GOD WITH US

A second edition of *God With Us* has been under consideration for seven years. When Dikran Y. Hadidian suggested reprinting a trilogy of Joseph Haroutunian's out-of-print books, to introduce them to today's theology students, no clear answer was known as to how relevant his theology was perceived to be by current theological thinkers.

A year later answers began to come. The first arrived in an enthusiastic letter from Stephen D. Crocco, a recent Princeton University graduate who had discovered Haroutunian while doing his doctoral research. In the following year, his article, "Joseph Haroutunian: Neglected Theocentrist" (*Journal of Religion,* Vol. 68, No. 3, July, 1988) revealed his knowledge of Haroutunian's writing, as well as his strong empathy for Haroutunian's point of view. Stephern Crocco's interest continues.

First published in 1965, *God With Us* was the author's last published book. It comes close to summarizing his theological preoccupations (excluding the subject of the Holy Spirit, on which he was working at the time of his death). The content is based on lectures, addresses and articles originally prepared for specific occasions during the preceding decade. Although out-of-print for several years, the book has continued to be used in theology courses.

Readers who have matured in consciousness of the "Language Revolution of the Eighties" may find models of "non-inclusive language" in the pages of *God With Us.* The most common "fault", the generic use of masculine nouns and pronouns, could be "corrected" easily, by the substitution of gender-neutral words. Beyond that, lacking an editorial policy appropriate to its content, the text resists further editing from the inclusive language point of view. For example, a good gender-neutral equivalent for *fellowman* and *fellowmen* is hard to find. The author coined and used those words repeatedly, to expound a favorite theological issue. His interpretation of the theme of *communion* unifies the chapters of *God With Us* and leans heavily on those words as keys to further insight. A similar problem arises when trying to edit the author's closely analyzed passages concerning "the Nature Of---" (the Church, Man, God, the Persons of the Trinity, etc) through the lens of inclusive language, especially when these passages are woven with quotations from or references to historical sources.

The decision to reprint the 1991 edition of *God With Us* in its original form was based partly on the above reasons, partly on practical reasons and partly on the desire to make the original work available, as he wished it. To refrain from editing an author according to linguistic standards he never held seems only fair, and pays respect to the integrity of the author and his text.

Joseph Haroutunian wrote and taught during the period between the late 1920's and the late 60's. He was multi-lingual, with English and Armenian his first languages. His prose style was modeled on the conventional academic rhetoric of his period and environment. It reflects the social and cultural attitudes of his time, when the generic use of man and mankind was traditional, following an ancient, universally accepted convention.

In *God With Us,* the author's exposition of the theme of *communion* unfolds gradually and can provide fertile theological ground in which new concepts can grow freely and abundantly.

April, 1991

Helen H. Haroutunian
Milbridge, Maine

xii

FOREWORD

The word "transpersonal" in the subtitle of this book does not appear in the text. It came to me while I was trying to find a word that might capture the point of the following chapters. For a while I considered the word "interpersonal," but finally had to reject it because that word usually implies the priority of persons to their interactions. "Interpersonal" does not indicate that persons come into being in the process of their conversation and cooperation one with another, or that they come to exist as persons by their transactions. The word "transaction" was used by John Dewey and Arthur F. Bentley in *Knowing and the Known* to state explicitly that both organisms and their environment acquire their characteristics in a process that is prior to either. I have used "trans" instead of "inter" to point out that the individual human being emerges by way of communion. In my judgment, this thesis, properly elaborated and understood, points to an image of man as fellowman that has weighty theoretical and practical consequences.

The second half-word in the subtitle—that is, "personal"—requires no lengthy explanation at this point. By combining it with "trans," I want to say that by our transactions in the human community we exist as persons; or that our transactions are such that they transform organisms into persons. Thus we become persons who are organisms, rather than organisms with personal traits. I wish to indicate that the communion of fellowmen is discontinuous with the transactions of organisms, although fellowmen are in obvious respects organisms. A person is a social and not a natural entity. On the other hand, he is a social and not a higher than natural, though still natural, entity. He is born with certain physical capacities for human life; but the actuality of his life as a fellowman or person is a consequence of communion. The point, however, here, is that by communion he is a person or a fellowman. I am sorry if the word "transpersonal" does not seem elegant. But it does suit my purpose in putting this book together.

The word "life" is quite vague, but it has a glory of its own, and I prefer it to such words as "relations," "existence," "process," etc., which I find no less vague and not quite so suggestive.

As for the word "theology," I used it instead of "theory" or "conception" because I take the transpersonal life of the Christians with Jesus Christ to be the paradigm, or model, of the life of fellowmen. As a Christian, I may not forget that all the life I have with my fellowmen is a life I have also with Christ, and that communion by which I exist is at once a communion with Christ and with my other neighbors. Wherever my neighbor and I are present, Christ is present with us and to us. Whatever goes on between me and my neighbor is determined by "the grace of our Lord Jesus Christ," so that I cannot understand our life together except under this grace. But the grace of Jesus Christ as the model of the grace in transpersonal life is the grace of God, because it is grace toward fellowmen as well as among them. Therefore, the title of this book is "God with Us," and its subtitle, "A Theology of Transpersonal Life."

I am grateful to many friends who have urged me, off and on, to publish the material in this book under one cover. Mrs. Esther Swenson, of Maryville College, and Professor John Burkhart, of McCormick Theological Seminary, both former colleagues at McCormick, have been especially persistent. I want also to thank Professors Joseph Sittler and Bernard Meland, of the Divinity School, The University of Chicago; Principal Stanley Glen, of Knox College, Toronto; Professor Seward Hiltner, of Princeton Theological Seminary; Dean Gordon Jackson, of Pittsburgh Theological Seminary, who have encouraged me with their kind responses to several of the lectures contained in this book. I wish to thank Dean Jerald C. Brauer, of the Divinity School, The University of Chicago, for giving me leave of absence during which I prepared this volume.

The Introduction and the Conclusion have been newly written. Chapter 1 is a lecture delivered at Bethany Theological Seminary, in July, 1964. Chapter 2 is an almost completely revised version of "The Spirit of God and the People of God," published in *Union Seminary Quarterly Review*, May, 1957. Chapter 3 is an extensively revised version of an address given at Pittsburgh Theological Seminary, in September, 1961, and published in *Pittsburgh Perspective*, December 1961. Chapter 4 is a lecture given at Princeton Theological Seminary during the Gallahue Conference on Psychiatry and Religion, April, 1963. Chapter 5 is a presidential address given before the American Theological Society, Midwestern section, in April, 1958, and published in the *Journal of Religion*, April, 1960. Chapter 6 is an expanded version of an address given at the Centenary Convocation of Knox College, Toronto. Chapters 7 and 8 are the Stephen Greene Lectures for the fall of 1958, given at the Andover Newton Theological School and published in the *Andover Newton Bulletin*, April, 1959. Chapter 9 is a revised and expanded version of an article published in Social Progress, in the November, 1958 issue.

J. H.

Chicago, Illinois

INTRODUCTION

Toward a New "Image" of Man

1. CRITIQUE OF WESTERN INDIVIDUALISM

It is no longer possible to do "business as usual" in theology without condemning it to futility. The same human condition that has made it necessary for economists and statesmen, moralists and philosophers, to forego obvious dictates of tradition and common sense makes it necessary for theologians to venture into new ways of thinking. The same setting of human life that has made people critical of laissez-faire capitalism, of the principle of national sovereignty, of "natural law" ethics, and of some traditional metaphysics, has also made people critical of traditional theologies, whether "natural" or "revealed." It is no longer a matter of common sense to believe that we live under the providence of a just and almighty God, so that we are destined for an "afterlife" that will be the solution of "the problem of evil." A man can no longer argue from nature to God, or prove that we are immortal, with the hope of being certain of his logic or persuasive to thinking men around. Such arguing and proving, which used to be a matter of common sense to deists and atheists alike, is today suspect both to believers and unbelievers. Reason and theology are today uneasy bedfellows. In fact, they have moved not only to separate beds but also to different rooms.

The time has come for the kind of thinking that will not take things for granted; that will reexamine deep-seated assumptions, and will consider new thoughts, no matter how strange or even unpromising; that will go slowly and laboriously from one thing to another, with the hope of some limited insight into "the human situation" and into the problems that have our backs against the wall. Theology is not excused from such thinking.

Since our embarrassments have grown out of concatenations of things obviously true and good, it is these things which require sustained effort at criticism and judgment. It is our common sense that has produced our confusion; therefore, every utterance of common sense today is suspect. It is suspect because it is precisely our common sense that has presented us with problems that have become our embarrassment, not to say our despair. Our common sense, for instance, tells us that the value of a thing varies with supply and demand. If a thing is plentiful, it will be cheap. If it is scarce and in great demand, it will be dear. But the fact is that in our society, advertising is a successful suspension of the "natural" law of supply and demand. Again, our common sense tells us that nations in possession of great economic and military power will be able to follow their interest successfully in their dealings with nations that are not as strong. But a power like Russia is unable to have its way with Albania, and the United States has not been able to change the regime in Cuba; and neither Russia nor the United States is able to have its way in our world. No nation today is sovereign. Again, it is common sense that a man should follow his enlightened self-interest and practice the Golden Rule as a way to both success and happiness. But, in fact, doing to others as we would have them do to us is a guarantee neither of success nor of happiness. It often completely dehumanizes our relations one with another and frustrates all parties involved in it. There is no principle of common sense, private or public, that does not enter into our private and public difficulties and our sense of helplessness with regard to them.

If there is one thing in our society that deserves to be called an unquestionable utterance of common sense, it is the principle of individualism. Everybody, as it were, knows that the given, atomic, primordially real thing among us is the individual with his mind and body, his birth and death, his impulses and desires, his thoughts and actions, his duty and destiny. We look in the mirror and see our own face, and not another's. If we see another's, we know that it is his face and not ours. We look around us and we see many people, each with his name. We confront a man and recognize him as this person, with his own clothes, gait, looks, and manner, his own five senses and his own seeing and hearing; his own feelings and emotions and actions; his own attitudes and purposes and sensibilities. He is this discrete body bounded by his skin and he occupies one space and not another. This is the individual who exists by birth and dies his own death, and between the two things is identical with himself and other than everybody else. It is obvious to him and to everybody else that he is an "individual substance" and subject of all his experiences and the agent of all his thoughts.[1]

Ever since the ancient Greeks defined man as a "rational animal" and Boethius defined a person as "an individual substance of a rational nature," Western man has seen himself as an individual substance endowed with certain powers and potentialities by virtue of his nature, which is his by birth. Even though man is clearly also a political animal and in all his doings exists in the society of his fellow man, his basic self-image has been that of an individual entity who interacts with others for the fulfillment of his own life and destiny. Although he belongs to the human species and exemplifies the human race in general, his own actions and passions are ultimate as his own and have their meaning as well as reality within himself. His characteristics may be universal to the human race and they may depend upon structures and functions he shares with all his fellowmen. Nevertheless, in some mysterious way he is this unique individual, having the principles of his being and action within himself as this "individual substance of rational nature." One may speak of individual men or of man in general. There has been much debate as to the reality of the one or the other. But it is a fixed thing in our minds that the individual exists by birth, and has his powers by birth, or that he is what he is by "nature."

Such individualism was deeply established in the Western mind by its tradition of thought and life since Augustine, or since the earlier fathers. One should not forget Socrates' discovery of the mind by subjecting thought itself to critical scrutiny; Plato's poetic construction of a realm of ideas open to contemplation by the human mind; Aristotle's view of substance as the principle of individuality; Stoic universalism, which turned the individual into or upon himself; the Hellenistic mind with its quest for salvation from the vicissitudes and sins of the world. When Christianity became the established religion of the Roman Empire, it was already self-evident that the end of religion is immortality and that it is the being with a "rational soul" that may seek it and hope for it. It would be hard to overestimate the effect of universal concern with "future life" and the promises made by the church concerning it upon the basic intuition of Christendom that the individual who is born and dies exists by creation and nature as a unique and ultimate entity. In any case, it became axiomatic that the individual, with his mind and body, with his spiritual and physical nature, with his supernatural destiny, is man and the bearer of "rational nature." When philosophers and theologians (Augustine, Aquinas, Calvin, Descartes, Locke, Kant, Bergson) sought to understand man, they turned their attention to the thinking, feeling, acting individual, with his nature and faculties and powers. And common sense itself was on their side in that "every man" thought of himself as this individual who had received his life and nature from God and lived with the hope of the Good now and hereafter. The characteristic institutions of the Western world, as they have developed especially since the sixteenth century—scientific, economic, political, industrial, educational—have been constant sources of the individualism characteristic of our culture and received by common sense among us as "God's own truth."

It is not necessary to speak elaborately of individualism as a momentous accomplishment of the Western man. Nature, as it were, does not care a straw about an individual living thing. It performs amazing feats of ingenuity for the preservation of the species, but in the process of breeding and feeding, it sacrifices individuals, in numbers large and small, without any regard for their own existence. It appears that in primitive societies, the individual is regarded as a bit of the corporate being of the clan or tribe, so that his life or his death is a matter of relative indifference to the ongoing reality of the group in whose existence he participates.[2] In noncivilized societies, neither god nor man appears to have regard for the private life, experiences, or destiny of the individual unless he is regarded as the bearer of the power and dignity of the tribe. In peace he is used for the well-being of the prince, and in war he is sent to fight, and perchance to die, for victory over the enemies of the prince, who embodies the destiny of the tribe. What counts is the existence of the tribe, and its power and security. The individual does not exist; he inheres and he is readily replaced in the tribe, which is an organism rather than a society. Such an attitude is so deeply ingrained in even so-called civilized societies that people are readily persuaded to shed off their existence as "individual substances" and to find happiness in becoming "mass men." Individualism is a priceless fruition of civilized life; a "new being" realized through centuries of struggle, both political and intellectual. The loss of it would mean the loss of humanity as the Western man knows it and the undoing of his culture. It would be the death of us.

Nevertheless, there is many an indication, from every phase of civilized life in the West, that traditional individualism is no longer viable either in theory or in practice.[3] Even while individualism was a salutary and immensely enriching overcoming of tribalism, and in its way gave us our civilization and way of life, it was, or is now, a distortion of reality that has become intolerable. The age of science, and age of power, the nuclear age, the age of world wars and dictatorships, the age of anxiety and frustration—this age of unfulfilled promises and dire threats—constrains us, willy-nilly, to reconsider that individualism which has dominated Western mentality and ethics to this very day. We are now forced to ask with a new seriousness whether the true and the good as envisaged by individualism are not to us a source of lies and evil that may become the undoing of the gains of civilized life in the West.

The thing in question is the traditional Western notion that the unit or atom of human society is "the individual substance of rational nature," who appears in this world endowed with traits and powers that go into the making of our common life. Is it true that the individual human being exists by birth equipped with a "human nature," which makes him the being he is and forms his conduct in our common life? Is it true that we are to see ourselves and others as the atoms of society and to deal one with another accordingly? Is this how we are to live together and to engage in our economic and political activities, trying to prosper and find our peace?

The question of truth comes first, and there are a number of ways we may argue that human beings exist as fellowmen, or that "human nature" is a matter, not of birth, but of our life together.

We do not know our "nature" except in our transactions with our fellowmen.[4] We do our speaking and thinking, our purposing and acting, in the process of our mutual transactions. Even our perceptions and emotions, our eating and drinking, and our loving and hating occur in a social process that makes them what they are. Whether we act by habit or by reflection, whether mechanically or freely, we act in the context of social institutions, and by reacting. In short, human behavior, in its interiority or exteriority, in its concrete occurrence, with all its aspects or dimensions, is a matter of transaction and response, without which we are not human beings. Psychologists speak of "field theory," "interpersonal relations," "dynamic interaction," etc. Sociologists see the individual in the context of institutions and common life in its various aspects. Philosophers have come to center attention on language as a key to human behavior and to recognize that language is a matter of signs, respondings, and communication. Ethicists are now aware that good and evil, right and wrong, freedom and responsibility, and even pleasure and pain, are to be understood, not in terms of action on the part of the individual, but in terms of interaction. Men of science, whether physical or biological, no longer deal with atomic entities but with the dynamics of a field or a whole in which entities have their being by virtue of their inclusion in a process. The point worth emphasizing, in view of the deep-seated prejudice of common sense, is that it is a distortion to see a space or field as occupied by preexisting and definable things, or the whole as made up of its parts. It is not true that the field or the whole is made up of interacting entities which are physically and logically prior to the process in which they interact. What is prior is the transaction or response by virtue of which each individual does what he does and is what he is, or is found to possess such and such a nature.

Nor is the situation a matter of "the hen and the egg." It makes all the difference in the world whether transaction or interacting things comes first. To look at a thing outside of the dynamic context in which it acts is to distort its reality, and leads to consequences that are frustrating both in theory and in practice. It is to misunderstand it, to misjudge it, to misuse it, and to abuse it. In the physical realm, it prevents comprehension and control. In human affairs, it leads to inhumanity and common misery. In economic life, it produces attitudes and behavior that obstruct public prosperity and common well-being. In political life, it leads to lack of intelligence in the ordering of our common life and results in injustice and confusion. In the ethical life, it produces prejudice against justice and faithfulness, which makes men bitter and inhuman. When people see themselves first and others second, when they give the "I" a logical and natural priority to the me," they do not merely put the hen before the egg; they kill the hen and crush the egg, and the outcome is hunger for which there is no food.

We have become sensitive to the priority of transaction to interaction, of context to entity, not because of a sudden outburst of intelligence in our times, but because of a common mind that is relatively new and peculiar to our age.

It is hardly possible to overestimate the influence of Darwinism upon our minds. Even perhaps more significant than the theory of evolution has been the Darwinian insistence upon seeing the organism in its physical environment, and as living and changing in its give-and-take with it. Thus, Darwinism has given a tremendous and irresistible impetus to the understanding of the organism in its context. Darwin tried to explain the structure and characteristics of herd and beast in terms of their survival in a milieu in which they lived and ate and fought. There may still be argument as to the relative effectiveness of "the nature" of an organism and the environmental conditions under which it lives in the process of evolution. However, Darwinism, with all the debates and discussions it has produced, must be set down as a major intellectual impetus against the kind of individualism that seeks to understand beast or man apart from its involvement in a transaction that is physically and logically prior to it. Darwinism in the above sense is a fact of our intellectual life and has taught us, indirectly perhaps, to see ourselves as fellowmen.

It is interesting that Darwinism appeared in the machine age. It may well be that the new dependence of the individual upon economic processes that characterize the industrial age was not without its influence upon Darwin's quest. In any case, we are now living in an environment that is dominated by technological organization and the economic and political processes that have grown out of it. The story of the age of "science and industry" has been told so often and so thoroughly that here we may be brief about it. Still, it is surprising how often men of "common sense" on every side, more or less cultivated, put on blinders when it comes to seeing and understanding the radical ways in which transaction in a humanly produced world of "men and machines" has made the traditional individualism of the Western world not only a distortion of reality but also a source of unrest and peril in our time.[5]

The transition from a physical environment to one produced by science and industry (which we shall call an artifactual environment) has meant a radical change in the transactions of human beings one with another and with their world. Once we recognize that the individual and his world emerge from transactions, we may well expect that the individual living and moving in the city built by man is not the same as the individual who lives and moves in the "nature" of physical forces.[6] He is a physical animal interacting, not with animals and vegetation, but with other men in a milieu of machines and goods. Both his dependence and his freedom take on new dimensions in his artifactual world. He has a new power with regard to the constructs of human mind and technology, and at the same time he is dependent upon social process in a new way.[7] In the physical world, good and evil are from "nature," and a man enjoys the one and suffers the other with those around him. In the artifactual world, good and evil arise within the social process. When a man enjoys good, it is in a social process, and when he suffers evil, it is again through the doings of man. He subsists, not so much in nature as an organism, as by institutions and in organizations as a citizen. Those around him are not so much people who happen to share with him a common physical world as they are agents of good and evil in a man-made world of things. If he is dependent upon them for his good, he also holds them responsible for his evil. Living in a world of human agency rather than of natural process, he both judges and is judged by his fellowmen with a new passion. His business, for good or evil, for hope or despair, is with his fellowmen; it is from them that he distinguishes himself as this individual who must provide for his needs and achieve his security. He is at one and the same time under the necessity of getting along with others and of pursuing his own "enlightened self-interest." The more he has to conform to instituted common ways, the more he has to protect his own being and space as this individual and the more he has to contradistinguish himself from his neighbor, who is engaged in a similar conformity and a similar practice of individuality. In the civilized life of our day, men exert among themselves a pressure that produces a peculiar variety of humanity and a peculiar type of the individual man.

The tendency of city life is to produce the "mass man," who has become a serious concern, if not the obsession, of many thinkers in our day. We hear about the lonely crowd, the other-directed man, the man who has lost identity, selfhood, freedom, and vocation and destiny.[8] We hear of men possessed by anxiety; of neurotics, paranoiacs, psychotics; of bondage to institutions, to advertising and propaganda, to images and attitudes induced by social forces of which nobody is master and everybody is a slave.[9] There is a "general will," a superego, an irresistible other, an It, which may well be a fiction; but it is a fiction with the quasi-divine attributes of omnipresence, omniscience, omnipotence, a god, a monster, a tyrant combined. It makes people ill, and it is the threat of destruction in our "Age of Power."[10]

The above characterization of our age will appear exaggerated to some, especially to those who are, quite reasonably, impressed by the goods and the promises of good in our society and by its overwhelming achievements toward the increase of prosperity and pleasure in the civilized world. There is hardly a perennial evil, such as poverty or ill health, that may not be removed through the powers of man available in our world. It is a fact that societies which possess the knowledge and power provided by science and industry have achieved human well-being that must be recognized as wondrous improvement over the condition of man in societies that were without them. No one in his right mind will be other than elated with the prospect of universal human participation in the benefits of the Power Age and therefore in the increase and spread of a civilized way of life in our world.

2. THE PROBLEM OF HUMANITY TODAY

Nevertheless, men of intelligence and imagination who have been prophesying evil must be heeded. Kierkegaard, Marx, Samuel Butler, Nietzsche, Freud, Heidegger, Berdyaev, and others cannot be brushed aside as false prophets. The wars, tyrannies, massacres, fanaticisms, frustrations, no-exits, of our age cannot be set aside as so many accidents or aberrations of wicked men. This is an age of fears and playing with fire, and of apparently inscrutable problems that turn our dreams of human happiness into nightmares of human misery present and to come. How can a man be blamed if he sees the travails of the age as symptoms of a deep-seated and chronic disease or the sign of a terrible failure in human intelligence and insight? What if, in fact, there has been some fateful oversight (or of course more than one) or fatal miscalculation while the civilized world, inebriated with its new powers, has rushed headlong with the overwhelming prospect of boundless power and felicity in a world of artifacts?

Could it be that in the process of organizing our common life for the creation of a world over which we would be lords and in which we would have all things at our disposal for performing endless miracles of "human betterment" we have, in fact, been losing our grip upon ourselves and our humanity? One may well be excused for suspecting that in our zeal for increasing knowledge and power we have lost sight of a "life together" which is the very source of human existence. If our troubles are deep and pervasive and we see no way of overcoming them, it may well be that there is a failure of intelligence among us, and with it a failure of our very existence as fellowmen. A whole dimension of humanity may have been obscured, and we may be like blind men groping in the dark, which is today a most perilous affair.

A vague but promising answer to the question posed by the above paragraphs is quite readily available. We have been told by men like Berdyaev and Buber, and may well observe for ourselves, that there is among us a breakdown in communion, or in human transaction as such.[11] Our way of life as civilized people, and our self-understanding that goes with it, has led to a preoccupation with the individual as he seeks his goods in the institutions that are his effective environment. We think readily in terms of the individual and society. We think of a man in terms of the economic, political, social institutions and organizations within which he lives and finds good and evil. We try to understand his place in these institutions, his problems, his prospects, his successes and failures within them. It is clear to us that his "life, liberty, and pursuit of happiness" depend upon the workings of social habits and ways of action.[12] These habits and ways in our society are extremely complex as well as crucial for human life. Therefore, we fix our attention upon them, and they occupy our minds to the full extent of their power. Who really understands the workings of the cluster or clusters of institutions that constitute our society, and who is able to comprehend the actualities of the ways in which they mold the life of the individual? Here is a field of endless observation and study, and one that is truly absorbing as well as illuminating. In fact, in civilized life the individual exists in the context and by the dynamics of organized, massive institutions; and it is only rational that he should understand himself as interacting with a "generalized Other" or Society as such.[13] It is no surprise that those who make it their business to understand man's ways should look at him as he lives and moves in our cluster of institutions: that is, as he is related to an "it" which we call Society.

In the city, the power that makes the difference between good and evil, a source of well-being or misery, is "the generalized Other." This Other is a potent abstraction that forms the attitudes and minds of the people. It is the ultimately Real, which determines men's judgments, their goals, and motivations. As the source of real promises and real threats, of life and death in the city, the Other takes on the quality of Power, of the Holy, of Deity. It acts as, or is, the superego that dominates the ego, and as the Dangerous Thing, it forms the individual's conscience and passes judgment upon him and holds him in its grip as a person in the ambiguous state of dependence and guilt. Thus at the core of his being the individual feels that his business is with It in the first place and with his neighbor secondly.

Thus the individual's neighbor becomes to him, first of all, not his fellowman, but the representative and symbol of Power, of the Other as It. Not only men of power and authority in the organizations that constitute It, but also any man, people as such and universally, become possible and probable means of the individual's weal and woe—not as neighbors or fellowmen, but as bearers of the power of the Other. As the vicars of Society in which the individual lives, moves, and has his being, they take on the quality of Society, and function not as fellowmen but as powers that are refractions of Power. Thus one's neighbors are powers before they are people, even though they are people who exist by the love of their fellowmen. It is indeed true that love still gives the community its being as a transaction of fellowmen. But Power takes priority over love and dominates the individual as "the determiner of destiny"; and the neighbor is felt and more or less acknowledged as Its functionary. It becomes a habit to look at another man not as a fellowman but according to his function and power in Society—so much so that thinking men see the person as the sum of the roles he plays in the cluster of institutions in the city. Men are known as businessmen, government men, doctors, teachers, "working men," etc., first, and as fellowmen secondly; and this means that it is their power and not their fellowmanhood that impresses those who have communications with them. It is not true that fellowmanhood becomes inoperative, because if it were, the common life itself would collapse. But still, it becomes habitual to see people as roles first and as fellowmen secondly. And here order makes the difference between fulfillment and frustration.

Institutions are organized habits of people engaged in a common life with common goals that have to do with the satisfaction of certain needs, such as food, clothing, shelter, security. In civilized life, institutions achieve a high degree of success in providing the people with goods that not only satisfy their needs but also increase and intensify their satisfactions. People have more things to enjoy, and develop capacities for enjoying new things. One would think offhand that the more civilized a society, the more the people enjoy themselves and the happier they are. But the truth is that enjoying things and being happy are not the same thing, and that one may enjoy much without being happy, and that one may be happy without having many goods to enjoy. It is also true that being unhappy, one may not enjoy the goods in one's possession. In short, there is no necessary congruity between possession and happiness.

The reasons for this difficulty are many and complex. Many city people may be unhappy with their goods because they work too hard and are tired; they may be too ambitious and are impressed with what they do not have and not with what they do have; they may be ill adjusted to their work; they may be involved with some struggle for power or advancement that drains their energies; they may suffer from fear, or guilt, or insecurity, etc. However, the problem usually is that common life and activity in institutions is characterized by common enterprise rather than by transaction as fellowmen. The plain, if vague, truth is that people attending to institutional purposes and processes, in their pursuit of the goods that institutions provide, may and do ignore one another as fellowmen, and in so doing, they frustrate one another. Their common sense dictates that they should be concerned with the business on hand rather than with their so-called "private lives." It is understood that they are engaged in an enterprise that may issue in a common good or the good of each man. The benefit each man derives from the enterprise is his own rather than the other's. A man is not expected to be interested in what the other person does with goods. He may well ignore whatever role the other man plays besides the one that goes with their economic activity in an institution. He need not be offensive in his ignoring, but it is understood that men's business one with another has to do with the roles they play in their common undertaking and that anything else which may concern them severally is a matter of secondary consequence. But in this way they do not meet as fellowmen; and since they are fellowmen, their meeting is a not-meeting and a frustration of humanity. Therefore, people commonly complain of a failure of humanity in civilized life and become quite bitter about it. That is one reason, perhaps the decisive one, for unhappiness in a society where many goods are enjoyed by many people, or for the failure of joy in an "affluent" society.

In truth, we are hardly able to speak intelligently about fellowmanhood. The very notion of fellowmanhood has become extremely vague and hardly intelligible among us. We can think with immense productivity about our engines and our institutions, about the manufacture and sale of our goods, about efficiency and improvement in our artifactual world. We are incredibly ingenious with the making of better goods, and our minds are reasonably devoted, with all the power of scientific method, to this end. It has become so that intelligence among us is identified primarily with ingenuity, and the use of it is nearly exhausted in calculations that make our economy of abundance possible. Add to this the correlative use of the mind in the pursuit of "enlightened self-interest" and there is neither the aptitude nor the intelligence left for the cultivation of fellowmanhood, which is a pity, since without it we are unable to meet and live as human beings. The "scientific mind" and the business mind dominate our common life. Neither of them can make much sense of fellowmanhood. Therefore, fellowmanhood is deprived of intelligence in our society. But if man is a fellowman, not to be intelligent about being a fellowman is an extremely dangerous thing and may well (logically, would) be the death of us.

3. TOWARD A NEW "IMAGE" OF MAN

In the pages that are to follow we shall be occupied with this matter again and again in different contexts. For the present it is sufficient to point out that in our judgment men exist in three dimensions, none of which may be ignored without distorting and imperiling human life. First, we are animals with our anatomy and physiology, our impulses and drives, our needs and satisfactions. We transact as natural beings within our physical environment, and eat, drink, sleep, and keep ourselves and the race alive. We live by our habits and meet the exigencies of life with whatever intelligence we may have. We watch our ways, trying to avoid evil and to come upon things that are good.

Secondly, as intelligent animals we form social habits that make up our institutions and form our common life. Intelligence enables us to find successful ways of satisfying our needs and of adding to our enjoyments. We engage in agriculture and manufacture; we improve upon our foods, clothing, shelter, and sundry tools and instruments. We establish political orders and learn to live by laws that make for common well-being. We arrive at sundry habits of association that increase the amenities of life and our enjoyments of it. We learn to care about "truth, beauty, and goodness" and to cultivate science, art, and morality. We also have our "religious" ways that help us to meet and cope with things unmanageable, of which the last is death. Our institutions serve ends that are rooted in our impulses and needs as animals and may be regarded, in this respect, continuous with "nature" in the animal's habitat.

In the third place, we have a "life together" as well as a "common life." We, in fact, are not satisfied when we cooperate for the satisfaction of common needs in and by our institutions. Food, shelter, health, order, morality, art, religion, even while necessary, are not sufficient for our peace. A man may have all these things and he may be unhappy and disturbed. A society, civilized and cultivated, may have all these things and it may be full of people who are not satisfied, who are, on the contrary, bitter and unwell and inhuman. What is lacking here is called humanity, or what we have called fellowmanhood. It has also been called friendliness, fellow feeling, sympathy, concern, caring, understanding, goodwill, love, etc. Language here depends upon tradition and insight. However, it is characteristic of humanity that men live by communion as well as by bread. They are together not only for accomplishing common purposes but also for being present one to another. The presence of men one to another is their very existence as fellowmen. It is their reality as human beings, their very being, without an end or purpose other than itself or themselves. It is a means of being that is altogether different from that manner of being which brings them together in their institutions. The common life with its habits and ways serves the ends of maintaining the life of the animal and of embellishing it. Life together with its dispositions and communications serves no end other than the presence of fellowmen to fellowmen. It is enough that my fellowman is there, that he is my neighbor and reveals himself to me in his speech and action. It is, of course, well and good that we have a business together and may well expect to be helpful one to another. It is good for both of us and good for something. But we are fellowmen who have to do business together, and it is not good that we should forget it, even though in our business together we may be sometimes too preoccupied to be ourselves as fellowmen. It is a want of truth, fidelity, justice, intelligence, for fellowmen to fail, to refuse to present themselves one to another in their common life. It is a bitter thing and a sign of death.

People deeply resent being treated simply as a means, even though we say that in being a means to others' ends, they serve themselves and their own ends. We all know, and admit not knowing with shame, that people are ends and not means. But what does this mean? In our institutions everyone is a means, and nobody may use others without being used by them. When we say that they are also ends, what we mean is that they are entitled to their own satisfactions. This is obvious, but it is also banal. In practice, what it means is that if they remain dissatisfied, they will not work with us. But the recognition of a fellow-man and the acknowledgment that he is not a means signify something else. They signify that his very presence as a fellowman is being itself and good in itself. People have a way, by their very presence, of demanding, not arbitrarily and willfully, but as a matter of truth and justice, that we set a peculiar value upon their being with us, that we acknowledge them and communicate with them and have joy in their presence without asking ourselves why we should do such a thing and finding reasons for not doing it. This is how they feel about the matter, and it is absurd and stupid to refuse to experience them as fellowmen, or to be blind to their reality as fellowmen: men who are men as our fellows and as such posit us as human beings.

There is here an "ontological question." Is it or is it not true that being at the human level is to be a fellowman? If each human being is what he is without being a fellowman, then my neighbor's demand that I treat him as an end and not as a means is arbitrary and groundless. But his demand is neither arbitrary nor groundless because a human being exists as a fellowman. He is human by virtue of his communication with me, a communication in which he exists as my fellowman. His very conversation with me, with its first and second and third personal pronouns, without which there is no human existence, indicates a manner of being in which neither he nor I exist except as fellowmen. He knows himself in his response to my response to him, and I know myself in my response to his response to me.[14] My very self-consciousness belongs in the context of a transaction, as I can say "I" because I can say "me" and "you" and "we." I exist by this transaction; rather, the transaction is my existence, even though by this transaction I do exist as my neighbor's fellowman.

There is, of course, a sense in which all things exist in relation. The beasts of the field and the birds of the air exist by transaction that posits them severally in their environment. People in their several institutions also exist in relation, and here communication by speech is an indispensable and decisive aspect of their relatedness to one another. However, our common life, both as organisms and as citizens, must be distinguished from our life together as fellowmen. In our common pursuit of goods, we attend, not one to another as "flesh," but to the benefits we expect to derive from our cooperation. When we speak one to another, we speak of means and ends, and our words signify goods and their relations one to another. Our transactions may be more or less intelligent, but they have to do with "the order and connection of things," and as such, they are factual. They have neither the nature nor the tendency to present us one to another as "living souls," or as fellowmen who exist by and for their communion one with another. Our transactions as organisms and citizens have purposes other than our hearing one another. Our words signify not ourselves but the things that concern us.

In our transactions as fellowmen the word becomes "flesh." Our words signify not our goods but ourselves. By them we present ourselves one to another as people whose communion one with another is their very existence one by one. Communion emerges as the very mode of our being, by which we posit one another and without which we nullify one another. Every man, as his neighbor's fellowman without whom he has neither life nor good, approaches his neighbor with a claim to his recognition and communication with him. He, at the same time, finds himself under a human necessity of loving him as himself, that is, as his fellowman. It is because men are thus bound with us in the bundle of human life that they oppose absolutely being used as means to the ends that we pursue in our common life with them. They certainly wish to cooperate with us. But in the process of cooperating with us, they will to be acknowledged as the existing individuals who are fellowmen with us. Thus they insist that as a matter of truth and reality, as existing by their communication with us, they are not at our disposal for use and exploitation.

There was a time when theologians spoke of man as created in the image of God, and philosophers argued that man's higher, spiritual nature endowed him with a unique and absolute value. Whatever the language used, there was a common notion of the dignity of man that kept people aware of our third dimension of human existence. It would likely be wrong to opine that in the past when the body-soul or body-mind dualism was commonplace, there was less exploitation than there is today. However, thinking men had a traditional notion of human dignity, theologically and philosophically explained, that was accepted as true and binding. This tradition is now largely dissipated. It is not dead, and we in a rather dumb way still have the notion that our fellowmen are not means to our ends. Still, "acids of modernity" are strongly at work among us, and we are neither theoretically nor practically impressed with our "idealistic" tradition as to the source and savor of human dignity. Our philosophers eschew dualism and speak of man as an organism rather than as a synthesis of body and mind or spirit. Our theologians still speak of man as God's creature and in God's image. But they too often eschew "dualism" and appear to use the word "creature" against "idealism."[15] Traditional dualisms are in disfavor, and there is no new image of man that has replaced them as an expression of "the dignity of man."

Meanwhile, in our city life dominated by institutional transactions, we think and live according to the principle of "enlightened self-interest." It appears obvious to us that people participate in a common life in which they follow their self-interest, that is, they seek, acquire, and enjoy the goods available in the city. To this way of life there can hardly be an objection, and were objections made, it would be futile. According to common sense, it is only necessary that the pursuit of self-interest be intelligent. We must know the means to our ends and must be critical of, as well as devoted to, our "way of life." We must have proper regard for the self-interest of others and must exercise justice and sensitivity in our common quest for the good things of life. There must be among us freedom of enterprise, equality of education and opportunity, keeping of contracts, considerateness, mutual help, and peace. Thus it is that the pursuit of goods will be enlightened and successful, and our common life both good and happy.

There is no question that it is better to have self-interest enlightened and intelligent rather than ignorant and stupid. Our machine age, by virtue of the goods it produces for consumption, demands that men pursue these goods or their self-interest. It also demands, being an age of human interdependence in an artifactual society, that the pursuit of self-interest be enlightened in the sense that men desist from standing in the way of others in the common pursuits of goods.

Still, the kind of human reality signified by traditional idealism as to the dignity of man must find a persuasive statement among us. The traditional dualisms of mind and body, spirit and matter, that have become not only obscured but also misleading must be replaced with images of man that do justice to the dignity of man which was signified by these dualisms. The idea of man as the seat of self-interest, enlightened or otherwise, will not do. It will not do because it is not congruous with the strange claim one man makes upon another to a dignity that will not permit him to use him, even in an enlightened way. Men are, in fact, furious when they are seen and treated simply as means to a common production and enjoyment of goods. They are, in fact, frustrated and hostile when they are addressed only as roles in our institutions and are made ill when they are ignored as "flesh and blood" or "living souls." They are disappointed, let down, and tempted to despair of their very existence.

If human beings are fellowmen and do not exist without acknowledging one another as fellowmen, our miseries themselves are signs that our third dimension is not a fantasy. Our very failure in joy in the city is a sign of our humanity, although we are threatened and anxious and have an "empty feeling" among us. Our very restiveness is a sign of life. Our "search for identity" is a sign that we still are fellowmen. Our complaints about the meaninglessness of our lives and works, our fears as well as experiences of boredom, our sexy-ness and intemperance, our fascination with violence and irrationality, the "existentialism" of the young and the not so young among us—all these are more like a disease or some madness that speaks to us of health and sanity.

Nevertheless, our situation appears grave. The temptation to substitute "enlightened self-interest" for an intelligent regard for one another as fellowmen is very strong in the city and is unresisted in civilized life. We appear no longer to understand effectively the meaning of fellowmanhood for our existence as human beings. The animal man is studied massively in our biological sciences. The man in institutions is studied elaborately in social sciences, in politics, economics, sociology, and social psychology. Philosophers and theologians muse about "man's place in the cosmos," or about man's relation to "ultimate Reality," Being, or God. But there is no commonplace of concern with fellowmanhood.[16] Men of public affairs assume self-interest as the principle of human conduct, and so do scientific students of society. We lack the very aptitude for weighing properly the importance of love as an exercise of humanity. It is admittedly doubtful that there can be a science of fellowmanhood, and the scientists may be excused from trying to ascertain its meaning in our common life. But it does not follow that we do not need disciplined reflection on the third dimension of humanity. Understanding is an integral part of the function of humanity, and understanding fellowmanhood may be integral to our existing as fellowmen. It may make the difference between good and evil in this Age of Power.

This volume represents repeated attempts at stating in a coherent way the quality of the existence of fellowmen. Although each attempt may be less than satisfactory, it is our hope that the book as a whole will impress the reader as an intelligible and suggestive exploration of a subject that is of crucial significance for our existence and peace in this "brave new world."

4. AN EMERGING "IMAGE" OF THE CHURCH

In one respect, the World Council of Churches was inaugurated with the Amsterdam Assembly of 1948 as a grand response of the Christian churches to the travail and peril of humanity in our day. From the very first, in the midst of their concern for "unity," the thinkers in the Council have been concerned also with the "nature and function of the church," seeking a new understanding of the church as a source of healing and health in our world. They have found it necessary to seek for a new understanding of "the church" in the light of the pressing need of our time for human well-being in a world of commotions and deadly strife. They have been moved inevitably to the conviction that "the church" which might act as a genuine force for justice, peace, and commonweal in our world cannot be the officialdom of the institutions called churches, or their intelligent leadership. It has become progressively and inescapably clear that the church which might be a light or haven in the world is the "body of Christ," of which all baptized Christians, "the laity" as well as the clergy, are members. From the first, there must be a new image of the church in terms of a new self-awareness of Christians as a *koinonia*, a communion, who severally exist as a covenanted people, to be and behave as fellowmen, as Christ's fellowmen and therefore fellowmen with all people.

It now appears that the Christian people are called upon to live by a new obedience, in a new freedom and responsibility. There is a new apprehension in the church that baptized and confessing Christians in many lands and scattered in thousands of places, with their various cultures and conditions, are severally a "servant" people who may bear witness to a truth and power that shall free the world from bondage or bondages toward universal disaster.

In spite of the reservations of the theologians who see God alone as Savior and are professionally sensitive to the pride and presumptions of "men," the fate of the modern world may well depend upon the response of the Christian peoples to the demand that is made upon them to become agents of salvation in the Age of Power and Troubles. It is now clear that we may not "leave it to God," nor hope without faith and love, expecting God to save the world while the people of God forego their freedom and opportunity to be lights in the world. The Reformation principle of "by faith alone," "by grace alone," even "by Christ alone," needs to be reconsidered so that it may not become a snare or stumbling block among us. If it is true that we are not to confuse and weaken our faith in God's sovereignty, it is equally true that we are not to confuse and weaken our freedom for which Jesus Christ died and rose again and sent forth the Holy Spirit.

The truth is that today we doubt alike the sovereignty of God and our freedom. The time is past for setting one of these against the other and limping between the two things. If we are to believe in God's sovereignty, it is not enough to say, "the grace of God, the grace of God." If we are to believe that we may do God's will, it is not enough to say "the freedom of man, the freedom of man." The total effect of the traditional dialectics on "grace and free will" has been the practical confusion of Christ's people, who have wavered between "Let God do it" and "I shall do it," and have, in our Age of Power, ended with "We shall do it." But neither God's doing it nor our doing it is impressive as we see "no exit" written on big signs while we rush from one trouble to another. What is desperately needed in the church is some notion of "grace and freedom" that will function properly in our—in people's—service of Christ in this age of anxiety. We are no longer denying God's grace and boasting of our freedom. In the Age of Power the problem is seeing ourselves as God's people who may live as fellowmen, with hope rather than in despair. Despair rather than pride is the condition of the Christian today. The doctrine of grace must be stated to speak to this condition, not so much to remove man's pride as to reveal his hope, even though despair goes in some way with pride.

It is a very good thing that there are Christian thinkers today who, more or less directly influenced by the thinking going on in the World Council of Churches, are teaching the church to be a means of grace in the world. We are now learning to think of ourselves, of the so-called "laity," as ministers, priests, servants of Jesus Christ in our world. Christians are learning not to say "Let God do it," "Let the church do it." They are coming to see that they are to do it; they are to live and act toward the increase of truth and justice in their troubled and perilous world. There may be less than one might hope of such awakening of the laity to their opportunities as the body of Christ. There may well be more of it than meets the eye. In any case, our duty is to reconsider grace and freedom in the church and to explain their possibilities for the ministry of Christ's people in this Age of Power.

The emerging "model" of the church as God's people and fellowmen may require us to rethink and restate the whole "body of Christian divinity." Christian doctrines are so interrelated that a new understanding with respect to one of them cannot but alter our understanding of all the rest. Hence, it is quite certain that the imminent acknowledgment of the Christians that they are the body of Christ, Christ's vicars in the world, will provide new ways of theology that shall be authentic expressions of the life and mind of the church. Once we fully understand that the church is a society of fellowmen under Christ, we are bound to have a new understanding of the Christian faith as a whole. The following lectures and addresses are essays toward such an understanding. They are inevitably tentative and doubtless inadequate. However, if they prove to be suggestive and encouraging, they will serve their purpose.

1 Reflections on the Doctrine of the Church

1. THE CHURCH AS SOCIAL INSTITUTIONS

The Reformation doctrines of the church are characterized by a fateful ambiguity that persists in Protestantism to the present day. The church was defined by Luther in 1528 as follows: "I believe that there is one holy Christian Church on earth, which is the community, the number and assembly of all the Christians in the whole world, the only betrothed of Christ and his spiritual body." [1]

In the 1536 version of the *Institutes of the Christian Religion*, Calvin spoke of the church as: "the whole multitude of Christians, joined together by the blessing of faith, and assembled to be one people, over whom the Lord Jesus is Prince and Captain; united into one body of which Christ is the Head; in which [body] God has eternally elected all who belong to him, in order to gather and add them to his kingdom." [2] There are numerous such definitions of the church in the early Reformation literature and they forcibly bring out the Protestant doctrine that the church is people, congregation, the multitude of those who believe in Jesus Christ as Savior and Lord.

On the other hand, the church is defined in terms of "the means of grace"; as the place where the gospel is purely preached and the Sacraments are rightly administered. Calvin stated the matter firmly: "Wherever we see that the Word of God is purely preached and heard, and the sacraments are administered according to the institution of Christ, we are to have no doubt whatsoever that there is the Church;

because the promise that he has made to us cannot fail."[3]

It was fixed in the minds of the Reformers that the people of God need "external means or aids by which God invites us into the society of Christ and holds us therein."[4] The multitude of believers are provided with the means of grace not only because they, being physical, need physical means of receiving God's Word, which is spiritual and too high for them, but also because they are subject to "ignorance and sloth" and are otherwise weak.[5] Hence, God accommodates his truth to them by giving them "doctors and ministers of the Church," who preach the Word and administer the Sacraments and other elders who administer discipline. These men are "ambassadors [of God] in the world, to be interpreters of his secret will and, in short, to represent his person."[6] Further on, Calvin says:

> Nothing fosters mutual love more fittingly than for men to be bound together with this bond: one is appointed pastor to teach the rest, and those bidden to be pupils receive the common teaching from one mouth. . . .The Lord has therefore bound his church together with a knot that he foresaw would be the strongest means of keeping unity, while he entrusted to men the teaching of salvation and everlasting life in order that through their hands it might be communicated to the rest.

In the next paragraph he adds:

> Through the ministers to whom he has entrusted this office and has conferred the grace to carry it out, . . . [God] dispenses and distributes his gifts to the church. Neither the light and heat of the sun, nor food and drink, are so necessary to nourish and sustain the present life as the apostolic and pastoral office is necessary to preserve the church on earth.[7]

Calvin is clear that the ministers are in the church. They are there for the upbuilding of the believers at large through the Word and the Sacrament and discipline. They are "tools" of the Spirit, but not vessels of infused grace. They have no power that is not God's, no authority that is not Christ's, and no dignity except as servants in the church. Nevertheless, the traditional dichotomy of those who preach the Word and administer the Sacraments and exercise discipline on the one hand, and those who hear the Word, receive the Sacrament, and undergo discipline is maintained as clearly and sharply as it was in the medieval church.

This is said, not by way of criticism, but as a matter of fact. The present point is that the Reformation doctrines of the church—with its insistence upon the external aids necessary for the salvation of the people—perpetuated the Catholic contradistinction between the dispensers and the recipients of grace, and thus between the clergy and the laity. The Reformation opposed the institution that was engaged in bringing the means of grace to the people, to the *laos* or the crowd to whom it was brought for their salvation. In doctrine, the Reformers did not identify the institution, with its personnel and cult, with the church. Still, Calvin could say: "The church is the common mother of all the godly, which bears, nourishes, and brings up children to God, kings and peasants alike; and this is done by the ministry."[8] The church is the mother, but the work of the church is done by the ministry. It has been by no means hard or farfetched for those who received the grace of God through the traditional means of the Word and the Sacraments to identify the church with the institution that dispenses the grace of God. No definition of the church as the people of God could undo the fact that the people received grace in the hands of an institution and regarded it as the place where God offered them salvation and eternal life—that is, the church. It has been inevitable in the nature of the case that the people have contradistinguished themselves from the clergy and identified the church in an obvious and effective sense with the ministers of God in their midst. It has been inevitable that the church should have been identified as a "sacred institution," with its officials and action, and the people should have regarded themselves as believers who are the beneficiaries of it. The priest has been done away with; the ministry is no longer a Sacrament. The means of grace have been declared to owe their efficacy to the Holy Spirit and "faith alone." Still, Roman Catholic institutions and organizations and their priesthood have been replaced by Protestant institutions and organizations and their "ordained clergy," and just as Catholics do, Protestants "go to church" rather than know themselves as the church.

The Protestant churches as institutions have certain characteristics in common with the other institutions of society at large. They are objectified in buildings, personnel, paraphernalia, habits of thought and behavior that mark them off as one kind of institution among others. One can tell them by their chancels with their crosses, pulpits, tables, Bibles, candles, choir benches, by their large colored windows and rows of pews separated by aisles. They are places where congregations hear the Word of God and partake of the Sacraments, sing, pray, and contribute to the collection. In doing these things, they are faced by ministers, elders, ushers, and the choir. They engage in worship, with thanksgiving, confession, petition, and sometimes intercession. They use a certain kind of language and do all things in stylized ways and with a certain solemnity. Thus it is impressed upon them that they are in church and not in the town hall or in school or in a store.

Institutions exist as habitual ways of doing things for the fulfillment of some public need. The state governs and protects; schools teach; factories produce goods, and shops sell them. The churches have inevitably claimed the support of the public on the basis of some palpable good they have been known to provide. The churches have, through their teaching, cult, and discipline, helped the people to meet the crises of their lives (especially the last crisis, which is death) with some strength and dignity, and to hope for the prevention and removal of the sundry evils to which men are exposed all their lives.

They have made available to the people a supernatural and all-efficacious Power against the natural and mundane powers that imperil life, health, property, peace in this world of uncertainty and surprise, or against evil beyond the control of men and their competency to overcome it. The usefulness of churches in keeping the social fabric mended has been obvious to the state and the public at large. As channels of supernatural Power, they have made for social stability, provided sanctions for public morality, and contributed immensely to public well-being. In doing all this, they have formed the image of the church as social institution and established the distinction between the officials of the churches as bearers of divine grace and the people of the churches as the recipients of it. It has been a deeply ingrained habit to contrast the church with the state and to conceive of both in institutional and organizational terms as against the people for whose benefit they exist and exercise authority. Thus, and in short, in spite of official doctrine that identifies the church as the multitude of believers, the people themselves recognize their several churches, whether denominational or local, as church, and themselves as Christians who believe their preaching and worship in their precincts.

For a number of reasons, the place and function of the institutions in our society called churches have become unclear and questionable.

a. In our "pluralistic society" the traditional cooperation between church and state, between religious institutions and others, has been largely disrupted. The state operates without the benefit of the clergy; political, economic, and educational institutions no longer appear to depend upon the religious institutions for their own efficacy. The churches among us do not enjoy the protection of the state, and the state, together with the school, the market, and the military, have their own autonomous beings and behavior.

b. The function of religion itself has become ambiguous and obscure. Religion as access to supernatural and sacred Power, although acknowledged in our society, is hardly operative in the lives and works of the people in our Age of Power. The "acids of modernity," compounded of science and secularism, together with our efficiency toward an economy of abundance, have permeated our total culture. Men prefer preventing and removing evils to having them made bearable through cultic performances; and the shocks they receive from nature, including death, are not sufficient to persuade them to take too seriously whatever religion they may have. Many still support religious institutions for one reason or another, sometimes for reasons having little to do with religion. But religion is not their ultimate concern, and religious institutions are, compared to political, economic, educational institutions, matters of secondary interest.

c. There is today an alienation between religion and reason that no amount of accommodation and apologetics on the part of religious officials is able to overcome. Even such master apologists as Reinhold Niebuhr and Paul Tillich have hardly been able to persuade unbelievers of the truth of Christian doctrine.[9] The mind of the officials of religious institutions and the mind of the officials of other institutions hardly meet one another. The clergy have become a race apart, with their peculiar language and ways, and their isolation from the common mind and life is almost complete. As representatives of religion, although not as good and helpful men, they have lost contact with the reason operative in our culture. The more they insist that reli-gion is a matter of faith and not a matter of reason, the more they fortify the wall that separates them from the people who must willy-nilly live by their good sense.

d. Even the contribution of the churches to public morals has become vague. The people still appear to believe that religion is good for the good life; but they also believe that they are good, not because of the church, but spontaneously and by habit. It is agreed that the churches contribute something to integrity, altruism, law keeping, etc., and therefore to democracy and prosperity. However, that "something" is rather indefinite, and the amount of it appears not to be crucial for public well-being. Since reli-gion among us is traditionally justified in terms of its social value, unclarity of mind with regard to this matter is a palpable source of indifference to the churches in the land.[10] Everybody, as it were, knows that atheists are often good citizens and churchgoers often do evil in our public life. Hence, once again the churches as institutions appear to be of doubtful value and are treated as second-class institutions.

2. THE CHURCH AS A PEOPLE

a. It is evident from all this that the traditional and present identification of churches as institutions engaged in some public service is no longer viable. Hence, there has been much effort made on the part of Christian thinkers in our times to "rediscover" the nature and function of the church, and the total effect of this effort has been a genuinely renewed understanding of the church as a people first and as an institution second. The ecumenical movement, Biblical scholarship, recent theology, have all contributed to a new awareness that unless the "multitude of believers" come to recognize themselves as the church, bearers of God's grace in our world, the church acts neither as the body of Christ nor as a light on earth.

The ecumenical movement has made us aware that the church transcends any denomination and its institutions and that it is characterized first of all, not by a variety of organizations, but by a common confession that Jesus is Lord and King, a confession that is made, not by ecclesiastical officials, but by the believing Christians throughout the world. Worldwide Christianity with its many churches is not readily seen as an institution. It is a multitude called, gathered, and established by Jesus Christ and the Holy Spirit, both being of God the Father. Thus the church has emerged as a community with its institutions rather than as an institution for the religious benefit of the people.

Biblical scholars, trying anew to understand the Bible in its own terms, have been impressed by the fact that the Bible is made up largely of accounts of dealings of the living God with his people covenanted to hear his Word and obey it. It has become clear that the people of Israel are logically prior to the institutions of Israel, and that the church of the New Testament was the new Israel with its institutions. The characterizations of the church as a royal priesthood, a holy nation, the body of Christ, the bride of Christ, vine, flock, building, etc., refer to God's own people. The church of the New Testament had its churches or assemblies; it had its apostles, overseers, elders, teachers, deacons, etc.; it had its cult and ways. But none of these was the New Israel. The church was the community of believers.

It is unnecessary to enlarge upon the evidence of recent theology. One has only to mention the names of Emil Brunner, Karl Barth, Dietrich Bonhoeffer, H. Richard Niebuhr, J. E. Lesslie Newbigin, Paul Minear, to be reminded that the doctrine of the church as a community created by Jesus Christ is today well established.[11] One might go so far as to say that a lively and articulate conception of the church as the multitude of believers is an outstanding contribution of present-day theology to the faith of the church. Renewed emphasis upon words and phrases such as "faith," "covenant," "the humanity of Christ," "the responsibility of the church," "ethics and eschatology," "reconciliation and service"—all point to a new awareness of the church as the body of Christ, whose members are the people. It is inevitable that our theologians will gradually reconsider all the traditional doctrines of the church in the light of this understanding of the church as human beings scattered throughout the world, believers in Jesus Christ living in our awesome world with its precarious future.

b. The new concern with the life and the responsibilities of the so-called laity in the world has brought to our attention the ethos of the church as integral to the nature of the church. It is becoming clear that the *esse* of the church is expressed not only in the sermon, Sacraments, and discipline of the churches, but also in the witness that Christians bear to the gospel in their life in the world. The church exists as a style of life, as indicated by such words as "vocation," "discipleship," and "service," which have come to frequent use in many quarters. The church's reality is known by the love of the Christians and the works of love that they do in their several callings. There is no faith in the living God, who reconciles the world to himself in Christ Jesus, that is exercised apart from the quest for justice, mercy, and peace in the world. The church is where God makes free for love and freedom is practiced as love. And both freedom and love are God's gift to his people and not institutional things or sancta.

The same thinkers of the church who have recovered the view of the church as a people have expounded Christian ethics as integral to "dogmatics." We still have theology that is worked out apart from ethics, and ethics that is discussed apart from theology. But the new style in Christian thinking is to bind theology and ethics together, to see the grace of God and the responsibility of God's people as belonging together.[12] There is no Word of God that does not at once make free and bind, that does not present us at once with the gospel and the law. The church is the place where God enables his people to love him as their God with all their hearts and one another as themselves.

c. Concern with the ethics of the church has produced a new view of the purpose or end of the church. The traditional characterization of the church as an institution having the means of grace went with the public notion that the purpose of the church is salvation from evil in this world and in the next. This notion was hardly qualified by the institution's condemnation of sin and its provision for the forgiveness of sins. Sin itself was understood as transgression of law, and the forgiveness of it was institutionalized in the churches. Moreover, the sting of sin was felt in the punishment of it with some evil. In any case, religious institutions have functioned mainly with the purpose of helping people meet the crises of life. As institutions they have been concerned more with "man's supernatural end" beyond this world and its evils than with the people's obedience to the law of Christ in the communion of saints.

According to the newer views of the church, its purpose is to enable man to keep the law of God, to hear his Word for justice, mercy, and peace in this world. The problem of man, according to this view, is not the evils he suffers in this world, but the sin that turns God's good creation into a realm of enmity and misery. God created man as fellowman, to enjoy the good by his love and justice as fellowman. By God's grace, man is a creature, at once finite and free: both finite and free so that he may find his life in love both given and received. But man turns against his finitude, and in so doing, he turns against God, his fellowman, and himself. He subjects himself to enmity and bondage; to injustice, misery, and death.[13]

The Son of God came to free man from his bondage and his death as a fellowman and to restore him to his God, his neighbor, and himself, to live in the joy of thankfulness, love, and peace. The Spirit of God came to gather together a people who are no people and to establish them in faithfulness and hope; to form a society where there are isolated individuals, and to create fellowmen where there are anxious and desperate egos; to open men to God, to their fellowmen, and to themselves, for intelligence and love. In short, according to the new view, both the nature and the purpose of the church are to be sought in love according to Jesus Christ. The purpose of the church is to bear witness to the love of Christ in the world today. Such witness is the opportunity of the people of God. Therefore, the church is the people.

3. CONSEQUENT QUESTIONS

The present-day views of the church amount to a new phase of the Christian understanding of the church. But they also raise a number of questions that are likely to command the attention of our thinkers in the years to come.

a. There is need to overcome the traditional individualism in Christian theology. We need to see the church neither as a multitude nor as a corporate unity or totality. We need to see it as a covenanted community of fellowmen whose lives consist of communion one with another and with God the Father, Son, and Holy Spirit. The individuality of these fellowmen is a function of their communion, and their unity is formed by communion. They are creatures under the covenant of the Lord with his people, and by this covenant. So also are they sinners and saved. They are sinners by breaking the covenant that posits them as fellowmen, and they are saved for the keeping of the same covenant. The riches of their experience as individual human beings, in their activity and passivity, in their interiority and uniqueness, in their mystery and awesomeness, in their very communion with God as free and responsible agents—in short, in all things peculiar to them as "God's intelligent creation," occur in their lives as God's Israel who exist by communion and for one another in the name of Christ Jesus.

Knowledge of God and of the works of God; worship of God and service of God; union with Christ and joy in his benefits; justification, sanctification, eternal life itself—these are graces and blessings in the church, that is, in and by the keeping of the covenant of faith among themselves, by twos and threes, in the presence of the living Christ. Man's business is indeed with God. But this man is a fellowman and he has no business except as a fellowman.

b. There is need to rethink the means of grace. Exclusive attention to preaching, the Sacraments, and discipline has established among us the notion that the church is the ecclesiastical institution. If we take seriously the view that the church is the people, we must recognize that the communion of believers as such is an indispensable means of grace, that without it the other means of grace are bound to function feebly, if at all. We must earnestly consider the thesis that the dubious efficacy of the traditional means of grace among us is due to failure in communion. The Word of God is not heard properly, the Sacraments are not received for the strength and comfort of the people, discipline is not conducive to edification among a people for whom faithfulness and forgiveness, received and returned, are not matters of constant and ultimate concern. If the people are not priests one to another, they have neither priest nor God. If they do not minister one to another, they have no minister and no ministry. If the church as the people is not means of grace, there is neither grace nor means of grace. The living God who saved us through a Man still saves us through our fellowmen. Preaching, Sacrament, discipline, are efficacious in the church or the body of Christ, and the body of Christ is made up of members who build up one another.

c. It is Biblical, Protestant, orthodox, traditional, to say that faith produces love and good works. It is also neoorthodox and in good style today to say it. However, who or what produces faith? The proper answer is, God and Jesus Christ. How, then, do God and Christ produce faith? The proper answer this time is, through the Word and the Sacraments. But the Word is preached and the Sacraments administered by the clergy, who are officials of the religious institutions. Thus, the Protestant thesis that love grows out of faith functions as a doctrine that establishes the primacy of the institution as characteristic of the church.

If we take seriously the church as a people, we might say that faith is the gift of God the Father, Son, and Holy Spirit; and that the Spirit induces faith in the process of communion, as well as by preaching and the Sacraments, by worship and discipline. Faith comes by hearing and by communion, and not by either one alone. And so does love. My brother the layman, as well as my brother the preacher, is God's minister or servant for my edification, which includes faith, hope, and love. My sinful brother's faith and forgiveness, which he receives from Jesus Christ in the church, are indispensable means of my salvation—my own repentance, faith, and forgiveness. My faith, hope, and love are three aspects of the grace of God that the Spirit indwelling the church in my brother communicates to me from God the Father and Jesus Christ. There is no faith before love and no hope that is not from love as well as faith. Even while in hearing, love grows out of faith, in communion, faith grows out of love. And the church that exists in and by communion is prior to both preaching and hearing. Faith, hope, and love are aspects of God's grace in Jesus Christ and the Spirit, and they are aspects of the same grace in the communion of believers being justified and sanctified by communion, rather, reconciled and reunited as brothers. Faith that comes by hearing and faith that comes by communion, with love and hope, belong together and together they are faith that comes at once by our hearing the preacher and our hearing our brother. The sermon presents us with the promise of God in Christ Jesus, and in communion the Spirit persuades us, by the faithfulness of sinners, that the promise is solid and true and to be believed. God promises our reconciliation and restoration by the ministry of preaching and of the forgiven brother, and the two together are the means of grace.

The time has come so to interpret the Reformation principle of *sola fide*, *sola gratia*, *sola Christi*, as not to make it a basis for contempt for the church, or our fellowmen, whom God has in his infinite wisdom given us to be means of his grace. It is indeed against the gospel and the Reformation to put up our "works" next to God's grace as justifying or saving. It is absurd that we who are sinners should set ourselves up next to Christ as our brothers' saviors. In this respect, the Reformation principle stands, and to deny it would be to deny the gospel.

But still, we have to answer the question, Why then did Christ rise from the dead, ascend to the right hand of God the Father Almighty, send the Holy Spirit, and create the communion of saints? Is it not because the Lord God himself intended the church to be the body of Christ, and his people to be members of the body for the actualization of his grace in the world? Is it not so that the people of God, by the name of Jesus Christ, are made the members of the body of Christ to become means of grace one to another and to all men, forgiving one another and all men in the name of Christ; and if forgiving, then justifying and sanctifying one another, as God's co-workers, knowing that their sufficiency is of God? Is it not their vocation in all their works to glorify God by their truth and justice among themselves and thus to be the members of Christ's body? Pitching the grace of God against the work of the Spirit in the communion of saints will not do. If pride before God who, *sola fide* sought to discourage it, is wrong, so is the denial of the body of Christ and the life of its members by which they exist for the building up of the church.

d. It is time to consider the Sacraments, which the Catholics consider as primary and Protestants as secondary means of grace. The Protestants gave up the sacrament of the priesthood as a channel of supernatural and superpersonal grace, but they retained the Sacraments as adjuncts of the Word. The Sacraments, although considered all but indispensable, were treated as visible signs of invisible reality, given in the main by way of accommodation to human weakness. As parts of the cult of the church as an institution, they were kept and confirmed as means of grace under the Word. But the administration of them was justified as an act of obedience to Jesus Christ who had instituted them. There has been, and still is, in spite of every apology for them, much doubt as to their meaning and efficacy as means of grace. They are, among Protestants, mainly sacred acts of churches as institutions, and the people receive them, with more or less fervor, as rites that belong to, and as parts of, the institutions of which they are members.

The Catholic doctrine of the Sacraments as channels of grace depends upon the doctrines of ecclesiastical orders and "infused grace." Once these latter doctrines are given up, it is hard to hold on to the doctrine of the Sacraments as visible signs of invisible grace, or as channels of grace. There is no intelligible congruity between grace as God's gracious will toward his people (which is the Protestant view of grace) and the visible signs of water, bread, and wine. God's grace and Christ's grace are signified logically by the grace among God's people, which is grace promised in the Word and received in the Spirit. The "elements" do signify Christ's death for us and our life in him. But such signification depends both upon God's grace and the grace exercised among us. Without the latter, the elements may signify Christ's death, but they do not signify God's grace.

When the church is characterized as a people with their institutions, the Sacraments may be regarded in a new light. They are means of grace as celebrations of grace by God's people. Baptism is a celebration of the gathering of the community in the person of the one baptized. The Lord's Supper is the celebration of the growth and establishment of the community at the Lord's Table and in his company. The Sacraments are celebrations, with thanksgiving, of the mission of Jesus Christ, of his victory over sin and death by his cross and resurrection and ascension, of the coming of the Spirit, and of the repentance, forgiveness, freedom, faithfulness, joy, and peace among God's people, and of the hope of God's Kingdom, which goes with faith and love.

But if the people are to celebrate God's grace and Kingdom in Christ Jesus and the Spirit, they need to know the joy of both grace and the Kingdom. The new Israel needs to exist as children of the fathers whom God brought out of a land of deep darkness into a marvelous light. They need to remember the victories of the Lord in their behalf, their present calling, and the promise given them of God's Kingdom. They need to know sorrow and joy, in repentance, forgiveness, and love, from Christ and before him, and among themselves. They need to be thankful, and fearful, and hopeful. In short, they need to rejoice in God, as he has shown them his grace and made them his chosen people, a holy nation and a royal priesthood, in this world and for the redemption of the world.

How are the people so to celebrate and rejoice both at Baptism and at the Lord's Table unless they assemble together as those who repent and forgive and love and hope? Unless they so assemble, how are they to know that the Lord of grace is with them and that they are gathered around him? And if they do not know the Lord's presence at the Font and the Table, then they do not receive the Sacrament properly, and it is to them no means of grace. In this sense and way, no people, no thanksgiving, no Sacrament. As the speaking and the hearing of the Word go together, so the administration of the Sacraments and the receiving of them go together. And in both cases, there needs to be a people who know their God.

In the light of the new views of the church, there is no way, among Protestants, of restoring the Sacraments to their rightful place as means of grace without a people who give thanks and rejoice. Thus seen, the Sacraments are ways in which God's people celebrate their salvation, and so it is that they are means of grace equal to preaching. The people celebrate the Word of God by baptizing their children and by eating and drinking at the Lord's Table. They do the one as they do the other, with joy, and not at a loss as to what they do; they both hear and respond with thanksgiving.

Thus it is that the Sacraments are signs. They are signs of

God's grace in communion, and as such, they are signs of the new life in the church by the mission of Jesus Christ. The Sacraments are signs of the presence of God in the church, but the presence of God is known by the communion of saints. We know no signs that are not at once signs of God's grace and of grace among his people. To celebrate God's grace is also to celebrate grace among us. It is this double grace that is celebrated in the Sacraments; and the water, the bread and wine, are signs of both. They are not the signs of the one without being the signs of the other, and we may not celebrate the one without celebrating the other. We may not celebrate the death of Christ without celebrating his resurrection and gift of the Spirit. But we celebrate the gift of the Spirit when we rejoice in one another as vicars of Christ in the church and in the world.

e. There is much said nowadays about "lay apostolate," about the responsibility of the Christian to bear witness to the grace of Jesus Christ in the world. In fact, the present insistence of Christian churches upon the doctrine of the church as the people is inseparable from the growing conviction that the mission of the church today is, in one primary respect, that the people fulfill their calling as Christians in their daily work and occupation in "the secular world." We now understand that unless "the laity" live and act as the covenanted community of Christ in the several institutions of our society, there will be no telling witness to Christ in our world, and God's will shall not be done on earth for peace.

However, the laity may well reply that they are not sufficient for their "apostolate," or that too heavy a burden is placed upon them by their well-meaning but not too understanding leaders. One cannot say to a businessman, or worker, or politician, "Go to, act as a Christian in your role in your organization." Hardly a man is brave enough and self-sacrificing enough to do battle against evil on his own, even by a supposed private help of God and under prodding from preachers.

"Lay apostolate" requires the communion of saints. In the matter of "doing the truth" in our world, the people need God who works his salvation in the covenanted community by the comfort and strength and hope one fellowman representing Christ is able to give another in his love of him and engagement with him in the mission of the church. The Spirit of God moves mightily in and by communion, and so it is that he makes each man free and able to engage in the warfare of his King with the world. Human flesh is weak and is no match against the spiritual powers in the world.[14] The Spirit alone is sufficient for this warfare, and the Spirit is the Spirit in the church that exists and thrives by the comfort the people give one another. There is no mission of the body of Christ, or of its members, without the communion of the believers in their making one another strong in the bond of life by which they severally exist and enjoy the peace of God in Christ Jesus. Everybody, as it were, wishes to see Christians show forth the faith that is in them by following "justice, mercy, and peace" in this troubled and imperiled world of ours. In a sense, this is the end for which we live in hope of reform, reunion, renewal in the church. Such, in a sense, is the meaning and the excitement of the ecumenical movements, of the councils and reapprochements, of the searchings and hopings in the church in our time. We live with the hope of the witness of Christ's people to the power of Christ for the peace and prosperity of the multitudes in our world, where hope and despair are making for a madness that may end in death. It is at this time as needful as ever to understand that the communion of saints is the church and the source of the church's witness to its Lord in the world; or that communion and mission are two sides of the work of the Spirit of God who, with the Father and the Son, alone is a match for the principalities and powers of this present world and will save the same world by the grace that is among the people of God, who may impart it to the world by the communion of saints.

2 The Spirit of the Living God

1. INTRODUCTION

In the main line of the Christian tradition, God is acknowledged as Father, Son, and Holy Spirit. It is this God the believers have worshiped, invoked, and trusted for their peace and every blessing. They have sung to the Trinity, prayed to the Trinity, and cleaved to the Trinity. This is the God of whom the theologian is called upon to speak intelligently in the service of God and his people.

Each person of the Trinity being God equally with the others is one without whom God would not be God. The Father is known as the Father of the Son, and the Son as the Son of the Father. The Father without the Son would not be God the Father of the Christian faith, and the Son without the Father would not be God the Son of the same faith. When the Father is detached from the Son, we have "natural piety." When the Son is detached from the Father, we have an idol and not the Christ of God. The Father and the Son are God together, and they can be neither logically nor in faith separated one from the other. They are in the same sense and way "Persons" of the Godhead, so that "Person" means the same thing as applied to both, as "person" would mean the same thing as applied to John and James.[1] This point was settled in the ancient church and has remained firm in the main line of the church's tradition.

It is important to remember that faith in God the Father and Son is not simply a matter of theological rigorism. In this case, as in any theological question, the life of the church or the Christians is at stake. A God called Father who is not the Father of the Son is a god who is not known through Jesus of Nazareth, who "suffered under Pontius Pilate." He is not a god who has revealed himself as the Father through the cross of Christ. He is not a god whose children are called upon to "take up their cross" and thus to walk in the way of life. It requires little reflection to acknowledge that a god presented to us in the cross of Christ is Father in a sense different from a god whom we must call our Father as protection against a cross. These are two different kinds of "Father." One is the "Father" of the Christian faith; the other is "Father" of "natural religion."

Now, this being true with regard to the Father and the Son, it may be true with regard to the Spirit as well. The Spirit whom the church confesses in its creeds is the Spirit of the Father, or the Spirit of the Father and the Son. In the church's faith as based upon the ecumenical Creeds, the Father and the Son are no more detachable from the Spirit than they are each from the other. The Spirit is the Spirit of the Father in such a way that the Father would not be the Father without his Spirit, and the same is true of the Son. On the other hand, the Spirit would not be the Spirit of Christian confession were it not the Spirit of the Father and the Spirit of the Son. When a Christian speaks of the Father, he speaks of the Father of the Son and of whom is the Spirit. When he speaks of the Son, he speaks of the Son of the Father and of whom is the Spirit. When he speaks of the Spirit, he speaks of the Spirit of the Father and the Son. And so speaking, he speaks of God.

Again, the logical inclusion of the doctrine of the Spirit in the doctrine of God is not a matter simply of theology as an intellectual enterprise. Here also, the Christian life may be at stake and there are countless statements in the church's tradition that indicate that this is the case. There is a solid line of confession from the apostle Paul to present-day theologians that one cannot confess the Father and the Son without confessing the Spirit, that the Christian mind and life in their totality, as they depend upon the Father and the Son, are the work of the Spirit. Henry P. Van Dusen and Karl Barth, to mention two theologians with quite different minds, are agreed on this point.[2] In introducing Book III of his *Institutes,* on "The way in which we receive the grace of Christ: what benefits come to us from it, and what effects follow," Calvin said with characteristic pointedness: "To sum up, the Holy Spirit is the bond by which Christ effectually unites us to himself."[3] And since the whole of the Christian life comes from the Christian's union with Christ, it is clear that there is no faith, or love, or hope, or any other blessing, without the working of the Holy Spirit. The Holy Spirit is regarded among us, more or less consistently, as the author of our knowledge of God and of obedience to him, and of "eternal life" itself. Therefore, Christians have perennially prayed, "Come, Holy Spirit," with the conviction that he is "the Lord and Life-giver."[4]

And yet, the doctrine of the Spirit of God is no longer theologically viable. Although the church continues to invoke the Spirit in its worship and prayer and although theologians continue to introduce the Spirit into their analyses of the Christian life, it has become all but impossible to make the doctrine of the Spirit integral to the doctrine of God. For the layman in theology, the Spirit is a ghostly entity that is associated with "spirituality," or a mysterious character vaguely related to "faith and practice."

The explanation of such weakness in our confession of the Spirit of God is a long story. Our failure in this matter has deep roots in the mind and life of the church. To mention only a few, it has to do with the identification of God with Being, First Cause, Creativity, and the like; with ascetical and mystical constructions of salvation; with Augustinian-Pelagian controversies in which the Spirit has been confused with grace on the one hand and with "moral influence" on the other; and with failure in the realization of *communio sanctorum* (about this more will be said later). When God is identified with Being or the Power of Being, and the Word or Jesus Christ is made the revelation of Being, what does one do with the Spirit?[5] Or, when one has a "personal God" and "the historical Jesus," again, what need is there for the Spirit?[6] When the work of the Spirit is identified with variations of "the experience of Pentecost," there is no cogent reason why such phenomena should not be referred simply to "God." The same is true of faith, "union with Christ," "fellowship with God," and other aspects of the Christian life that have been spoken of interchangeably as works of grace or the works of the Spirit.[7] Since in the individual's experience of God it is hard to distinguish between Christ and the Spirit, and Christ has the advantage of being a historical figure, the Spirit is put in the shade.[8] In short, in terms of traditional theologies, orthodox or unorthodox, the doctrine of the Spirit is intellectually and practically superfluous. We know we cannot do without God the Father Almighty and Jesus Christ, his only Son our Lord, but what are we to do with the Spirit, except perhaps use him for Augustinian ends (as in the Reformation and Barth)[9] or confuse him with "spiritual experience" of one sort or another?

A chapter of this length is not sufficient for clearing up this confusion of long standing, which goes deep into the history of the church. The writer can only make a few suggestions that might eventually lead to a clearer and more meaningful confession of our faith in God the Father, Son, and Holy Spirit.

2. THE SPIRIT IN THE HISTORY OF ISRAEL

The Spirit of God has been made synonymous, roundly and commonly, with the immanence and the power of God. There is, of course, ample excuse for this identification. The coming of the Spirit upon a warrior or a prophet suggests, at least to a modern reader, that we have to do with a God who is neither distant nor inactive. When the Spirit comes upon Gideon (rather, clothes him), or Saul, the living God himself seems to be present with his power and sufficiency. (Judg. 6:34; I Sam. 11:6.) Or, when the Spirit comes upon Saul, or Elijah, or a band of prophets, so that they become ecstatic and prophesy, once again we might say that God is present among them with his transforming power. (I Kings 18:12f.; II Kings 2:15 .) Jesus himself receives the Spirit in his baptism, and thus God's presence and power enable him to fulfill his mission of mercy and peace. (Mark 1:9-13.) He is raised from the dead by "the Spirit of holiness," which shows that God has neither forsaken him nor withheld his power from him. (Rom.1:4.) So also, God is present in the church with his power, in that the Spirit of God enables his people to prophesy and bear witness to Jesus Christ. (Acts 1:8; 10:44f.; 11:27f.) In short, where the Spirit works with power, God himself is present, so that one may reasonably, though vaguely, say that the Spirit of God is the immanence of God with power.

However, the identification of the Spirit with the immanence and power of God is not unquestionably right. Certainly the Spirit presents us with the living God, and this God is not otiose, or removed from the world in some supernal abode. He is present in the world. However, the presence of God may be indicated in a variety of ways: by references to his face, and angel, and the Ark, and word, etc. The Spirit is one of a number of signs of God's presence and has no exclusive title for designating the immanence of God. It is commonplace in Scripture to refer to God's presence, with his work and action, without referring to the Spirit. In short, the Spirit does signify God's presence, but it is not God's presence. God's presence among his people is indicated through a variety of signs.[10]

As to the "power of God," there is no question that usually the presence of the Spirit signifies the presence of God with power. The living God is God having the Spirit, and he is the mighty God. But it does not follow that the Spirit is God's power. *Rûah*, even as wind, is not synonymous with power. When *rûah Yahweh*, the Spirit of the Lord, comes upon a man, God reveals himself as *hayil*, or powerful. Where there is *pneuma theou*, there is also *dynmis*, power.[11] But power, in Hebrew or in Greek, is not the same thing as the Spirit of the living God. The Spirit is the bearer of power, not power itself. The Spirit draws our attention to the living God who performs mighty and saving deeds, through—or, rather, by—his servants and in behalf of his covenanted people. "The Spirit of God" in Scripture is predominantly a soteriological phrase and can be spoken of properly in that context. To say that the Spirit means power is to leave out what is characteristic of the Spirit: namely, that it comes upon the servants of God, and that by its coming upon them they fulfill God's ends for his people.

This is not to deny that the word *rûah* may have been in use outside of this context, as was the word *pneuma* outside of the New Testament. There is ample evidence in the Bible itself that *rûah* meant wind, and also breeze, air, spirit. *Pneuma* itself means life, air.[12] Hence, etymology itself suggests that "the Spirit" is to be associated with an invisible, dynamic quiddity that is manifest in natural and organic vitality in general.

However, the word "spirit" as used in many Biblical texts, especially those having to do with God in his dealings with his people, cannot be referred to simply or generally in terms of wind, power, and the like. In Biblical material, especially in narratives that tell of God's mighty deeds in behalf of his people, whether among the old or the new Israel, the word "spirit," as the Spirit of the Lord God, acquires meanings and connotations that must be seen in the context of these narratives. The same is true, of course, of other words such as word, angel, face, presence, etc.

We are dealing with the action of God who has entered into a covenant of righteousness with his people. God saves his people and reigns over them to the end that they may know and obey him in a common life of justice, mercy, and peace. This point is important for our argument. If salvation were from some evil like enemies and oppression as such, if it were from hunger, disease, or some other physical evil, if it were from finitude, or finally from death as such—then the actions of God would have been a manifestation of supernatural Power, as often credited to the gods of the nations, Greek or Scandinavian. But the end for which God delivered his people from Egypt and scattered their enemies before them was that he might be their God and they his people under the covenant of righteousness. There is, of course, much in the Bible that, when detached from the history of Israel, lends itself to a supernaturalistic, rather physical conception of God's action and of his power. But if the theme of the Bible is God's *hesed* or gracious loyalty to his people under the aspects of law and gospel, then it is inappropriate to include the action of God under the general notion of supernatural power. A God whose speaking and hearing and will to be heard are essential to his action with regard to his people cannot be identified as power in general. When we consider the mission of a Gideon or a Saul and the manner of its accomplishment, when we consider above all the mission and the cross of Jesus of Nazareth, leading to the appearance of the church, we realize that we have to speak of God's power as well as of his wisdom in a way appropriate to the history of redemption.

In the stories that involve the Spirit, salvation is the establishment of Israel as the people of God under the covenant made with Moses, for the people's faithfulness to him and one to another. The history of God's people, as produced by God's saving acts, is a history of their turning to God and to one another as beings who exist as fellowmen. It is not, as such, a history of salvation from the sundry evils that beset human life in this world of vicissitudes and pains. It is not a history either of overcoming the physical world or escaping from it. It is a history of the making of a people, and the action of God in it is congruous with his purpose in the creation and preservation of man. In short, God was engaged in a commerce with human beings living with one another in this physical world toward the realization of a "holy nation." It is in the history formed by this commerce that the Word and the Spirit of God alike belong. There is no understanding of the Biblical language about the Spirit outside of this commerce and its consequences, which form the history of God's people.

3. THE SPIRIT AND GOD'S SERVANTS

There is no denying that in the Bible and in the religions of man in general the word "spirit" goes with ecstatic phenomena; with possession and exorcism; with sudden influx of power and exhibitions of power; with visions, dreams, and divinations; with violent emotions, babblings, and mysterious utterances; with ecstasy, rapture, and mystical union. Such phenomena, commonly associated with the experience of the sacred or divine, are woven into the warp and woof of religion, both Christian and non-Christian. Hence, it has been commonplace in the church to associate the Spirit with "mysticism" of various kinds, and people have expected the Spirit to give them religious experiences that clearly satisfy a deep and universal need for power and fulfillment.[13]

Yet we cannot but be struck by the reserve and sobriety of the Bible with regard to the traditional manifestations of the Spirit. Indeed, there are stories such as those of Samson, Saul, Elijah, and Elisha in the Old Testament, and references to speaking with tongues, prophecy, ecstasy in the New Testament, that unmistakably point in the direction of universal "spirit possession." It is probable that both in Israel and in the early churches people were much more impressed with spiritism than our Biblical material indicates. Nevertheless, it is clear that dervishism was frowned upon by the teachers and prophets in Israel, and glossolalia was subordinated to faith and love by the leaders of the early churches (I Cor., ch. 14). What is decisive is that in the Old Testament spiritism is placed in the context of God's dealings with his people according to his covenant of justice with them. And in the New Testament, the Spirit is inseparable from Jesus Christ and the new covenant established between God and his people by the mission of Christ.

Nevertheless, it may well be that the imagination in the context of the history of God's people entertained the notion of the Spirit as a ghost, an ethereal being in human form and with human will and passions, although this may be putting the matter in too sharp an outline. (I Kings, ch. 22.) It may be that there was no fixed notion of the being called the Spirit and that it was often thought of as windlike or as a fluid. Our texts do not permit us to reproduce a *conception* of the Spirit that might be valid for all of them.[14] The truth is that an understanding of the doctrine of the Spirit in terms of an imagined entity is not only hopeless but also fruitless. What or who is the Spirit who falls upon, pounces upon, envelops, enters, fills, lifts up, is drunk of, speaks, hears, guides and teaches, intercedes, etc.? All these verbs cannot be logically attached to the same imagined subject. The theologically significant thing about the Spirit is not that he or it produces certain psychic and physical effects (as in religion in general), but that he or it is the Spirit of the living God, of the God of Abraham and Moses and Jesus and Paul, who is in commerce with his covenanted people for their life and peace. The Spirit may be imagined as a ghost, or wind, or fluid. But he or it is *conceived*, not in itself, but as the Spirit of God who is the Lord of his people. And conception here is not a matter of entertaining an image, but one of understanding the manner of God's dealings with his people through his servants. The Spirit of God is the Spirit of the Lord who delivers, commands, provides, directs, his people by the agency of his servants. The constant thing about the doctrine of the Spirit is not that he or it causes "spiritual" phenomena, but that by the Spirit of God there is in Israel and in the church victory, prophecy, peace.

In Scripture the phrase "the Spirit of God" has its place in narratives or expositions in which the characters are the Lord, his servants, and his people. The Bible constrains us to modify the general religious notion that a spirit enters an individual and causes some sort of ecstatic exhibition. God's business is not with certain individuals as such, and his Spirit does not enter anyone for his private benefit. God's business is with his people, and with his servants the kings and prophets and priests for his people's sake, for the sake of their life together as his covenanted people. The point of the narrative in which the Spirit appears is not possession as such, or any particular experience or type of ecstasy that may ensue from it. It is, rather, that those upon whom the Spirit of God comes are enabled to do the will of God for his people, whether in prophesying or in fighting. For instance, Elijah was perhaps an "ecstatic prophet," but we are told nothing definite of the nature of his ecstasy. We are told that the Spirit took him hither and thither in the fulfillment of his prophetic mission. (I Kings 18:12.) Jesus received the Spirit in his baptism, but here again his "experience" is not reported except insofar as it marked the beginning of his mission. (Mark 1:10-11.) The visions of Stephen, Peter, and Paul are clearly significant, not as private ecstasies, but as they concern the future of the church. (Acts 7:54f.; 10:9 f.; 9:3f.) In short, the Spirit of God belongs in narratives that have to do with the Kingdom of God, in the sense of God's reign over his people, in their knowledge of him and faithfulness to his covenant of righteousness with them. It is the distinguishing characteristic of the notion of the Spirit of God in Scripture that its activity belongs in

Israel and in the church.

In postexilic writings there are texts which prophesy that God will pour his Spirit upon his people as such. (Isa. 44:3; Joel 2:28f.) It is acknowledged by Ezekiel and other prophets that God's covenant with his people, their fulfilling his law and obeying his voice, shall be fulfilled at a time when the Spirit shall be poured upon them or when it shall work within them for a new heart and a new spirit. (Ezek. 36:26) It has become clear that it is not enough for the prophets and kings of Israel to receive the Spirit; a holy nation shall come into being only when the young and old in Israel shall drink of the same Spirit and shall thus be enabled to walk in the ways of peace. Once again we may notice the reserve of our texts with regard to matters of ecstatic experience which readily fascinate the human mind. Doubtless in the new age there will be dreams and visions. Yet the hope of the writers is that the people will hear the Word of the Lord for obedience and peace. But the point here is that the Spirit shall be poured upon all flesh. (Isa. 44:3; Joel 2:28 f.)

4. THE SPIRIT IN THE CHURCH

This hope becomes established and clear when we turn to the New Testament where the coming of the Spirit issues in the formation of the church, the new Israel of God. The Spirit comes upon the disciples of Jesus in a manner not unlike its rushing upon the servants of God, the kings and prophets of old. (Acts 2:1f) The people find them acting as though "filled with new wine," and the prophecy of Joel is fulfilled among them: "I will pour out my Spirit; and they shall prophesy." (Acts 2:18) As Paul expressed it, "For by one Spirit we were all baptized into one body—Jews or Greeks, slaves or free—and all were made to drink of one Spirit." (I Cor. 12:13) Even though God continues to endow his servants, the apostles, teachers, miracle workers, and others in the church with sundry charismata or gifts, he has now made his people members of one body by baptism in the name of Jesus and by the outpouring of the Spirit among them. Thus, "there is one body and one Spirit, just as you were called to the one hope that belongs to your call, one Lord, one faith, one baptism, one God and Father of us all, who is above all and through all and in all." (Eph. 4:4-6) The Spirit is the Spirit of God and the Spirit of Christ. But he is the Spirit poured upon God's people, so that to speak of the Spirit is also to speak of the church. The work of the Spirit is the life of the church, and the Spirit is now inconceivable apart from the "life together" of the people of God the Father and the Lord Jesus.

The doctrine of the Spirit and the doctrine of the Christian life belong together. This is a statement to which the church's theologians as well as the people at large have perennially borne witness. As it were, nobody doubts that a holy life is the work of the Holy Spirit. However, we have been prevented from thinking this thesis out adequately by a failure to do justice to the church as a communion of believers. Our habitual individualism or social atomism has kept us from a proper understanding of our life as fellowmen and therefore from a proper understanding of the work of the Spirit in the church. In line with the usual introversion of the religious man, Christians have thought of the Spirit working in them but hardly among them. Their common language has been, "Spirit of God, descend upon my heart." They have imagined themselves as beings who exist and live, not by their life together, but by a "nature" physically and logically prior to their existence and life as members of the body of Christ. They have thought of their bodies and minds and hearts as their private property, received from God or nature. They have imagined themselves as originators of thought, feeling, and action, and as having the springs of their lives within themselves. Hence, they have sought their power within themselves, and as related to God, and not to the church or their fellowmen. With such notions of their own givenness and their private priority to their life together, they have thought of the Spirit of God as working within them rather than among them. They have fancied that their communion with God, their knowledge of God and peace with God, are matters of private interaction with God. Thus, they have construed the life of the church, not as a communion among themselves, but as common commerce with God. Thus, they have separated what Scripture has bound together, and obscured the work of the Spirit, who works mightily among us and in us at once. But we know no love of God for us without our love for one another, no forgiveness of God without our forgiving one another, no faith or hope from God, except as we have faith toward one another and hope in one another. We hear no good news from God or from his Son, except as we speak it one to another. Such is the church, and the Spirit of God is in it for the Kingdom of God.

What is needed for proper doctrine of the Spirit is a proper doctrine of the church as a "communion of saints." We are to seek the Spirit, not in some private ecstasy, or even in a private power or virtue, but in the presence of our fellowmen and their life with us. The insepa- rability of the Spirit and God's people, as well as the inseparability of the Spirit from the Father and the Son, means that there is a sense in which the Spirit is the Spirit of the church. It cannot be in every way right to associate the Spirit with Christ and not with his church, even though there is no Spirit in the church that is not the Spirit of the Father and the Son. In the Bible, God, his servants, his people, go together, and the Spirit upon his servants is also the Spirit upon his people. As we know no Spirit without the servants, we know no Spirit without God's people, that is, without our neighbor who is under covenant with us.

Thus, it is not quite unobjectionable to allow our imagination to present the Spirit to us as wind, or fire, or oil, or water, without the confession that the bearer of the Spirit is the Son and our brother. To associate the Spirit with a ghostly being in preference to our flesh and bone brother is a confusion of thought that has had not only dire theo- logical consequences in distorting the doctrine of the triune God but also dreadful consequences in our misunderstanding the life and the meaning of the church, of God's people, for our knowledge of the glory of God upon the face of his Son and among his people. If the Spirit is among God's people, then our fellowmen belong with our conception of the Spirit, and we may not think or imagine the Spirit apart from the human face. Hence, it is incongruous and profoundly misleading to speak of the Spirit as "it" and not as " he."

It is true that the Spirit is not my brother and my brother is not the Spirit, or "the Spirit" and "my brother" are not interchangeable words. The Spirit is he without whom I would not have a brother; or I have a brother who is God's servant to me by the working of the Spirit between me and my brother. I have no way of imagining the Spirit without my brother, or when I imagine the Spirit, I am not to imagine a ghost or a fire, and not my brother. The bearer of the Spirit is my broth- er. We do not say that the Word of God is an " it "; because Jesus is the bearer of the Word, we refer to the Word as he. So also we should not say the Spirit, or wind, or breath is an "it," because my brother is the bearer of the Spirit. We should say "he." Indeed, we say Jesus is the "Word incarnate," but we do not say that my brother is the "incarnate Spirit." Jesus is my brother's and my Savior, and my brother is not my

Savior in the same sense. Still, in the company of Jesus, in the church, I am not saved without the service of my brother. If my brother is not the Spirit as Jesus is the Word, still, he is the bearer of the Spirit so that without him I do not receive the Spirit of God. We must properly reserve the word "is" for Christ and the Word. However, it does not follow that we have to say my brother is *not* the Spirit. Or if we say that, we have to find a manner of speech that states the case of my brother as well as possible. We have to so state the case that we express the reality of the church as the locus of the Spirit, or our faith that God by his Spirit enables my brother to be his agent for my salvation from sin, the devil, and death.

Perhaps we should say that the Spirit indwells my brother. (I Cor. 3:16.) It is better to say that the Spirit interdwells my brother and myself for our communion with God and with one another in Christ Jesus. But "interdwells" is the language, not of imagination, but of conception (which is true also of the incarnation), which has to do with the process of the Christian life, and it is to be used to speak of the grace of God whereby my brother is God's servant in my behalf, and I am the servant of God in his behalf. We are speaking of God and his servants, and when we speak of these, it is not proper that we should speak either of the Word or of the Spirit as "it" in preference to "he." Our business is not with a word or with a spirit but with the living God and his people. We do speak of the Word or of the Spirit as "it," but when we speak properly of God and Christ and Christ's people, we say "he." The point is that according to the nature of the case and to the Christian doctrine of the triune God, it is not proper to speak of the Word as he and of the Spirit as "it" because our business is with God, with his Servant, and with our covenanted fellowmen, his servants.

Our imagination in this matter is misleading. Although it is true that "the Father" and "the Son" invite us to imagine these two as persons, whereas "the Spirit" does not do so with equal clarity, the doctrine of the Trinity does not permit us to think of the Father and the Son as persons and of the Spirit as impersonal. It constrains us to use the word "Person" in the same sense for all three, who are our God. It would not be correct to say that the first two Persons are personal, whereas the third Person is impersonal.[15] The fact that our theologians have perennially wavered on this point has been a source of much confusion in the church. The theologians' ambiguous language in this matter has been a reflection of the confusion of the Christian people who,

even while confessing God the Trinity, have thought of the Father and
the Son as Persons, and of the Spirit as a spectral presence known
mainly in terms of extraordinary "spiritual" experiences. But this confusion has been due to a failure in the communion of saints. When the
brother is rejected or even ignored as the bearer of the Spirit, the Spirit
is indeed imagined as a ghostly Power.

In traditional theologies, the assumption, in its way fully justified, has been that the Spirit is the bearer of God's power. The doctrine
of God has been frequently "demythologized," and the spectral Spirit
has been turned into God's grace, or wisdom, or presence, or action, or
especially power. Thus the doctrine of the Spirit has been theologically
superfluous, because the Spirit, as wind or air in motion, has become a
characterization of God's action. The Spirit has then become an adjec-
tive rather than a noun, or if a noun, an abstraction.[16] Such a way or
ways of thinking have made it difficult to understand the doctrine of the
Spirit as a Person of the Godhead.

Our thesis is that this difficulty is due to the Christian's failure
to recognize—rather, to think out—that the presence or action or power
of God are known among God's people. The work of the Spirit, whether
in illumination or in sanctification, whether in ecstasy or in obedience,
occurs in the communion of saints. There has been no servant of God,
no prophet or king, who has not been called in, as well as for, the
church. Not even the baptism of Jesus and the descent of the Spirit
upon him occurred outside of Israel and the life together of this covenanted people. We know no Spirit of God, or the manifestation of his
power, outside of the body of Christ. There is no "vertical dimension,"
communion between God and a man, apart from a "horizontal dimension" in the Christian life, that is, from human intercourse. It is right to
say that the Spirit came upon such and such a servant. But it is wrong
to forget that this coming occurred by the prior presence of the Spirit in
the church. Moses and Elijah, Jesus and Paul, are no more God's people
than the people of God to whom they are sent. If they prophesy by the
grace of God, so they prophesy by God's grace which they receive from
Israel and the church. They have no word of God without the word of
their fellowman. They speak as they hear the word of God, but they do
so as they hear the word of men and speak men's word to them. Their
business is with God as those who have business with their fellowmen.
Even as they are rejected of men, they are their beneficiaries, and they
serve God as they are served by their fellowmen. By the grace of God,

who has called them to be his servants, they receive grace and truth by
the service of their brothers whom they serve. In short, they are servants by the service of the church.

Therefore, one has to speak of God, Jesus, and the people (cor-
respondingly one has to speak of God, Christ, and the Spirit). One has
to speak of God and Christ, and of Christ and the church. It is not
enough to say God; one has to say the Son of God. It is not enough to
say the Son; one has to say the Spirit. As there is no Jesus without the
church, there is no Word without the Spirit. Without the Christ, there is
no church. Therefore we say, the Spirit of Christ. But without the
church, there is no Christ. Therefore we say, the Spirit interdwelling the
church, or, in this sense, of the church. As Christ is the Word of God,
the church is the place of the Spirit of God. One can no more logically
say the church without saying the Spirit than one can say Christ without
saying the Word. Christ is the Word of God; as the Word, he is of God.
The Church is the habitat of the Spirit; as the habitat of the Spirit, my
neighbor is of God. In our usage, the Spirit signifies that the knowledge
of God and obedience to God and every grace a Christian enjoys is in
"the communion of saints."

According to Scripture, the business of the living God is with
his people for their faithfulness to the covenant by which they exist to
him and one to another for peace and good. It is in the transaction of
this business that the Word of God is uttered and the Spirit of God
comes upon his servants. But Abraham, Moses, Aaron, Joshua, Gideon,
Saul, and David; Elijah, Amos, Isaiah, Jeremiah, Ezekiel; Barnabas, Peter, and Paul: all these servants of God— prophet, priest, or king—are
presented to us as men who are not sufficient for their calling and the
work imposed upon them. There was, for all their virtues, a chasm between their power as human beings and the power required by their duties as God's servants. The case of Jesus Christ was no different. He
was like all the other men of God, a human being, with the limitations
of a human being. This is not the place to enter into the mystery of
Christology. What is clear is that in him the wisdom and the power of
God were revealed in the obedience of a man who "suffered under Pontius Pilate."

All this confronts us with the peculiarity of the work of the living God that contradistinguishes him from the supernatural beings of
natural religion. The latter wield lightning and thunderbolts; they hurl
big things and turn nature upside down. They have no servants because

they do their work by "miracles" and exhibit their power, not through the weakness of men, but by overwhelming it. They have neither Word nor Spirit, and their power crushes everything before it because they neither create nor redeem a people. It is even said that they are idols and vanities.

It is not so with the living God. Since his business with his people is their communion with him and one with another in justice as his "intelligent creation," he reveals his deity, not by overthrowing the creature who is "flesh," but by calling him to rise up and serve him for the peace of his people. Men rise up in obedience and go forth in power, for all their weakness and insufficiency, and the Word of God is heard and his will is done in his having a people and in his people having a God. This is the miracle that has occurred among God's people: the very sign and signature of the living God in all his superiority and perfections. This is the miracle of the Holy Spirit, the miracle of Jesus Christ, the miracle of the one and only living God of his people. If a person is not impressed with the servants of God, if he does not recognize them and receive them, if he is not surprised by them and does not rejoice in them, he knows neither the Word nor the Spirit and has turned his back to the living God.

In our judgment, what has perennially obscured the doctrine of the Spirit and confused Christians as to the signs of the Spirit among them is the failure of the churches to exist as communions of God's people, bound one to another as forgiven sinners and human beings. Because of certain soteriological and theological preoccupations indicated at the beginning of this paper, Christians have failed to acknowledge that the saving work of God is done in the context of a living society in which the people of God acknowledge the responsibility to become a "priesthood of believers," doing what they must do as human beings who are bearers of the Spirit of God, approaching one another to give and to receive the humanity for which Christ died and was raised from the dead. The bond that binds the Christians together in the church is unthinkable apart from the work of the Spirit, who reveals to every man his neighbor and establishes the true bond of fellowmanhood in a common life, where all the gifts of God for our salvation are received by the exercise of humanity in liberating and uniting grace, which men must give one to another and receive one from another if they are to live as God's people and according to their proper destiny.

The work of the Spirit has been traditionally identified with

ecstatic experiences induced by enthusiasts and often generated in mass
meetings. People have "spoken with tongues," quaked and ranted, and
have otherwise undergone deep emotional upheavals. Today "spirituality" is identified with mild and temporary ecstasies that people expect
from worship, prayer, and Sacraments. Since God is free to influence
men's emotions in any way that befits them, it is not for a theologian to
pass judgment upon the many varieties of "religious experience" that he
finds in the history of the church. On the other hand, he cannot make
ecstasy of any kind normative for the church and therefore he cannot
identify the work of the Spirit with it. Therefore, he also cannot make
the language of ecstasy and inebriation decisive for the doctrine of the
Spirit. The work of the Spirit, as the work of Christ, is no more and no
less than our restoration to the Creator as a society bound to him and to
one another in freedom and love proper to creatures. If we find the
Word in Christ, we find the Spirit in our neighbor, without whom we
know neither God nor ourselves, neither Christ nor redemption, neither
sin nor salvation. For we do not know Christ except by the Spirit, who
reveals him to us in the communion of saints as they bring one another
before Christ in their common strivings against the devil and all his
works *among* them.

3 The Knowledge of God in the Church

INTRODUCTION: THE CHURCH AND THEOLOGY

The purpose of this chapter is to explore the significance of the church for our knowledge of God. The question is, what difference does it make for our knowledge of God that we are a people who exist and therefore may think as the people of Jesus Christ?

This is not a traditional question in the church, and we receive no ready answer to it from traditional theologies. If the question had been asked, the answer to it might have been as follows: There is a common knowledge of God, a *sensus divinitatis*, which goes with our being "rational animals." Any sane man who considers the world, the given physical world and the things in it, knows by direct apprehension that there is a God who is the Creator of the world and of all the things in it. This fact is evident both from the universality of religion and from our own reason and conscience.[1] When the Deists presented belief in "God, freedom, and immortality," or some similar list, as a matter of "common sense," they expressed a traditional conviction that none but exceptional unbelievers would have denied. The Christian philosophers, with their several versions of "proofs" for the existence of God, have in their own way confirmed this traditional and common notion.[2] We are not concerned here to examine the validity of this attitude to our knowledge of God. Our point is that the existence of the church is irrelevant to it.

The Christians, of course, realized that natural theology does not include the peculiar doctrines of the churches. It says nothing about the Fall of man and original sin, the incarnation and the atonement, prophecy and miracles, the Sacraments and the resurrection of the body. It was evident that the knowledge of God, insofar as it involved such doctrines, is attained not by reason but by revelation, not by nature but by supernatural oracles. It is for this reason that the questions of the authority of Scripture, and of the church which taught the supernatural origin of the Bible, were crucial for Christians and formed the basis of any exposition of the Christian doctrine. The function of the church traditionally was to act as the authority whose teaching is the ground of the believer's knowledge of God in the full sense of the expression. It was commonly known that the church's authority is derived from Scripture, which in turn was known as revealed truth on the church's authority.

Both natural and revealed theology have ceased to be a matter of Christian common sense. Good churchmen, of course, continue to believe in God. But they do not always rely upon their "sense of Deity" or "religious experience." They believe in a personal God (the God of whom the churches speak and in whom the people think they are expected to believe) rather than know him by intuition and reason. They may still intuit and argue that there is a "First Cause," or "Power behind the universe." But their "Father God" is one in whose existence they believe in spite of at least occasional protests from their reason and experience. "The problem of evil" is a lasting and serious impediment to their certainty with regard to a God of love. It constantly obscures the presumed benignity of God and leaves their minds in such a state of confusion as to make it necessary to believe in spite of the light of evidence to the contrary. Hence, it is commonly accepted among us that a man's belief in God is a matter of his will rather than his mind and that it is his private affair. It is understood among us that there is no constraint of reason or intuition that makes belief in God a question of common sense. Belief or unbelief is a matter of private judgment, and everyone is entitled to his own convictions with regard to religion.

Men's attitude toward revealed religion, "the Trinity and the incarnation," is strictly a matter of "orthodoxy." Everybody, as it were, knows that men believe in the Trinity through the teaching of their churches and by habit formed through their participation in their liturgy. Everything depends upon whether they belong to a "right-wing" or a "left-wing" church—not quite everything, because a man may belong to a right-wing church without being too convinced in his beliefs; and he does not find himself in difficulty if he is discreet and quiet. For after all, a man's belief is his own private affair, and his neighbors respect his privacy.

In short, religion or belief in God, the personal God of the churches, is no longer a matter of common sense. It lacks the force of a public intuition or reason. The same is true of "revealed" doctrine. Faith is a private matter of the will rather than of reason, and it is hardly proper to speak of "knowledge of God."

We must observe that believing which is other than knowledge, being a thing of authority rather than reason, commonly occurs in churches that are social institutions. In principle, and usually in fact, authority is exercised by institutions through their officials, and belief is a response to the teachings and ways of institutions. The traditional problem of "faith and reason," or the contrast between believing and knowing with regard to God, has its setting in churches as institutions and derives its seriousness from the exercise of authority by such churches and the reason of those who live under them. The perennial tension between belief and knowledge in the Christian churches is a function of the reality and definition of the churches as institutions which through their cult and officials provide the people with certain supernatural benefits received by "faith" or by believing that indeed such benefits are at the disposal of these institutions.

The traditional theologies of the church, including the doctrine of the knowledge of God, which is our present concern, are to be understood in the light of a deep-seated image of the church as a sacred institution which goes with the traditional practice of the churches as the means of grace for the benefit of the believing community. Where the bearers of grace are the clergy, and the people are its recipients, it is hard for the latter to recognize themselves as the bearers of grace as ministers of Jesus Christ in a weighty sense. It also follows that for the knowledge of God, they have to depend upon the clergy, as they do for grace in general.

If there is anything that is characteristic of theology during the last three or four decades, it is the effort to apprehend and comprehend the church as "the multitude of believers" first and as a cluster of institutions secondly. As though under a new pressure from God and the world alike, the World Council of Churches, Biblical theologians, systematic theologians, and many in the leadership of the churches have together been proposing a new and living awareness of the church as "people of God," "the household of God," "the covenanted community," "the body of Christ," "the servant church," etc., which have the aim and purpose of impressing upon the Christian public the image of the

church as a community committed to Jesus Christ as "the light of the
world." This day of promise and peril for our "one world" has become
the day of the church's self-examination and thus of a sustained concern
with the theology of the church, so that we may well call ours "the age
of ecclesiology."

This new preoccupation with the doctrine of the church is an
inevitable and inescapable response to the need of the church in our
time. The ecumenical movement and the World Council of Churches
have shown that the Christian churches as institutions led by a minority
of officials are not competent to fulfill the responsibilities of the church
in our day. It has become increasingly clear that unless the people of
the many congregations of the church take their membership in the
body of Christ seriously and learn to think and act as Christ's people,
the words and actions of their leaders and supposed representatives in
the councils and sundry organizations are less than adequate as the
"church in action." There is too much of a hiatus between the church as
a cluster of institutions and the church as the "multitude of the faithful,"
and so long as this hiatus exists, the church's witness to Jesus Christ remains confused and abortive. It is not possible to have a living church
with dead members, no matter how well organized and ably led.

When theologians today call the church the people of God,
what they intend more or less clearly is to teach that the people themselves are responsible before God to act as the church: in love and justice in a manner relevant to their situation and the need of the world in
our day. Love and justice are modes of grace among the people and
subsist only in the people's actions toward one another. Institutions cannot love for the people, and their leaders cannot be just for them, and
there is no peace except among the people.

The Christian responsibility to obey the will of God, to love
and to do justly, has always been recognized. But it has not always
been clear that love and justice belong to the *esse* of the church, so that
without these there is no church. There has been a more or less confused notion in the church that since we are "justified by faith alone,"
love is neither primary nor crucial. People have been encouraged to
make sure that they believe, and to do the best they can in the matter of
love. Concessions have been made to sin, human nature, self-love, limited loyalties, and the like, and love, as the very essence of the Christian life, has been pushed out of its central place. But what is faith without love and without hope? Without love, there is no faith, and there is

no faith without hope. If the church exists by faith, it also exists by love and hope. Hope and love are no more and no less "works" than faith. All three are gifts and all three are responsibilities in Christ's company. Our life is a communion, and communion is by faith, hope, and love.

2. THE TRADITIONAL APPROACH TO THE KNOWLEDGE OF GOD

The church as the communion of saints is the setting of the knowledge of God as well as of obedience to God, of theology as well as of ethics. There is today a new understanding of the church as the life of God's people together, by which they believe in God as well as obey him. This understanding is the possibility of a new approach to theology itself as disciplined thinking in the knowledge of God.

The new ecclesiology will not permit us to carry on with our theological work in the traditional way. It is no longer feasible to relegate the doctrine of the church to the latter parts, say the fourth part, of a theological system.[3] One may no longer proceed from the doctrine of God to the doctrine of man, and then to the doctrines of Christ, the Christian life, and the church, in this or a similar order. One may no longer start with discussions of reason and authority, of nature and Scripture, of revelation and experience.[4] It is not that these matters are to be forgotten, but that they are to be approached in a new context and newly understood. We must continue to learn from our predecessors but we have to do our own thinking in the light of the self-understanding of the church today and in view of our special responsibilities as the church in our world.

Our difficulty with the tradition is that it did not take the communion of Christians seriously as the context and condition of the knowledge of God. The knowledge of God, whether through reason or through faith, was regarded as an act or state of the mind as possessed by the individual as such. Since it is this or that person who thinks and believes, it was assumed that knowledge occurs in a subject with regard to an object. Thus in the knowledge of God, the knower was a man and the known was God. The existence of the knower as a fellowman was irrelevant to his knowledge of God. Thus the communion of saints was irrelevant to the faith by which people knew God. Faith required not communion but authority, not "life together" among God's people, but their common life in an institution. For this reason, revelation was construed as a creed and consisted of a series of statements that were believed on the authority of Scripture and tradition. Scripture was taken as a repository of statements about God and man, and tradition was taken as a repository of Scriptural doctrine with regard to the faith and the life of the people. Scripture and tradition alike were in custody with the church as an institution, and the knowledge of God available through them was received by the people severally as individual minds participating in the cultus of the church. Given the existence of the Christian man as a beneficiary of the church, in the knowledge of God and his will, faith took priority over reason, and credulity took the place of intelligence. A man—assuming he used his mind at all—had to choose between believing and thinking, and since he lived and hoped by the grace in the church, he did not permit his thinking to interfere with his believing. In any case, in the knowledge of God his business was with the church and not with his fellow believers. Hence, what is strangely lacking in traditional theology is a fruitful attention to the communion of saints as the context of our knowledge of God.

Consequently expositions of Christian doctrine by theologians had little or no connection with the church. The existence of God, his nature and attributes, his relation to the world, his providence, were discussed as though the Christians' life together had nothing to do with their knowledge of God and his way. When theologians considered the doctrine of creation, they attended to the physical world and to man with his peculiar nature and powers. They reflected on the creative act according to the analogy of causality or construction, and on the end of creation according to the analogy of human purpose. In any case, communion was no significant clue with regard to either the nature or the meaning of creation. Whatever the theologians might have been talking about, they were not talking about the church, or the nature and meaning of the existence of fellowmen.

When theology inquired about man, it was concerned with Adam and his descendants, with Adam's original righteousness and his fall, with his nature and faculties and powers, with his sin and salvation. The mind of the theologian moved from Adam to his descendants and back, from Adam to Christ and back, from the Fall to original sin and back, from Man to mankind and back. And through all, fellowmanhood was hardly allowed to illuminate either the nature or the sin of man, either his life or his death, either his origin or his destiny. Theological anthropology might have been influenced by Christology, but ecclesiology was not even within the horizon when theologians argued about the Christian understanding of man.

What shall we say about the doctrine of Christ? Whoever Jesus Christ was for traditional theology, he was hardly a fellowman. The man born of Mary, who ate with sinners and argued with Pharisees, who suffered and was crucified, was known as the Son of God and the son of man, but not as the author of the communion of saints and as himself having his existence by communion. The theologians discussed and argued about the pre-existence of Christ, about the two natures of Christ, about the incarnation and the atonement, and even about the resurrection and ascension of Christ, with hardly a flicker of light from his communication with his people in their justification and sanctification.

In its consideration of the Christian life itself, the main line of theology in the West, following Augustine, was preoccupied with the problem of "grace and free will," or "grace and nature." The basic question was, What roles do God and man play in salvation and a righteous life? In medieval theology no effort was spared to establish man's responsibility for good works, although the sovereign grace of God was upheld. The consequence was some synergism that sought to do justice both to grace and to man's freedom. The Protestants came forth with *sola gratia, sola fide.* Thus they opened the way for the deistic insistence upon substitution of the human will for the grace of God in man's practice of virtue. Once again, it is not our intention to pass judgment upon a matter that remains a bone of contention. What concerns us here is that whichever horn of the dilemma was grasped, the common position was that the Christian life, with regard to its possibility, is an affair between God and the individual, that it is the individual agent who is able or unable to fulfill the law of God. A combination of jealousy for God's supremacy and the *idée fixe* of the individual as the moral agent made it impossible to see both God's grace and a man's will as functioning in the covenanted community, or among men as well as in them.

The locus of grace was seen in preaching and the Sacraments, and nothing was made of the church as the means of grace. Regeneration was obviously an act of God, and not man's, which occurred by baptism. The man who had sinned was forgiven, or justified, through the institution and not through his fellowmen. Sanctification was regarded as the work of the Holy Spirit within the Christians, with or without cooperation on their part severally. And obviously "the resurrection of the body, and the life everlasting" could have been seen only as a work of divine omnipotence. Indeed, Christians might have exercised "justice, mercy, and peace" toward one another and they might even have edified one another for piety and good works. They might have been good examples one to another, more or less. However, grace was from God through the institution. With regard to the means of grace, everyone existed as an individual agent under the preaching, the Sacraments, and discipline of the church.

In short, whether for the knowledge of God or for the salvation of his soul, a man depended upon the church as an institution and not upon the church as the communion of saints. And theologians said nothing to lead him to think otherwise. Presumably the Christians' life together had little to do with either faith or life.

We may not overlook the improvement made by Schleiermacher when he interpreted Christian doctrine as a disciplined statement of "feeling," or, as we say, "experience." The Pietist and Evangelical attention to the source of doctrine in the religious man's communion with God, or his experience, gave Christian thinkers a new perspective upon the origin and nature of our knowledge of God. It produced a profound modification of the traditional problem of authority and reason by making revelation itself a thing that is experienced rather than taught by the church and received by an act of submission. Faith was thus freed from credulity, and the knowledge of God was made a matter of the individual's experience, a certain intuition of "divine realities." The object of faith was recognized as an "empirical reality," even though it was commonly understood that the individual also made faith a leap of the mind beyond experience.

However, theologies based upon Christian experience have not been conspicuous in their attention to the communion of saints. It has been assumed that the knowledge of God is an affair between God and the person who experiences him.[5] Since the individual is the subject of the experience of God, as he had been the bearer of reason and faith, once again it was assumed that the church is a multitude of those who have experienced God rather than the locus, as a "covenant community," of their experience. Theologies based upon Christian experience minimized the church as an authoritative institution, but they were unable to see it as a communion of saints or to understand the knowledge of God in its living context in the church.

The tradition of individualism has been so firmly entrenched in Christendom that not even the so-called neoorthodox theology has been able to explore adequately the significance of the church for our knowledge of God.[6] "Faith-knowledge" continues to be regarded as a consequence of God's self-revelation which impinges upon the believer and becomes the source of "life together." There has been much argument as to *sola fide*, "grace and nature," revelation and response, with more or less Augustinian rigorism. But the tradition of seeing knowledge as private is so strong that Christian theology continues to ignore the church as the context of our knowledge of God.[7]

In short, traditional Christianity and its theologies have been dominated by an individualism that has made the church theologically all but irrelevant.

This is not to overlook the fact that Christians have always been taught to love one another. Christian faith has always been expected to bring forth fruits of righteousness in good works. Since Augustine, it has been axiomatic that there is no faith without love and no love without good works.[8] In spite of much argument and misunderstanding, Christians have, as it were, always known that faith without love and the works of love is dead. Nevertheless, the requirement of love and good works has left the individualism of traditional Christianity intact. For after all, good works are what the individual believer performs. Doing good is a movement from the doer of the deed toward the object of his love. It is not so much an act of communion as the way one gives evidence of his faith and salvation.[9] Good works with a minimum of communion among justified sinners have followed logically from the impregnable individualism which has formed the mind of traditional Christian piety. Thus, neither the faith nor the life of the Christians, neither their knowledge of God nor their obedience to him, has done justice to the reality and the responsibility of the church as a communion of saints.

3. COMMUNION AND THE KNOWLEDGE OF GOD

a. Communion and the Love of Jesus

If the church, which is the mother of the believers, is the communion of saints, as we today are inclined to believe, then we have no life without the church; if we have no life, then we have no mind or will as Christians, and therefore, without communion, we have no knowledge of God. It is not enough to say that "outside the church there is no salvation." It must be clear that the church in question is a communion with its institutions and not an institution with its adherents. Outside the church there is no salvation because salvation is communion and communion is the church. Salvation is life. Human life is communion. Communion is the church. It is in this sense and way that the church is our mother, and the clergy are her servants entrusted with the preaching of the Word and the administration of the Sacraments. But if preaching is to be heard and the Sacraments are to be received, there has to be a church in the sense of communion. Hence, communion, no less than preaching and the administration of the Sacraments, is a means of that grace by which is the knowledge of God.[10]

What, then, is the communion without which there is no knowledge of God? Communion is the meeting of fellowmen initiated and continued by Jesus Christ, including faith, hope, love, peace, joy, and every blessing of the Christian life. At the center of it is the love of Jesus for his fellowmen, who are sinners, and their love for him and for one another. It is the reunion of forgiven fellowmen in mutual recognition as neighbors and brothers who are bound together in the bundle of life and exist by caring one for another as members of the body of Christ.[11] Communion is the coming together, by the approach and call of Jesus Christ, of men who have fallen apart. It is the reconciliation of enemies who have been destroying one another by each one turning his back to the other. It is the justification of each man by the other's dealing with him as a fellow creature who deserves his favor rather than his malice. It is the sanctification of each by the love of his neighbor. Communion is justice in the form of mercy and mercy in the form of justice, bestowed and received, with all the deeds that are justice, mercy, and peace. Communion is Jesus' knowledge of us and service of us, and our knowledge of him and service of him, and one of another, so that these three make one thing, which is communion.

There is a knowledge of man that is our response to Jesus Christ and with it one to another. There is much that we may learn from the sciences and the "humanities," much about our bodies and souls and social existence. But when it comes to our existence as fellowmen, Jesus is our light and our truth. We exist by his grace as his brothers, and as his brothers we know ourselves. It is always Jesus and I, my brother and I; Jesus, my brother, and myself. There is no leaving this twoness and threeness behind for a knowledge of man in general and in particular. We have to do first neither with universal human nature nor with the unique and spontaneous individual. We have to do with Jesus and those he loves, and with ourselves as loved and loving. The concrete man is the fellowman, and it is as fellowman that each man knows himself as one of Jesus' people. So it is that he exists, and so it is that he properly knows himself. He cannot know himself properly as a creature or as a sinner, as body, mind, or soul, unless he knows himself by Jesus' meeting him in the company of those whom he knows, by this meeting, as his fellowmen. In short, the Christian man knows himself as he is known by Jesus in the company of Jesus' people.

b. Communion and the Creature

This knowledge is by forgiveness, and by forgiveness a man knows himself as a creature who is a sinner. A man's knowledge of himself as a creature is inseparable from his knowledge of himself as a sinner. A man sins by denying that he is a creature, that is, by rejecting the love and forgiveness of Jesus. The "Pharisees," the scribes and lawyers, around Jesus, were farther from the Kingdom of God than the "sinners" because they rejected Jesus, because they rejected the forgiveness of sin he offered to them as well as to the publicans and harlots. They rejected him because it was unbearable for them to receive the grace of Jesus, to acknowledge their dependence upon him for their peace, that is, their life as fellowmen. Their zeal for the law and the "righteousness of works" was an insistence upon their own self-sufficiency and, therewith, a denial of their existence as creatures. Their piety by which they declared their dependence upon God and their independence from Jesus and their fellow sinners around them was the great deceit that justified them before themselves but not before God. When they turned their backs to Jesus, they turned their backs to God and no longer knew themselves properly as creatures.

A man exists as a fellowman. He is a creature as a fellowman.[12] He exists by the love of his fellowman, and, being a sinner, by the forgiveness of his fellowman. When he rejects the love of his neighbor as the means of his existence and turns away from the forgiveness of his neighbor which restores him to his existence as a fellowman, he denies that he is a creature. A sinner knows himself as a creature when he will allow his neighbor to forgive him. (And the first neighbor of the

Christian is Jesus Christ.) Our self-knowledge as creatures is by way of
our self-knowledge as sinners, but this knowledge is by the forgiveness
of sins in the church, which is Christ's people and body.

We do not deny the traditional view that the creature is a finite
being, in time, space, and power. It is true that a man is a creature as a
being who is born and dies and between birth and death is subject to
every sort of limitation. It is true that if a man did not die, he would
hardly have his peculiar sense of creatureliness. It would be foolhardy
to say that in this matter the tradition from Augustine to Tillich has
been wrong.[13]

Nevertheless, it must be pointed out that a Christian exists by
the grace of Jesus and as his fellowman, and he does not exist otherwise. Since man exists as a fellowman and is a creature as a fellowman,
he knows himself as a creature in the company of his fellowmen. In the
presence of Jesus there is no knowledge of ourselves as creatures except in our communion one with another as forgiven sinners. Even our
knowledge of ourselves as mortals grows within and out of our communion one with another. The sting of our death is sin. The misery of
our anxiety about life is from sin. The power of death over us is by
temptation which occurs in our communion as fellowmen. The quality
of human finitude emerges within communion; human creatureliness is
a quality of communion.[14]

By the love of Jesus, it becomes clear that we are creatures
who sin one against another. Since sin is the rejection of our dependence upon our fellowmen for our existence, we must understand the
creature as a being who exists by communion.

Creation as seen through sin is not simply a making. Many
things are made, or manufactured. But the fellowman is created. Physical, technical, and even artistic analogies to creation are profoundly
misleading.[15] Creation presupposed in human existence is an act by
which we live as fellowmen, and this act is communion. The proper
analogy to the creative action of God is the communion of Jesus with
sinners and the sinners' communion one with another. If we are restored
to our knowledge of ourselves as creatures by the communion of our
fellowmen, it stands to reason that creation itself is by such a communion. Salvation is not creation. But since creation is intelligible through
salvation, and salvation is by communion, communion is the proper
clue to creation. As the agent of redemption is a fellowman, so also the
agent of creation is the same fellowman. But the fellowman both

creates and redeems by speech. Hence, we say that creation is by the Word of God, who is Jesus Christ. We say this in the church, where under Christ we exist by the love and forgiveness of his people and our fellowmen.

c. The Knowledge of God

In the company of Jesus, God is known by the forgiveness of sins. He is known by the love of Jesus for sinners and by the sinners' love one for another. He is not known by the love of Jesus without the love of sinners. If sinners were not surprised by their love for Jesus and for one another, they would hardly be surprised by the love of Jesus for them. It is as we know how hard it is to be forgiven and to forgive that we are astonished at the forgiveness of Jesus. The miracle of Jesus and the miracle of the people of Jesus are inseparable one from the other.

At Jesus' Table, joy and glory occur among sinners who turn one to another in hope because of Jesus' presence. And their turning one to another amazes them as they are amazed at Jesus' turning to them. They are amazed at each other and they are amazed at him. They cannot take each other for granted and they cannot take him for granted. As they know that they themselves are not competent to forgive, they know that Jesus' forgiveness is of the living God. (Mark 2:1f.) When they see Jesus, they glorify God; they do this logically enough, although not by deduction but by faith, which is their response to God among them. God reveals himself by miracle, in miracle, as miracle; but the miracle is communion. The communion of Jesus and his people is the miracle, and the miracle is the act of God whereby he reveals himself as our God.

When we start with the concrete situation of the Christian, that is, with sinners around Jesus, we know God by the forgiveness of Jesus and of his people. God reveals himself as the Father by the love of Jesus in the church. He distinguishes himself from Jesus in that the love of Jesus is a miracle. The love of Jesus is not an instance of human love, but the very possibility of it, and as such, it is not the love of man but the love of God. But God does not distinguish himself from Jesus in that we are saved by a love other than the love of Jesus. God distinguishes his communion with us from that of Jesus in that he creates us by communion. But he does not so distinguish it that we may commune with him and not with Jesus. He presents himself as our Creator, but

not as though we could live and move without the love of our Fellowman. Thus, God reveals himself and hides himself, so that we may not
depend upon him without depending upon Jesus and the people of Jesus. He constrains us to cleave to him as we cleave to Jesus and to our
neighbor, and thus declares himself the Creator who is known by communion.

God is the Creator of communion, and not of being in general,
or of individual being.[16] He is the Ground and Power of the existence
of fellowmen, the Creator of fellowmen in communion. But the creation of fellowmen in communion, as against the "creation" of things,
whether visible or invisible, is thinkable only as itself an act of communion. The Ground of communion is God who communes, as the
Ground of Being is a God who *is*. The Ground of Being may be known
apart from Jesus, or even apart from men's life together. The Ground of
communion exists by communion; and we have no knowledge of him
apart from the communion of Jesus with us and our communion one
with another. We are not to leave Jesus and our brother aside and commune with God. But when we commune one with another, God communes with us and we with him, who is the living God. We must distinguish between God and man, but we may not think of them apart. We
cannot say that God forgives, but not man; or that man communes, but
not God. God who forgives communes, and man who communes forgives; but God as God and man as man. Forgiveness and communion
are inseparable. God and man are inseparable. But we know this as
Christ's people. This is the mystery of Christ, and after him, the mystery of the church. The living God is the Lord and Father of Jesus and
his people, and he has not at any time been without them.[17] It is incongruous with the character of the God we know in Jesus Christ and the
church to think that God, in his aseity, in his eternity and superiority,
ever willed to be without Christ and his people. We know God as the
God of his people, and another God we do not know.

This is why the Christian church, following Scripture, has always denied the bare unity of God. Monarchianism is a heresy, even
though it has been widely held, especially in the Western churches. The
living God is the triune God who is not above communion but, rather,
has his being and joy in it. Monarchian names of God, such as the First
Cause, Absolute Being, the Ground of Being, the Power behind the universe, and the like, are misleading, and even pernicious, insofar as they
obscure the name of God as Father, Son, and Holy Spirit. God the Crea-

tor and Redeemer is God who communes, and as this God, he is with the Son and his church.[18] The traditional doctrine of the Trinity has been repeatedly reinterpreted, and no doubt will continue to be reinterpreted. But the living God we know in Jesus' company remains the Father of the Son and the church in the Holy Spirit.

Here we must avoid a mystification and the bad logic that goes with it. When we say that the Ground of Being in general *is*, but the Ground of communion himself communes with his creation, we do not mean to imply that God communes with us as do our fellowmen. We are not saying that there is an experience of communion with God that is the same as our experience of communion with our fellowmen. God is not a "rational animal" next to others, and he does not make sounds in his speaking as do our fellowmen. He does not exist as another man and he does not commune as one. We have to express ourselves in these negatives, not because God is a being altogether different from man, but because he is the triune God, and Jesus Christ and the Holy Spirit, no less than the Father, are God. The communion of Jesus Christ with us and our communion one with another are the communion of God the Father with us. God the Father does not commune with us as a being separate from the Son and the people of the Son. He communes with us as the Father of the Son and our Father in the Spirit. We distinguish the Father from the Son and the church because we know the communion of saints as a miracle. When we speak of God who communes, we speak, not of the Father as such, but of the triune God. There is one communion, which is the communion of the Father, Son, and Holy Spirit with us. And this one communion is none other than the communion of Jesus with sinners and the sinners' communion with him and with one another, which is the communion of the triune God with us in his mystery and power.

d. Of Faith-Knowledge

According to traditional Protestant theology, we know God by faith, and faith has been contrasted with reason. The relationship between faith and reason has been endlessly debated, and it is today. The "Reformation position" has been that we know God by faith and not by reason. The "Anglican position" has been that we know God by both faith and reason, which supplement one another. The "liberal position" has been that the knowledge of God is a matter of experience that includes both faith and reason. And it has not been uncommon to credit the knowledge of God to some combination of intuition and reasoning that convinces us that there is a Being behind and beyond the world in which we live. In general, it is not common sense but faith that goes beyond reason and believes in a God who is man's helper in his quest for peace in a world where life is perilous and evils abound.[19] Since "the problem of evil" resists solution, faith is characterized in terms of trust, venture, leap, if not against reason, then beyond it. Faith has become a passionate opinion that is held for the sake of tranquillity and hope in a world where troubles are often, if not always, present or around the corner.

Once again, we must point to the irrelevance of the church to such ways of believing or thinking about faith. Faith or belief, justified by experience, or as a venture, is an act of the individual in a world that is a bewildering mixture of good and evil. The subject of faith is the individual organism as he suffers the vicissitudes of life, and its object is a supermundane Power which or who might enable him to overcome the evils lurking in his world. The business of the believer, in his believing and doubting, his trusting and rebelling, his hope and despair, and all the turbulences of his mind and spirit, is with an unseen Being, beyond the world and with power over it, who shall intervene in the perilous goings-on around him for his well-being and peace. That there are people around him who share his concerns and contribute to his weal and woe is not unimportant. But they are not his God, and his passion and prayers are not directed toward them. His "ultimate concern" is with the Ground and Power of Being, with the Supernatural and the Ultimate, with the Holy and Wholly Other, who alone is able to be his help and comfort in life and in death. If he associates with his fellowmen in his religious quest, it is not for communion with them but for communion with his God. His faith is an affair, in his spirit, of the alone with the Alone; a private affair and business with "the Power behind the universe."

But faith in the presence of Jesus has a different character. It is the acknowledgment of God in the forgiveness of sins. There is no faith in the church apart from the recognition of miracle in Jesus' company. Here we know that we are sinners who are forgiven and forgive one another. We know that although it is we who forgive, it is God who forgives so that sinners are in truth forgiven. There is no logical congruity between one man's forgiving and another man's being forgiven. Man plants and waters, but God gives the increase. We do plant and water, but when the plant grows we know that it is not our doing; we know that it is of God. Faith is the knowledge of this miracle, and it is knowledge in the church. It differs from other knowledge, not in its lesser rationality or in being an experience, but as a response to God's self-revelation in Jesus Christ and his people. Where the miracle of forgiveness occurs, there is faith.

One is always tempted to deny that the miracle occurs. One is tempted to deny that what occurs is miracle. One may not forgive and be forgiven. One may "forgive" and deny that it is God's doing. God does not force a knowledge of himself as does a man or a thing. Hence, it is always possible to deny him by rejection, either by refusal to forgive or by pretending to forgive. Hence, faith is an act of the will as well as an act of reason. But it is not, therefore, an arbitrary and illogical act. It is a response to the grace of Jesus in the church and a matter of knowledge proper to its object, who is God. It is the knowledge of God who at once reveals and hides himself in the forgiveness of sins, reveals himself in that we are forgiven and hides himself in that he forgives as his people forgive one another in the presence of Jesus.

Our knowledge of God is unique knowledge, not because he is transcendent Being and therefore cannot be known as we know other beings, but because we know him by forgiveness, because God, in revealing himself, hides himself, because God's forgiving us and our forgiving one another are inseparable one from the other.[20] If God forgave apart from the forgiveness of Jesus, we would know him as we know a man. We would say, "God forgave, and not Jesus," as we say, "John forgave, and not James." We would know him by an action that is his and not another's. But since God forgives by the forgiveness of Jesus and by our forgiving one another, and in so doing reveals and hides himself in a way peculiar to himself, we know God by a unique knowledge, which we call "faith." Everything either discloses itself or hides itself. We know it or we do not know it. God alone is known in his revealing himself and in his hiding himself and by our receiving or rejecting him as we receive or reject the forgiveness of Jesus and our neighbor; so that in receiving we know and in rejecting we are ignorant. As Augustine, and after him Calvin, insisted, humility is the first prerequisite of the knowledge of God, but the humility in question is the miracle of willing to be forgiven and to forgive, which is the gift of God in

Christ Jesus in the church.[21]

Christ Jesus reveals himself in the church as the faithful and
constant man with whom "there is no variation or shadow of turning
due to change." His forgiving is the very exercise of his faithfulness; of
his knowledge of us as his fellowmen, of his turning to us, and of his
putting himself in our place as sinners who are creatures. Faith is the
exercise of fellowmanhood on his part toward us first, and on our part
toward him secondly. It is his faithfulness as our fellowman; his being
present to us as our neighbor, and his loving us as himself and his hope
in us for our presence to him. Faith as we meet it in Jesus is none other
than his truth toward us in the truth of his humanity and ours, in his
truth toward us which restores us to him and one to another. In short, it
is his knowing us as his fellowmen, by which knowing he forgives us
our sin or turning away from him and from one another. The faith of Jesus is his fidelity which overcomes our infidelity, that is, his forgiving
us. He forgives us by remitting or covering our sin. But his forgiveness
is true, that is, forgiveness which issues in our salvation, because it is
an act of a fellowman's fidelity by which he presents himself to us as
our fellowman. It is an acquittal that renews the bond of humanity in
the communion of fellowmen, acquittal that sets us free for Christ and
for one another and makes peace among us.

Thus, Christ Jesus knows us as fellowmen, as his fellowmen,
who exist by their communion one with another. He knows us as "flesh
and blood," as "body and soul," as the living who are anxious for our
lives and bitter for our losses. We are to him indeed "empirical objects"
who can be seen and touched. But we are known to him also, in our humanity, as his fellowmen who present themselves to him in our speech
no less than in our eating with him. In our presenting ourselves to him
in our speaking and hearing, He knows us who exist by communion, no
less in hearing us than in seeing us, so that did he not hear us, he would
not know us. He knows us as his respondents, in the self-knowledge he
induces by his knowing us, in our guilt and freedom in hearing him and
speaking to him. His is a knowing in which seeing and touching, speaking and hearing, although distinguished, are inseparable one from the
other. As a knowing by hearing, it is a knowing that is from and toward
faithfulness, so that, were there no question of faithfulness, or turning
toward or communion, it would be no knowing at all. In this sense, it is
faith-knowledge. It is knowing because by speaking he is present to his
fellowmen as such, and by hearing he has his fellowmen present to

him. But it is also faith because neither is he present without faithfulness nor are his fellowmen present without their faith and sin. Such faith-knowledge is not beyond reason; as a matter of speaking and hearing, it is the exercise of rationality by fellowmen.

But Christ Jesus is not visible to us as we are to one another. For this reason it is said that he binds himself to us by the Holy Spirit.[22] The sign of Christ's presence in the church is the faith of the Christians whereby they, as the members of Christ's body, forgive one another, rather, are themselves faithful one to another for their very existence as fellowmen. Faith is by hearing the word of Christ, but our fellowmen are given to us as Christ's vicars, so that when we hear them and speak to them, we hear Christ and speak to him. He is present to us, among us, as one of us, as we are present one to another and thus present to him.

Thus we know him and one another as fellowmen. This knowledge comes by hearing and speaking and is from faith to faith, which is inseparable from the works of love. Faith is to be distinguished from knowledge and knowledge from love. Yet where the one is absent, so are the others. How is one to be faithful unless one hears and speaks, unless one is present to his fellowmen? How is one faithful except as one loves and does the works of love? Still, one knows by the faithfulness of another and for one's own faithfulness, and one is faithful by the love of another and for the love of him. There is no knowing without hearing and speaking. But since it is one's fellowman that one knows by hearing and speaking, there is no knowing that is not fulfilled in faith, love, and hope.

But what of our knowledge of God? He who does not know his brother, as explained above, does not know Jesus the Christ, and he who does not know the Son does not know the Father. In "the order of knowledge" everything depends upon the Spirit, who reveals us one to another in our faithfulness and knowledge of one another. The miracle of the presence of our brother is one piece with the miracle of the presence of Christ with us, and the presence of Christ signifies, and is, the presence of God. The knowledge wherewith I know my fellowmen (a knowledge bound to faith and love) is the same wherewith I know Jesus Christ and the Father. The same knowledge that is by "the communion of saints" is the knowledge of God the Father, Son, and Holy Spirit and the knowledge of the church, my fellowmen. The Father we do not see. The Son we do not see. The Spirit we do not see. Our brothers we

see. But when it comes to knowing, he who knows his brother knows
God, in the same way and sense. We know both God and our fellowmen in such a wise that without faith, there is no knowledge, and without love, there is no faith. But love is justice, mercy, and peace in our
works in the church.

Faith and knowledge, as we have tried to show, are, in communion, inseparable one from another, but, one asks, how are they related to each other? The answer is that to know is to hear, and to hear is
to have a fellowman present to us. But our fellowman's presence puts
us in the position where we may be faithful. To know one's fellowman
is to have him present in his addressing himself to us, present as one
who has a claim upon our faithfulness. In this sense, knowledge comes
before faith. It produces faith in that we know One who is faithful to us.
But it does not produce faith in the sense that there is physical connection between our knowledge and our faith. Knowledge is acknowledgment, and faith is faithfulness, and the first may not issue in the second,
although the second does not occur without the first.

However, there is a sense in which faith comes before knowledge, that is, the faith of him who is known. Christ's self-presentation
to us as faithful is logically and actually prior to our knowledge of him.
Our neighbor's self-presentation to us as a sinner in Christ's company is
logically prior to our knowledge also of him. But in neither case is *our*
faith prior to our knowledge of the other person. Our faith is a response
and not the condition of our knowledge. It is illogical for us to think
that either Christ or our neighbor is present to us by virtue of our faith.
He is present to us by his Word, and we know him by that hearing
which is a consequence of his self-presentation of himself in his Word.
Of course, we do not know him "merely" by hearing, because he does
not "merely" speak to us. He is present to us by his Word, and we acknowledge his presence in our hearing him. In communion, speaking is
self-presentation, and hearing is the acknowledgment of the presence of
the speaker. And it is confusing to call (acknowledgment or) knowledge faith. One may speak of faith-knowledge, not because this knowledge is by faith (trust, faithfulness, etc.), but because here the present
one claims our faith.

But how may we speak of God and Christ, whom we do not
see? Are they not known by faith and not by sight? According to the
above discussion, Christ and God present themselves to us in and by
the communion of our fellowmen with us, and we know them by their

self-presentation to us in the word of our fellowmen. Our faith is no more the ground or reason of our knowledge of them than it is the ground of our knowledge of one another. God reveals himself (and hides himself) by the Son and the Holy Spirit, the Son being Jesus and the Holy Spirit interdwelling the communion of saints. The unseen present themselves by the seen and heard, this being true not only of God and Christ but also of our fellowmen. And in the case of all three, we know and are to be faithful. Faith is not an alternative to knowledge, but an element in communion inseparable from knowledge. Knowledge is by hearing a man in his word; faith is faithfulness to the man who is present to us by his speech.

It has been asked, especially lately, whether our language about God is literal or metaphorical. Some say it is analogical, others symbolical, and still others mythical. Those who deny that our language about God is literal think of him as transcendent Being who "exists" differently from beings in time and space, which are objects of literal denotation. Since, according to them, God is infinite Being, language we use to signify finite beings is inappropriate to God and is used about God metaphorically, or symbolically.[23]

The answer to such positions is that the living God is known by his grace and speech, and the language we use about him is literal and not metaphorical. We do not speak of God's forgiveness on the analogy of man's forgiveness; there is in the church no human forgiveness prior to God's forgiveness. Forgiveness is first God's act in Christ Jesus and literally refers to it. There is also a subordinate forgiveness which is man's doing, Christ's first and ours secondly. This is literally man's forgiveness. God forgives as God; Jesus forgives as our faithful Fellowman; we forgive as sinners being forgiven. God communes with us by our communion one with another, and he forgives us "our debts, as we forgive our debtors." There is no place here for metaphor.

Our communion one with another is a sign for God's communion with us, not in the sense that we infer the invisible from the visible, but in the sense that God reveals and hides himself in our communion among us. The words and deeds of truth among us may be signs of our communion among us, and when they are such, they are also, by the very logic of communion, signs of the presence of the triune God among us. Our communion as forgiven sinners is a sign in the sense that it is the miracle by which God communes with us. The miracle is a sign, not by a movement of our minds from the visible to the invisible, but by God's forgiving us our sin and uniting us with Christ and his people. In the knowledge of God we are to stay with the visible, or with our fellowman. Our problem is not to see invisible reality by the things visible, but to receive the forgiveness God offers us by the hand of our sinful brother. There is, of course, a sense in which forgiveness itself is invisible. But as an act of communion, its invisibility is not that of ultimate Being which we are said to know by an ascent of the mind from the finite to the Infinite, or from the many to the One.[24] Forgiveness is invisible as the action of God, who reveals and hides himself in the mutual forgiveness of his people.

Among sinners gathered around Jesus, God is known by the faith that receives one's brother as the angel of God and the bearer of God's forgiveness. Thus we know ourselves as fellowmen, as fellow creatures and fellow sinners, and we know our God as the living God, the Creator and the Redeemer, who is Father, Son, and Holy Spirit. There is indeed a literalism that is idolatry and not faith. But the answer to such literalism is not a set of negations and metaphors. There is nothing obvious about the notion that God is the In-finite, the Un-ending, the Un-changing, the Un-spatial, etc. Indeed, the living God is not a creature. He is the Creator. But he is the Creator by his Word and Spirit, the Creator who is the Redeemer, and the Redeemer who is the Creator, and he is known as both in the company of Jesus and his people. It is not through our negations but by God's speaking and our hearing, by our speaking and our hearing at the Lord's Table, that we know the living God. We must indeed shun idolatry. But we must do this as forgiven and forgiving sinners who have no God but the Father of the Son in the church and by the Spirit. When we leave the people of God, we find not God but idols, not life but death, not knowledge of faith but the ignorance of sin. In short, God is the living God of communion, as we ourselves are alive by communion, and our knowledge of God in all his perfections is by communion, in communion, and for communion. In this sense, the church is the presupposition of the knowledge of God as it is of our life as fellowmen.

PART TWO—*HOW GOD ACTS*

---

4 *Three Dimensions of Will and Willing*

1. A LOOK AT THE HISTORY OF IDEAS

It is traditional in the Christian church to discuss the will and willing in connection with the ability to choose between right and wrong and with the ability to act according to one's choices. In the ancient church, especially among the Greek fathers, this ability of man to choose and to act accordingly was accepted as essential to moral conduct. It appeared to them as self-evident, as it did to Aristotle, that unless men are able to choose between alternative actions proposed by the mind, there is no such thing as good and evil conduct.[1] It was evident that God had created man as a rational being and that rationality included willing. This is how Clement of Alexandria saw man as created in God's image, and he did not consider the fall of Adam as having resulted in the loss of either rationality or the freedom of the will. He attributed sin to weakness and ignorance as well as freedom, and he saw Christ, above all, as instructor and preacher. This axiom of man's freedom was modified by Origen, and later by the Cappadocian fathers, but it was not denied and it remained characteristic of the mind of the Eastern churches.[2]

In the West, there were long and complicated discussions of our subject. For our purposes here, I shall lift out several themes that remained basic to these discussions.

a. Augustine bound his doctrine of the will to that of love, and

love he regarded as *pondus animae*. He saw man basically in terms of
his love of the Good. The whole life of man, according to Augustine, is
the pursuit of goods, and ultimately of the Good itself. It is in this
movement toward the Good that man has a will or, rather, is a willing
being, and here it is that he exercises "free will." For the movement of
the soul toward the Good is a free movement in which man chooses between good and evil, as proposed by the intellect, and against desires
that move him away from the Good toward evil and finally the loss of
being itself.

   We need not go far into Augustine's denials of the freedom of
man to do God's will, which he made in his anti-Pelagian writings. He
did insist that because of the fall of Adam and original sin, man is incapable of righteousness without the grace or power of God. He maintained man's ability to distinguish good from evil and to choose between them. But he denied the power of the will to do the good without
God's grace. He did not deny man's love for the Good, but he did deny
his power to attain it, especially to do the will of God whereby he might
attain it. The point, however, is that Augustine regarded the will as freely tending toward the Good, and love he regarded as the basic exercise
of human nature as created by God and possessed by a man by birth.[3]
Human nature, as constituted by soul and body—by the rational and
voluntary action of the soul and the desires and passions of the body—
was to Augustine, as to the Greek fathers, a creation of God with which
he sought the Good and did good and evil.

   b. In Scholastic theology, attention shifted to the question of
the relationship between reason and will, the two elements of man's rational nature. Controversy was mainly with regard to the ability of the
will to resist and work contrary to reason. When, as in the writings of
Thomas Aquinas, the emphasis was upon the will as the bond between
reason and action, it appeared that the will chooses and acts according
to good as envisaged and presented by the mind. When, as in Duns
Scotus, the emphasis was upon the fact that the will does act contrary to
reason, the will was seen as free in relation to reason and, as in Augustine, as the more basic element of the soul. Reason was seen as at the
service of the will, and the will as the lord of reason. But whether the
one or the other was given the greater weight in moral action, reason
and will were treated as elements or faculties of the soul, possessed by
the individual person by creation, and as constitutive of human nature.
A man was born with reason and will and exercised them by a power

inherent to his soul as that particular person.

c. We need not tarry with the views of the soul held by the Protestant Reformers and Protestant scholasticism. The scheme of reason, will, passions, was maintained. It was agreed that man should choose and act according to understanding and should thus be the master of his passions.[4] Calvin described the misery of man, psychologically as we would say, in terms of the ruin of both understanding and will through bondage to the passions that filled man's life with sin and confusion. Calvin denied free will with respect to righteousness before God, even while he recognized man's ability to enjoy more or less of peace or order in his political life. He was impressed with the havoc played by the lusts of man in his daily life and took a dim view of man's ability to live justly with his fellowman. Above all, he adhered to Augustine's thesis that without grace man does not have the power to obey God's law as summed up by the great commandment. However (and this is pertinent to our argument here), Calvin continued the ancient tradition of seeing man as endowed with a soul by creation and a "nature" by his birth and inheritance. The same is true of Luther and the Protestant theologies of the time.

d. In modern philosophy we find no radical change with regard to the soul, its origin and faculties, especially as it affects our argument. For instance, Descartes continued to regard the understanding and the will as the two faculties of the soul, which he sharply distinguished from the body. He saw the will as possessed of freedom, and freedom as the ability to choose among acts proposed by the understanding.[5] It was evident to him that the will freely follows the dictates of the understanding and gives a man the ability to rule over his passions and to set them in order.

e. To turn to British philosophy, John Locke regarded the understanding and the will as two powers of the mind or spirit and distinguished them from the "modes of pleasure and pain," which go with sensation, bodily and mental.[6] As for "liberty," he says: "The idea of liberty is the idea of a power in any agent to do or forbear any particular action, according to the determination or the thought of the mind, whereby either of them is preferred to the other. . . . Liberty cannot be where there is no thought, no volition, no will; but there may be thought, there may be will, there may be volition, where there is no liberty."[7] Locke thought in terms of activities and powers rather than in terms of being and faculties. It is therefore all the more impressive that he regarded the understanding and the will as the powers of the human soul by nature or as such. He sees the individual person as the bearer of these powers, and his refusal to hypostatize the will does not lead him to question the traditional theory of the soul, which regarded the will as a natural endowment of a man. To him, the will is a power of a man.

f. When we turn to Kant we find that in him the Western theological and philosophical tradition has come to an impasse. The discussion of the will in relation to reason has become impossible because "pure reason" knows no freedom of the will; in truth, it does not know the will. It is not true that we can know ourselves as free in the sense that we know the objects of scientific thought. The soul as envisaged by "pure reason" has one power and not two: the power to see the world, or the things around us, in terms of causality. The soul of man who has the two powers of reason and volition does not belong in the world of science. It is a noumenal, autonomous reality: man as confronted with the "ought," with the moral law, with duty and responsibility. It is as moral agents that, by "practical reason," we assert our freedom and accountability. We "know" we are free because we are under an "ought"; we are under an "ought" as having freedom of will. This will is not a power among powers or a faculty among faculties. It is the power of the noumenal man to act autonomously as by a law apart from all laws of the physical world, and even apart from his psychological drives and passions.[8]

Kant asserted the autonomy of the will without arguing properly how it is that the will acts freely in producing effects that belong in the empirical and physical world. For indeed a man comes and goes, rises and sits down in the world of "pure reason," and he does all this "freely" in the line of duty. It would appear that the "real" man is free, and that "the phenomenal man," enmeshed in the systems of causality, is less than "real." Kant can be interpreted this way. But the word "real" has no clear meaning in this context. How is the world of morality more real than that of science?

Perhaps we have here a new vision of "voluntarism." In any case, Kant gives us man as a soul endowed with a theoretical and a practical reason and he both asserts and denies man's freedom in a way that states rather than solves the dilemma of "freedom and determinism," which suggests that it is wrong to treat will and willing in terms of the nature and actuality of an individual man.

g. Even though we are not able at this time to examine theology and philosophy since Kant, we may well be justified in making the general statement that in our intellectual tradition as a whole, will and willing have been attributed to human beings as their native possession and action respectively. Theological, metaphysical, psychological, ethical, discussions of the will and willing, in spite of great differences among them, are continuous in that they work with an idea or image of man, according to which each man, by virtue of his created or natural constitution, is a moral agent in the sense of being responsible to choose the good as against the evil and to act accordingly. This idea is, in our judgment, behind, or at least involved in, our traditional and common difficulties both with the idea of the will and with the paradox of freedom and causality, which continues to cause much theoretical and practical confusion.

2. WILL AND WILLING IN SOCIAL INSTITUTIONS

Let us begin with the fact that a man as a moral or responsible agent has little concern with, or even awareness of, the problem of "free will" that has exercised the theologians and philosophers of our tradition. There is to him no question of his freedom to act as a moral agent. As Kant saw clearly, moral law and freedom are inseparable one from the other. As a member of society, a man is responsible to do certain things and he is responsible not to do others. He ought to do this and not to do the other. He ought not to kill, steal, commit adultery, lie, and cheat. He ought to pay his taxes, obey traffic laws, and respect the rights of others. He ought to do useful work, military service, and at the right times go to the polls and vote. He ought to obey the law and play properly his roles in various institutions. In general, he ought to observe liberty, equality, fraternity. In fact, a large part of a man's duty and responsibility belongs in the republic to which he belongs, and he is to do his duty both intelligently and voluntarily. His duty is to obey the laws that enable people to live together for their common good and their good severally.

Will and willing occur as men take their place in the several institutions of a given society and do their part in them. Men do not will the right or the good outside of their social and common life. They neither know their freedom nor exercise it except as they make decisions for or against actions demanded by the common life and its institutions. A father, a student, a businessman, a soldier, a churchman, a citizen, are confronted with their particular moralities and duties. They will as father, student, churchman, citizen. Institutions have their customs, mores, laws. Customs, mores, laws, are things one wills for or against. Where there are laws, there is will and willing. Where there are no laws, there is no will and willing. It is true that physically there is a potentiality in man for willing. But we do not know that this potentiality, in organic terms, in terms of organic impulses, is for willing. The willing occurs as response to social habits and laws, and what characterizes it is not a subjective phenomenon but an objective demand made upon us. The nature of willing corresponds to the nature of an institutional demand, and we can speak about it intelligibly only in terms of that demand. The very vagueness of the words "will" and "willing," when considered in themselves and in relation to "reason" or "passions," indicates that it is impossible to give them definite meaning except in terms of definite duties and responsibilities that we meet in our participation in society as a cluster of institutions.

All this means that the soul as the bearer of reason and will is an abstraction. The individual soul as thinking and willing belongs in culture and does not occur by nature. There is no soul by a divine creative act or by physical generation prior in logic and as fact to a man's existence as a member of society, which is not a natural but a cultural entity. We know no moral law, or duty and responsibility, or freedom corresponding to duty and responsibility, in a "human nature" unformed and uninformed by our common life in which we are parents, teachers, citizens. "Human nature" is a contradiction in terms in the sense that there is no humanity, no reason and will, in a natural condition apart from a culture with its institutions, language and laws, rights and freedoms. Human nature without human society is a matter of opinion and not a matter of knowledge, and knowledge is more reliable than opinion.

In its institutional context, the phenomenology of the will does not simply present us with the freedom of the will. What is certain and prized is not the freedom of the will but its consent to the ways and laws of social life. And this consent is given by habit rather than by the conflict and resolution implied in freedom. The character of a man is more reliable for civic virtue or goodness than his ability to choose between alternatives that present him with a more or less difficult problem for conduct. For this reason, moralists as far apart as Thomas Aquinas and John Dewey gave a prominent place in their ethics to habit as an established disposition to action.[9] Freedom to choose appears when habit presents the agent with a problem, and the outcome of choice may be good or evil. Freedom introduces an element of uncertainty in the common pursuit of the good. Hence, habitual action is preferred to the exercise of free will, and the more so when there is a conflict among equally strong impulses for and against an acknowledged duty.

Willing, as a strenuous effort, appears when character is insufficient. The law insists upon the will and its freedom when an agent fails to conform to it. Our freedom is impressed upon us when we are strongly moved to disobey the law, and especially when we have disobeyed it and are guilty of transgression of the law. In the context of our common life and its institutions, free will is evident above all in our accountability for wrongdoing. Free will means, in one clear respect, our punishableness. It corresponds to the right of the custodians of the law to exercise distributive justice and to deal with an agent according to his violation of the law and the guilt incurred in doing it. This is not to deny that a man of good character obeys the law voluntarily or willingly. He wills to obey the law. But in his case conflict in an act of decision is reduced to a minimum. He hardly has an impulse to disobey the law or not to conform to it. He does not consider seriously an alternative to conformity. He conforms readily, without deliberation, voluntarily, to the demand made upon him.

The traditional conjunction of reason and will, favored by philosophers, is not real in willing the right as proposed by the institutions and laws of our common life. Intelligence has no certain role to play in willing to conform to the law. It is, rather, a matter of demands and compliance. Here a man acts, not as a deliberator and maker of more or less difficult decisions, but as a man of habit who is a will or has a will in not opposing the law. Reasoning in this context is not needed. It is irrelevant to the moral act. To be willing is what is right and properly prized by the law. The question raised by the law with regard to conduct is not whether it is rational or intelligent, but whether it is right. The failure of the tradition of moral philosophy to do justice to the institutional setting of our language about right and wrong has led to discussions of this language that are not adequately illuminating. Willing is not a natural doing of man, but an institutional phenomenon, and as such, an action not of the rational soul, but of the soul as will.

But, of course, the tradition of moral philosophy that conjoined the will to reason in the soul is not sheer error. The mind does present us with alternatives for action. We do deliberate as to what we are to do in a given instance. We do choose between apparent goods, and in so doing we follow one impulse rather than another. We do entertain proximate and approximate goods; we do entertain means and ends. We do seek satisfactions.[10] We exercise what is called "self-love" and enjoy the use of our powers and the "self-fulfillment" that accompanies our success in achieving our ends through proper deliberation and action. We choose the greatest apparent good, and in so doing, we act as souls endowed with reason, will, and passions. Thus we act as individual agents and as "rational" beings. It is this kind of thing which men commonly do that has led moral philosophers perennially to point to the individual as the bearer of reason and will.

However, this individual participates in the institutions and ways of a given society, and it is in so doing that he is an individual who exercises reason and will. His self-love and pursuit of the good with his deliberations and actions, as envisaged by our philosophical tradition, correspond to the goods and opportunities presented to him by the institutions in which and by which he exists as this individual. He is posited as an individual by these institutions, and his self-love, his exercise of reason and will, rather his deliberating and choosing, are done as inspired by the same institutions. Human self-love is a response to society, and the bearer of self-love, the human being of traditional moral philosophy, exists not only in but also by the common life of society. It is not a natural phenomenon, but institutionally social. Willing that follows deliberation, in its tending toward satisfaction and enjoyment, belongs in the same context as that other willing which is habitual and nonde-liberating. It is the willing of an individual with his needs and desires as formed by the common life of a given society. Individualism in this sense and political life go together, and its ethic is hedonism, which is in principle, in the above views of willing, insurmountable. The individual formed by a common pursuit of satisfactions may be more or less intelligent, but he is a hedonist and he does his duty as a hedonist.

3. WILL AND WILLING AMONG FELLOWMEN

Now, it is quite evident that hedonism is unacceptable as a complete theory of morals. Self-love, the seat of hedonism, is interpreted even by its advocates, be it Epicurus or Bentham or Dewey, so as to make room for altruism in some form or another. Everybody, as it were, knows that a man's life does not consist of his possessions and his enjoyment of them, even though no man can live without them. It has always been recognized that there is such a thing as friendship.[11] Although men have a common life and live it as individuals, they seek the recognition and respect and goodwill of their fellowmen. They meet as fellowmen, by twos and threes; they look at each other, and, more seriously, listen to each other. Although they may be engaged in some business together and in the pursuit of some common good, they may find among themselves a happiness that has no logical connection with their common life and interests. There is an exercise of humanity that is logically independent of any kind of role a man may play in the common institutions of society. It is not derived from self-love and the common pursuit of satisfaction, either physically or logically, nor from the family, or church, or school, or profession, or polity. It has nothing to do with the quest for any good, whether life or a thing in life. It has nothing to do with advantage, benefit, or prospect, or anything involved in self-love. It is inexplicable in terms of laws and customs. It is useless to the individual and irrelevant to institutions. There is a humanity that consists of the communion of fellowmen, of their recognition of one another as fellowmen, of looks, gestures, words, and deeds that belong to the existence of fellowmen as such without which there is no being in the human style.

There is a logical continuity between nature and institutions in the sense that certain needs of the organism are satisfied by our common life. This is clearly true in the case of the family, the state, the market, the school. But it is also true in the case of religion, which provides security and sanctions in innate terms. Of course, the continuity of institutions with nature is not always evident, as in the case of signs and symbols and in the "higher" needs of man by virtue of civilized life. Yet in spite of obvious difficulties, naturalists are able to argue more or less plausibly in favor of a continuity between nature and society.[12]

There is, on the other hand, no logical continuity between the satisfaction of organic need and communion of fellowmen. Communion, with respect to nature, is *sui generis*. The quality of communion and the quality of organic life are discontinuous, and there is no way of interpreting the life of fellowmen as an extension of nonhuman life. Fellowmanhood is a way of being that is peculiar to fellowmen and is constituted by communion itself. It is a mode of existence by speaking and hearing and one in which the individual fellowman is created in the speaking and hearing. Of course, speaking and hearing are done with the mouth and the ear of the organism. But the speech and the hearing of the organism are physically, not logically, prior to the existence of fellowmen. The fellowman is created *ex nihilo* in speech and hearing, so that with the speech and hearing of organisms engaged in a common life there is the speech and hearing of fellowmen, not for satisfaction in the common life, but for communion and for the existence of fellowmen.

It is not, therefore, proper to speak of the fellowman as a soul with reason and will. The reasoning and willing of the fellowman belongs in his communion with his fellowman and not in himself or in his soul, or as "an individual substance of a rational nature" (Boethius), or a "singularity of rational nature" (Thomas Aquinas).[13] The soul of the fellowman does not inhere in him as of his own nature, and his reason or will has no reality except in communion. If his will belongs to his existence as the partaker of a common life, it also belongs to his existence as a being in communion. Both the reason and the will of a fellowman are, as it were, there by his thinking and willing as a fellowman. Or, it is fellowmen who think and will as they commune one with another. Willing belongs with speaking and hearing, and there is no willing without communion. Fellowmen will as they commune one with another.

Fellowmen exist by communion, but the act of communion is by willing. They demand recognition one from another, and recognition is given or withheld. The authentic meeting of fellowmen in each case is one in which a right is claimed, a demand made, for faithfulness. When the claim is ignored and the demand not met, there is a violation, a breaking of the bond, which is bad faith and a cause for anxiety proper to fellowmen. Such ignoring and turning away is a willed act, and this is how fellowmen know will and willing. The will thus known is distinct from the will that operates under law and institutions. A fellowman does not will to acknowledge his neighbor by habit, and he does not exercise free will in choosing among impulses and goods.

It may be well to refer to willing in this context with regard to decision rather than choosing. Decision is not between projected satisfactions, but between hearing and not hearing a fellowman, between acknowledging him and not acknowledging him, between caring and not caring. Here the whole scheme of goods and evils under a transcendent and ultimate Good is irrelevant. One decides between turning toward and turning away from one's fellowman. So it is that one decides between good and evil, right and wrong, life and death. One decides to be faithful or to be unfaithful by a willing that is consequent, not upon the weighing of goods, but upon a response made to the demand of a fellowman for the justice of love. Decision occurs—rather, a fellowman decides—not by deliberation toward the solution of a problem (for choosing between greater and lesser goods), but by engagement or by facing his fellowman.

Deliberation and choosing indeed are indispensable for action that follows upon decision. It is unintelligent to acknowledge one's fellowmen without considering their rights and needs in the common life and its institutions. One has to be rational, as Aristotle and Dewey knew so well. But one must distinguish intelligence that goes with decision from intelligence that goes with choosing. There is a deliberation of fellowmen and another of organisms, even though a fellowman is an organism and must think as an organism who is a fellowman. The former belongs in the context of life together, the latter in the context of a common life. The organism deliberates toward satisfactions in view of impediments in the way of satisfactions. He thinks toward solving problems. The fellowman deliberates as one tempted not to act as a fellowman. He thinks as one confronted with the claim of a fellowman upon him to acknowledge him and to act accordingly. He thinks toward faithfulness as well as from faithfulness. He acknowledges himself as tempted to violate his fellowman by ignoring him and thinks as a repentant sinner. He thinks as a man of faith.

There is a will and willing that goes with "the communion of saints." Here both reason and will are subsumed under faith, and faith is the bond of the church, and is exercised by faithfulness among fellowmen. The soul of which reason and will are elements is not the property of the individual human being but the locus of life together. Reason and will are elements of a soul derived from communion and subsisting by faithfulness. As such, reason is concerned with a truth that is by faith, and willing is decision for or against it. Reason does not present the will with goods or with duties. It presents the will with the fellowman who calls upon another for truth and justice.

In this context, it is not clearly right to raise the traditional questions with regard to the freedom of the will in relation to reason on

the one hand and emotion on the other. Since the fellowman is not presented with the goods of the organism or with the duties of the citizen,
there is no question of the freedom of his will in relation to goods or
duties. In the context of life together, the traditional dilemma of determinism and free will does not belong in the center of moral life.

The fellowmanhood with regard to which a man must decide
is not so much an object of the mind as its logical presupposition. It is
not a thing to be conceived, but rather, a way of being and life that is
logically prior to all things conceived, and the goods and duties entertained by reason. In this respect, it is not proper to say that fellowmanhood is an idea of the mind that it presents to the will for decision, with
regard to which decision or willing might or might not be free. Fellowmanhood is the quality or "howness" of communion and is acknowledged as a response, which itself is at once a matter of reason and will,
rational as acknowledgment and volitional as decision. The question of
the freedom of the will arises, not in relation to reason, but with regard
to acknowledgment itself. Acknowledgment is by decision and places a
man in a position where he is to decide. There is no knowledge of one's
fellowmen without decision, even though decision presupposes acknowledgment. Even though at any given time a fellowman is in a position in which he has to make a decision-in-response as to whether he
will acknowledge his fellowman, his being in this position presupposes
that he acknowledges the claim of his fellowman to his recognition of
him as fellowman. The point here, however, is that the mind which
presents the fellowman with his responsibility to acknowledge his fellowman has its logical antecedent in the communion whereby this responsibility and with it the will subsist; and this communion is the human manner of being as such.

Communion is ontologically different from a life in common.
It introduces us into a realm of being different from that in which we
exist under law and in a causal nexus, under legal obligation or natural
necessity, as minds and bodies moved by reason and impulse. Neither
judgment of guilt before the law nor judgment of innocence before nature is congruous with judgment of righteousness or sin that is passed
upon fellowmen in communion. The debate between the lawyer and the
doctor with regard to guilt in violation of law does not belong in the
context of communion where decision is made for or against acknowledging our fellowmanhood. Neither the "guilty" of the lawyer nor the
"not guilty" of the scientist is the kind of judgment that either establish-

es or illumines the nature of the transaction that occurs in life together. The lawyer's insistence upon the accountability of an individual citizen before the law, and the doctor's insistence upon the origins of misdemeanor in disease, and the social psychologist's insistence upon the "social" sources of the same are, all three, incongruous with the existence of fellowmen in communion. One's insistence upon free will and another's insistence upon physical or social necessity are irrelevant to the character of decision that belongs in the intercourse of fellowmen.

The willing that occurs in decision is *sui generis* in the transactions of fellowmen in which one calls upon another for mutual acknowledgment, in which organisms and citizens put up a claim with regard to one another, to be heard by one another. There is a word which a fellowman utters to another that is other than the word by which men live a common life and pursue common goods, a word that is neither of the law nor of nature. This word evokes a response that either justifies or violates a fellowman, and the willing that goes with this response is neither free in the legal sense nor unfree in the medical or psychological sense.

Since this is a willing neither in relation to law nor in relation to organic impulse, it is not even willing as this act is understood in law and medicine. As a willing in communion, as response to a call to be a fellowman and to decide for or against it, it is constituted as willing by the call and as response to the call. As a willing in response to the call of the fellowman, it is not (guilty or not guilty) liable to punishment but, rather, sinful or righteous, making peace or evoking wrath.

The question is whether the use of the words "freedom" and "necessity" in connection with willing in communion are proper or illuminating. In relation to law, freedom is the ability to obey or not to obey it. In relation to an impulse, freedom is the ability to resist it. In both cases there is the assumption that an individual exists endowed with an ability to do one thing or another. But this is not the case in communion. The fellowman exists by the call of another and by his response to it. If he does not exist without communion, he has no will, free or otherwise, without the call of his fellowman. His ability to respond to the call appears with the call, or he makes his decision for or against hearing the call as he hears it. There is here no individual whose existence is logically prior to communion. Therefore, there can be no question of his having a will prior to communion or a will free to respond to his fellowman's call prior to the call itself. Indeed, he exists as a fellowman who may hear the call, but he exists by a society of fellow-men. His will is a gift, and so is his ability to respond to the call. He has as he receives, and he responds as he is called. It is equally true that he receives as he gives, and calls as he responds.

The fellowman is not free with regard to his fellows as he is with regard to the law. He is not free with regard to his fellows as he is with regard to impulses. How, then, is he free with regard to his fellows? His fellows do not *cause* his response as his impulses may be said to do. In this respect he is an agent whose action as fellowman does not belong in a nexus of causality. On the other hand, he is not a moral agent confronted with a law. Hence, he is not free and culpable as the lawcourt judges him. He wills in responding; thus, he is free. He wills as responding; thus, he is not free or autonomous in the legal sense. The word freedom in the context of communion has a meaning peculiar to this context. A man acts freely in the sense that he responds, and in responding he *may* acknowledge his fellowman. Yet the call of his fellowman posits this same freedom and puts him under a constraint all its own to acknowledge it and with it, his fellowman. Although this constraint is not the same as the forcing of a powerful impulse, it has a compelling quality of its own since the call that exercises this constraint comes with the authority of a fellowman whose communion with him is his very life as a fellowman. The law compels in common life. Impulse is imperious in the organism. The fellowman by his call exercises authority in the life together or in human life as the life of a fellowman. This call posits a fellowman, but it posits him as a responding being, by his responding to the call. The call creates, yet it creates by the response it evokes in the creature. The call and the response create the fellowman in communion, and communion is logically prior to the existence, and therewith to the freedom, of the fellowman.

The individual who is posited by communion is absolutely dependent upon it for his very existence. A fellowman exists by the grace of his fellowman and absolutely depends upon it for his existence as this individual. His fellowman may not acknowledge him. He may turn his back to him, and he may destroy him. The grace by which he is this individual is not at his disposal and as this individual he resents the freedom of his fellowman that places his own existence beyond his disposal. The individual thus dependent refuses to live by grace and seeks an autonomy that is as impossible as it is absurd. He nevertheless seeks it, and in seeking it he turns away from his fellowman and refuses him the grace by which his fellowman must himself exist. In so doing, he violates his fellowman and induces him to violate him in return. Thus human life is turned into death, and the joy of being is turned into misery. In this *massa corruptionis*, freedom is turned into bondage, and despair replaces hope as the quality of human existence. Fellowmen, in the language of a well-known cliché, cannot live with each other or without each other. Communion becomes mutual laceration and is full of the savor of death.

It is in this hell that Jesus Christ appears as the Son of the Father and bestows the Spirit of the living God upon the people of God in their bondage to sin and death. Fellowmen are restored to communion by the grace of God—the Father, Son, and Holy Ghost—by the grace that abounds among the Christians, so that they live by the grace of God in imparting grace one to another, in forgiving one another even as God forgives them by the forgiveness of Christ in the Spirit (Eph. 4:30-32). So it is that we know and acknowledge grace and with it the freedom of the Christian man in his willing to live and to give life by the grace of communion that is the life of the church and the life of the world.

In short, *human* willing is first of all, logically, a function neither of life in common and its institutions nor of the life of the organism with his impulses and pursuit of an apparent good. It does not lord it over reason, nor is it subservient to it. It does not rule the emotions, nor is it driven by them. It is not reason ready to act, and it is not emotions organized for action. It is neither the individual with his desire and power nor an element or power of his "soul." It is not he by nature or anything of his by nature.

Human willing as such is an element of the communion of fellowmen. It signifies that fellowmen may acknowledge their existence by grace, in their dependence one upon another, in their ability to turn toward or from one another, by which turning they live and see good, or die and see evil. But freedom in this willing is by grace, the grace of God among fellowmen, and bondage is by sin, by turning away, which is a mystery of the human spirit under temptation.

5 *Grace and Freedom Reconsidered*

1. CRITICAL

The traditional paradox of grace and freedom has become academic. When a man sets out to achieve a given good, he looks for the suitable means to do it, and "grace," the favor and agency of God, is not one of them. What a man needs is a certain combination of knowledge, skill, opportunity, power, and the freedom to make use of them. No man will trust his good to grace, and no man will question his freedom provided he has ability and is not prevented from using it.

When we are able to do what we will, we know ourselves as free, and when we are free, we need no grace. When we are unable to achieve our ends, we do not turn to a supernatural power but try to devise some new means that will give us success. Failure is a call, not to prayer, but to renewed calculation and effort. If success appears beyond our reach, we prefer to "accept the facts" rather than resort to "faith," which savors of superstition. If a miracle were to give us the success we seek, we should be greatly surprised and even discomfited. Hence, grace as supernatural or divine power is not what we live by, and freedom, the opportunity to act, has nothing to do with it.

Our way of life is not conducive to faith in God's power. It is no longer natural or rational for the human mind to meditate upon nature as a scene of good and evil emanating from a power or powers beyond man's knowledge and control. Given our physical and biological sciences, our experimental methods and mathematical explanations, together with our miraculous and extensive successes in manipulating nature and creating a second world of artifacts that dominate our effective environment—given all this, there is something incongruous about talking of the power of God and being concerned with it. This is not to say that we do not still have to fight natural evil and suffer from its ravages. But we have to fight it with our science and machines. We may still speak of a "Power behind the universe" or of "an immanent Deity" acting as "First Cause" through secondary causes. But such notions are of no use for understanding the order and connection of "facts" and are of no practical consequence comparable to the knowledge that comes from our scientists and engineers. In short, "the supernatural Power" of traditional religions and their pieties is no longer "real" and sought after. This, I think, is our situation, and in it God's grace is replaced by man's power, which explains to a large extent the triumph of moralism in our churches in spite of recent and petulant outbursts of Augustinian propaganda.

a. Here we must attend to reasons for our moralism that have grown out of the churches themselves, out of the life and the mind of the Christian institutions over a period of time. It is our thesis that the problem of God's grace and man's freedom, as well as the meticulous but indecisive solutions that traditional theology has offered to this problem, grows out of the church as an institution that claims to possess "the means of grace" necessary for the salvation of its membership.

It is traditionally recognized that God's grace operates in us by means of the Word and the Sacraments. Our churches are places where the Word of God is preached and the Sacraments administered by authorized persons, where people gather together to hear the Word and to receive the Sacrament, believing that in so doing, they receive God's grace. Our churches are the means of grace primarily in that they dispense grace to a gathering or assembly of people. The churches as institutions, with their equipment, personnel, organizations, and practices, stand in contrast to the "church people," who receive from the churches the benefits of their services. The point is that, insofar as churches act as institutions which provide the grace of God for the people, whether the emphasis be upon preaching or upon Sacrament, grace is received by the people as assembled individuals. Grace is from God through the institution to the man who hears or eats or both.

Institutionalism, that is, the notion that grace is available through an organization and its officials, is individualistic. Each man, as this or that man, goes to church or an assembly of believers and receives grace from the mouth or the hands of sacred personnel and in this way above all he is saved. The receiving of grace becomes a private affair between man and his God under the aegis of the clergy. Corporate worship reassures the individual rather than enables him to move out of his private selfhood. Ecclesiasticism and individualism are quite compatible one with the other. "Corporate worship" or corporateness in general is not a transcendence of individualism. By means of institutions, each man receives the grace that works in him and "saves " him.

The Augustinian version of the working of God's grace in us has gone hand in hand with institutionalism and individualism in our churches. Insofar as theologians have made it their business to elaborate and defend the ideology of the churches as institutions, they have favored, as Catholics and Protestants, seeing grace as a power from God dispensed by the churches to the people. So it turns out that *sola gratia* and *sola fide* mean also *sola ecclesia*. And, negatively, care has been taken to make it clear that no man is saved by his "works" without grace. A man's incapacity to save himself leads, in this context, to the conclusion that he is saved through the means of grace provided by the churches. Semi-Augustinians and semi-Pelagians have not disputed this point.

Of course, traditional theology insists that the true agent of grace is God the Father, Son, and Spirit. Catholics and Protestants believe that the cause in means of grace is Jesus Christ. It is understood by traditional theology that grace in us is inseparable from grace for us shown in the incarnation and the atonement and that grace in us and grace for us are the same grace—the grace of our Lord Jesus Christ. Theologians, Catholic and Protestant, often have been absentminded enough to discuss grace in us apart from grace by Christ for us. But they have insisted upon "the real presence" of Jesus Christ at the Lord's Table, and Protestants have emphasized that, in preaching also, we have to do with the Word speaking to the people.

However, the Christ in question has been the Son of God who saves us through the preaching of the Word and the administration of the Sacraments. The emphasis has been upon the indissoluble bond between Christ and the churches as institutions. How does the believer hear the Word or receive the grace of Christ? By hearing the sermon preached from the pulpit by the preacher. How does he receive, eat or eat and drink, Christ? By eating the bread, or eating the bread and drinking the wine or grape juice, served by the clergy in the church. Jesus Christ is the Son of God who saves us corporately and individually through the church.

Institutionalism and individualism go together, and the doctrine of grace is determined by both. The doctrine becomes that when a man hears a sermon or partakes of the Sacrament: God, the grace of God, or the Spirit of God, or the power of God (and these expressions are used interchangeably), works within him, upon his mind and heart and will, regenerates and sanctifies him, illumines his mind, cleanses his heart, and bends and redirects his will toward a godly and sober life. It is taught and professed that God himself, Father, Son, and Holy Spirit, by the instrumentality of the institution, gives the believer life and power to obey the law of God. This working is understandably said by the teaching of the church to be supernatural, mysterious, secret, and known only by faith.

The grace of God working in a man by the traditional means of grace is a supernatural Power. According to the mind of the churches as institutions dispensing grace, the people do not have the power to obey the Word and commandment of God. Their minds are in darkness; their wills perverted; their affections corrupted. They are subject to pride, rebellion, sloth, sensuality, dishonesty, ignorance, and the like, which constitute a corrupted nature in mind and body. Thus human nature is found incapable of attaining the good unless a supernatural Power works through the means of grace within the individual, restores it to health, and endows the will with a new power of godliness. So it is taught and understood that grace is a secret, supernatural power working from above, behind, under, within, infusing the mind, will, and affections of a man and empowering him for righteousness. The orthodox teachers of the churches have insisted that men are saved by the working of this power alone and they have agreed that without the prevenient power of God, *ab extra* and *ad extra*, available through *sancti* and *sancta*, there is no salvation.

But such supernaturalism confuses the situation of God's people under his judgment and mercy. Is obedience to God through the infusion of a supernatural power obedience at all? Either man's response of consent is by obedience and love or it is not the response of "God's intelligent creation." The whole point of man's existence is that he shall glorify God, not by infusions of power, but by a consent to his Creator in the proper exercise of his mind, will, and affections. Either man himself obeys God or God is not obeyed. Therefore, obedience by a power *ab extra* is no obedience. But man, this man or that, is not able by his own power to obey God. From this comes the dilemma that has agitated the mind of the church through the centuries and has ended in the fiasco of Augustinian talk and Pelagian attitude and action.

The distinction between *gratia operans* and *gratia cooperans, gratia praeveniens* and *gratia subsequens,* is no help in overcoming this dilemma. If man's ability to cooperate with *gratia cooperans* is the result of *gratia operans,* then such cooperation on the part of man is the operation of grace. If it is not the result of *gratia operans,* then it is not by grace. If man's consent to God's will in the working of *gratia cooperans* is due to *gratia operans,* is it really man's consent? If the consent is not due to grace, is it by grace? The doctrine of cooperating grace only conceals the paradox of "grace and freedom." If obedience is caused by a supernatural infusion, it is no obedience in consent. If it is not caused by such an infusion, the traditional doctrine of grace must be given up.

The doctrine of "cooperating grace" corresponds to nothing in our experience of God. The notion that the grace of God cooperates with man's will already turned to God by grace is an ideological solution to our problem. The power of God and the power of man cannot be juxtaposed because God and man cannot be juxtaposed. A man may cooperate with another man or with the power of some other creature because the two have the same kind of power, which can be multiplied through their cooperation. When this takes place, a man knows that he is being helped by another man, or by a beast, or by a machine. But God is not a man, or beast, or machine. We have no experience of his power as cooperating with ours, adding to our weight or pull. Christians have indeed confessed the grace of God as directly working in them and enabling them to do the work of righteousness. We do not deny the validity of such confession. But it is our judgment that in this matter they have been prejudiced by the ideologies of the institutions that claim to be the means of grace. The experience of God's grace is one thing, and the traditional interpretation of the manner of its working as a supernatural power in the individual is quite another. It is such an interpretation that produces the paradox of grace and freedom and ends up either in quietism or activism, either of which is a denial of God's grace.

b. Pre-neoorthodox "modern theology," as represented by John Oman and the "personalists," was an attempt to correct traditional Calvinism with its subpersonal doctrines of "irresistible grace." In this movement the repudiation of orthodox Christology and the affirmation of the humanity of Jesus Christ at "the core of his being" went with a new regard for the integrity of personality as a clue to the working of God's grace. God's grace, according to this theology, is to be seen in the grace or graciousness of Jesus Christ, who moved and moves people to love God and neighbor, not by an irresistible power, but through the influence of his own free and persuasive love. Our response to the grace of God as seen in Jesus is itself free. We may accept or reject it. In either case, under God's grace or love we are in a position of freedom and responsibility and we respond to God as intelligent and free creation, not as beasts or robots. In this way the dignity of God and the dignity of man, both as persons, are upheld, and any "mechanical" view of grace is ruled out of theology. We trust that this contribution of modern theology will be permanent in the church.

Unfortunately, this improvement, or perhaps clarification, which has found favor also in neoorthodox theology, was achieved at too great a price. In this scheme, Jesus responded freely to God's love. God loved Jesus as a person, and so also Jesus loved God. Jesus loved men as persons, freely; and so those who love him, love him as persons, freely. Love evokes love, and in love are involved God, Jesus, and men, loving one another, attracting and attracted by love. God, Jesus, and Christians are included in the classification of persons, and their loves are identified as in one class.

The difficulty is that God's role in the making of love is no longer clear. If Jesus loves us freely and spontaneously as a human being, and we respond to him in kind, what does God have to do with this interchange? If the love of Jesus evokes our love, as the love of one man evokes love in another, or as love evokes love, why do we have to consider God as another party to love, unless of course he is love and love is he? What is needed to evoke love in us is not the love of God, but the love of Jesus.

Of course, it has been felt that we need God's help in order to love; otherwise "theism" would end in "humanism." But the nature of God's help is by no means clear. If the power of God be superhuman, it does not act by the love we know in Jesus, and the scheme of "ethical theism" cannot be maintained. We may confess that the matter is a mystery—that God acts in a way unknown to us, without violating our freedom.[1] But we know no action that does not violate freedom except the love we find in Jesus. Therefore, we need no action but the love of Jesus. If we say we do, we are on the way back to Augustinianism. If we say we do not, we are on the way to nontheistic humanism. "Modern theology," concerned with our ability to respond to God's grace of love seen in the man Jesus, leaves us with our problem. We are still unable to think of God's grace and man's freedom together.

c. We may not close the critical part of this paper without referring the reader to the work of Karl Barth, whose *Church Dogmatics* may well be said to be a tremendous disquisition upon the grace of God as revealed and communicated in Jesus Christ, the head of the church. Barth himself has said: "The election of grace is the sum of the Gospel—we must put it as pointedly as that. But more, the election of grace is the whole Gospel, the Gospel *in nuce*. It is the very essence of all good news."[2]

The conjunction of grace with election and of election with Jesus Christ in Barth's thought is a decisive repudiation of any subpersonal doctrine of grace. In this, Barth is in line with contemporary theology in general. No one in our time has fought, as it were, as persistently and elaborately as Barth to vindicate the doctrine of the Person-ness of God as given in Scripture and proclaimed by the church. God's grace, for Barth, is expressed in the love and freedom of God and is to be understood as exercised by Jesus Christ, in the love and freedom of Jesus Christ. Therefore, "there are also no effluences, emanations, effusions or irruptions of God into the world, in virtue of which, apart from God Himself, there are in a sense islands or even continents of the divine in the midst of the non-divine."[3] In short, we know the grace of God by the grace of our Lord Jesus Christ, and any doctrine of grace known otherwise is excluded.

According to Barth, God himself reveals his grace in Jesus Christ. In the revelation the Revealer reveals himself as the Person who is a person, and this revelation is effected in us by the Spirit through the signs in the church or the means of grace: preaching and the Sacraments. So God reveals himself as Father, Lord, *origo*, the free and loving, or living, God. In Christ Jesus, God has, "in the sovereignty of his omnipotence and lovingkindness," as the eternal God, elected each man for "forgiveness and renewal."[4] This act of grace has been accomplished once for all in the atoning work of Christ, so that the sinner is saved quite apart from his accepting or rejecting this grace. "It is not for his being but for his life as elect that he needs to hear and believe the promise."[5] A man is in a position to reject his election partially and even wholly. In this sense he is free and responsible, and God does not force him to *live* as a Christian. But his *being* a Christian is altogether apart from his decision. It is by God's election and is grounded in Jesus Christ. Apparently, for Barth, there is a noumenal Christian, bound to the grace and will of the noumenal Deity as revealed in Christ Jesus. And there is a phenomenal Christian who lives by decision for or against Christ.

Barth's treatment of the paradox of grace and freedom does not appear promising to us. To say that under and within God's "eternal predestination," "under God's decision which precedes everything," God's "election becomes actual in man's own electing of God, by which he is made free to do the will of God, and achieves and possesses individuality and autonomy before God" does not overcome the paradox in question. One does not get far by replacing a doctrine of the temporal priority of God's election with a doctrine of its dynamic priority.[6] Barth's criticisms of the traditional doctrines of predestination are well made and extremely important. But he does not escape the dilemma of "grace and freedom." In the encounter between God and man, God is still presented as the source of the power of man to respond to God, and his grace, exercised in love and freedom, is still presented as the only ground of man's freedom or power as "intelligent creation." We are still confronted with a First Cause and secondary causes, and the First Cause is presented to us as working within the individual at the core of his being, *ab extra* and *ad extra*, as a supernatural and ontically overwhelming power exercised in freedom and operating on love. It is by no means evident that "the grace of election" and the freedom it creates in man present us with a lesser dilemma than does traditional Augustinianism. I do not see how Barth's exposition of this matter will keep the church from talking grace and practicing free will.

2. CONSTRUCTIVE

a. I think that the grand error of the traditional discussions of this subject is in the anthropological assumptions behind them. Since Augustine, our theologians have spoken of "human nature" or "nature" as a fixed entity that can be ascertained by a study of the individual, of his parts and traits. The mind was scrutinized by the Greeks as a man's possession, his by nature or birth; the will was scrutinized by Augustine as belonging to the individual human being, as inborn and having or not having the power to follow the good. A man was simply, or had, a will, and his will either did or did not have the power to do God's will. Pelagius said that it did; Augustine said that it did not. But both they and their successors have thought of the will as that with which the individual human being faces the law of God in obedience and disobedience. Augustine's contention was that without God's grace or power the will cannot but sin. Pelagius argued that unless the will has the power to obey God's law, a man cannot be held responsible to do it.[7]

Our thesis is that such individualism is at the root of the failure of traditional theology to speak illuminatingly about "grace and freedom." The individual with his reason and will, as a thinking and willing animal, is an abstraction and an unintelligible entity, and any discussion of his relationship with God is bound to be unfruitful and conducive to misunderstanding. As Barth himself has insisted eloquently and persuasively in other connections, there is no such thing as the individual human being except in the community of human beings.[8] There is no *Mensch* except as *Mitmensch*, no human being outside "the covenant" that binds him at once to God and to his neighbor, no Christian outside the "community." This might be said to be a particularly Protestant insight, the meaning of which has been far from fully explored. It was, as it were, discovered in the Reformation and Anabaptist polemics against the institutionalism of the Roman Catholic Church and rediscovered by Schleiermacher in his polemics against Protestant scholasticism.[9] It was insisted upon by Josiah Royce in *The Problem of Christianity* and elsewhere and became basic to the "social psychology" of George Herbert Mead and his disciples.[10] Unfortunately, the preoccupation of much modern theology with "science and religion," especially in Britain and America, diverted attention from "the communion of saints," and Christian thinkers continued to speak of "Nature, Man and God," as though *Mitmenschlichkeit* were irrelevant for an understanding of God's relation to man.[11] The time has come to correct this error.

We must take another look at "human nature" upon which the grace of God or God himself is said to act. It is not at all obvious that *human* nature or humanity is what a man is born with, so that one can

study and describe it as the individual's private equipment. We know
human beings in actual intercourse with their environment and in their
actual communion with their fellowmen. Characteristic activities of human beings, such as speech, thinking, willing, loving, and hating, do
not occur and are unthinkable apart from an interpersonal setting. Even
perceptions, feelings, emotions, and actions occur in a social context,
and these are what they are as responses in the common life men have
with their fellows.[12] Men's bodily functions are also involved in their
commerce with their social and physical environments and are understood concretely and properly as processes that are included in this
commerce. When we consider especially understanding and willing,
which have been regarded as characteristic of humanity and treated as
primary expressions of human nature, we can hardly fail to recognize
today that they neither occur nor are intelligible and describable except
in terms of communion among "God's intelligent creation."

If we take it, with Augustine, that love is *pondus animae*, that
it moves the will and motivates the understanding in its search for the
good, it is clear that there is no such thing as humanity except in love
given and received; but giving and receiving love is what goes on
among people.[13] The individual who expresses his nature by his love is
an abstraction. Love is not a response of one individual to another but
the communion of creatures whereby they are severally posited as human beings. The actuality of love, or the existence of the human being
with his "human nature," occurs as a response to the preexisting community of human beings. Of course, it is true that love presupposes the
loving individual, but there is no loving individual prior to the community that exists by love reciprocated. Every man possesses a human nature, not because he was born with one, but because he is born into a
human community.

"Human nature" is the specification of communion among
people. We come to have it and to know it as such in that communion
among creatures that is called "love." It is the manner of human existence and action. Human beings, at once as subjects and objects, acting
and acted upon, emerge and become aware of others and of themselves
in a continued communion that is the condition of each man's *existence*
as well as of his "nature." The loving and not-loving of my fellowman
is to me literally a matter of life and death as this human being. I continue to exist as this man because I am loved as this man—not as one

who has been loved, or is loved occasionally, but as one who draws his life constantly from the recognition of his neighbor and the communion that goes with it. It is my neighbor's speech and actions that evoke in me the response I call my "nature," so that in this way and sense my "nature" is my response and is unintelligible except as such. His nature is his speaking to me as this creature. My nature is my speaking to him as this other creature. And our common "nature" is that we are creatures by and in communion.

Since human nature is known traditionally as a conformation of traits physically inherited, it would be better not to speak of human nature at all. Communion is the being and nature and destiny of man. We have no ontological status prior to and apart from communion. Communion is our being; the being we participate in is communion, and we derive our concrete selves from our communion. The old controversy between the realists and the nominalists about universals and particulars is incongruous with the ontology of communion. We have to do, not with universals, but with our neighbors, not with particulars, but with particular fellowmen. We do not participate individually in Being, and Being is not by our own being individually. There is no individual to participate in Being or to make Being to be. In the beginning, by God's creation, is the *fellowman*, and the fellowman is by loving his neighbor. The apparently universal notion, at least in the Western world, that *one* man can *be* and that he can have a nature suggests an alienation that gives us, not a *human* ontology, but one from which the human manner of being is excluded. In the beginning is communion and not being or Being. For this reason, in Christian philosophy, traditional ontology is a source of misunderstanding and confusion. Before one speaks in the singular or the plural, one must have learned to speak in the *dual*. But, if one is to learn to speak in the dual, it is better not to begin by speaking about either being or nature.

b. Man is the living being who exists by being loved and loving. His neighbor's action by sign and speech posits him as a human being. Thus he becomes aware of himself as this individual person. He, in fact, acts as a person in responding to his neighbor and to his own response.[14] When his speech is directed both to his neighbor and to himself, he exists as a man. When his response to himself inspires his response to his neighbor, he exists as this individual man. His response to his neighbor, as inspired by his response to himself, posits him as a responsible being and becomes the basis of his intercourse with his neighbor. It also becomes the basis of his own existence as a private self and of all his thoughts and feelings, attitudes and emotions, with all their movements and interactions. Thus there emerges the unique person without whom there is no neighbor or humanity. The more persistently and effectively a man responds to his response to his neighbor, the more clearly there are both communion and individuality, both of which are indispensable for human existence.

All this is nothing new. What I would like to point out is that when by communion the individual man comes into being, there comes into being also the man who in his selfawareness becomes aware of his creaturely limitations in time and space, in duration and power. Communion posits him, and in so doing, it also leads him to posit his world in which he is evanescent and subject to alien powers. There is an inevitable and endless conflict between the environment and himself, and in this conflict the last word is not his own. He is marked for a defeat of which his own removal from "the land of the living" is a permanent and immovable sign. He is tempted either to overcome his existence as a limited being or to renounce it; that is, he is tempted toward either pride or sensuality or both.[15] In this situation, arising from his individuality, he lives by communion with his neighbor. The communion that posited him must also sustain him. Otherwise he perishes. But this communion, which occurs between and among individuals, is love. The temptation that besets the individual to escape his limits as an individual, to seek, as this individual, either to attain immortality or to renounce his individuality is bound to quicken his malaise. The sting of finitude is neutralized only by the communion that has posited the individual, and this communion is the substance of *human* love in its many manifestations.

The living tend to live or to have a "will" to live. This will, or rather impulse, to live is seen in much that the living do, such as eating and drinking, mating, fighting, laboring, etc.[16] That men have a will to live is clear. But it is not clear that the will to live makes men human beings. Men are human beings when they will to live in communion. The individual's will to live presupposes communion or love. He wills to live as he is loved and loving. As a human being, his will to live is inseparable from his willing to respond to love with love. Since his life is his communion with his neighbor, he derives the will to live from love—from the love of his neighbor for him and from his love for his neighbor. His "willpower" is his ability to love, and this power, without which he knows no will, he knows only in communion. In human life the will has no reality except from and for love. The will to live, to know, to act, and to achieve any good whatever—these are abstractions from the human act of communion. They occur in a context of communion, and the ability to do anything, as a human action, is received by way of love. The will, in short, is not a faculty born in the animal, but a characteristic of loving that occurs by way of a response. The animal as the animal does not have the will of a man because it does not speak and does not love as a man. Therefore, we will, not by nature, but by communion. We do not know that we have a will except as we love, except as we will, which means as we exercise power. But the power to love is one we receive from our neighbor. A man's neighbor gives him power or takes it away. He gives him power as he loves him and takes away his power as he does not love him. So a man knows himself as willing as he loves and responds to his neighbor's and his own love. In short, the will is a function of the individual's *Mitmenschlichkeit*.

I do not, of course, overlook that there is such a thing as a will that is asocial or even antisocial. Men exhibit great "willpower" in the pursuit of goods, domination, security, prestige, status, etc. They do these things with indifference to, or even disdain of, what others think or do. They may even do them in hatred of their fellowmen or "society." Thus, willpower appears as a man's private possession, exercised as his "nature" rather than as a gift. Insofar as a man is alienated from his neighbor, the will and its power appear as his own, as instruments of his own existence and expansion. And since alienation is commonplace, so is the notion, common to our tradition, that willpower is inborn and exercised in a hostile world. But this, I think, is a delusion. Asocial and antisocial willpower goes with alienation, which in turn arises from the refusal of neighbors to love one another as themselves. When love is refused, the individual either loses his willpower or transmutes it to lust. As men usually have a degree of "willpower," what we commonly observe is lust, which is a corruption of love and the sign of sin. The neighbor's rejection of a man is as potent toward sin as his love is toward love. The actuality of a willpower that manifests itself in "selfishness" is to be explained in terms of communication between human beings and not in terms of the individual's "natural" equipment.

In this context it is incongruous to ask if the will is free or not free. If there is no humanity by birth and no human nature with a will, it is not helpful to inquire whether the will is free. A free will is a will able to love, but such ability is a gift through our neighbor. An unfree will is a will unable to love, but such inability we know only in the failure of love among us. The question is not whether the will is free, but how we come to love. It is not whether the will is unfree, but how we come to desist from love. And the answer is to be sought, not in inherited nature, but in our existence as fellowmen. Since we are individuals posited by communion, we do not have free will, or rather the ability to love, except as a gift from our neighbor. A man loves as he is loved. Without the love of another, we are not free. On the other hand, since we are these individuals (being posited by communion), we are responsive and therefore able to respond. But the ability is a gift by way of our neighbor. Where there is love, there is ability to love. This is a situation in which the question of the freedom of the will, in the traditional sense, does not arise, because the primal reality is the communion that posits the individuals and not the individuals about whom we may ask whether they are free and able. We have to learn to think in a new way. The will is a gift being given, and as such, it cannot be said to be free or in bondage. Such an alternative in this context is nonsense. A man is free as he loves; he is unfree as he does not love. But neither his freedom nor his unfreedom is prior to communion or makes sense apart from it.

The neighbor's love by which a man exists is not a natural affection. It is a gift, and the giving is the act of a person who *may* give, not *must* give. Love is a gift precisely because the neighbor might not give it; in fact, he does not truly give it except as he decides to give it. Without this decision of my neighbor to enter into communion with me, there is no love and no gift. If I accept his love as love and come alive by it and rejoice in it, it is because my neighbor has acknowledged me as his fellowman, opened himself to me, and sought my response as his fellowman. He might not have done all this. He might have shut himself up and turned away from me. He could have found very good reason for such an act of rejection in that we have met as aliens and enemies. But (and I should never cease to be surprised by this) he has instead received me as his neighbor, not to be my benefactor, but as an act in which he posits at once himself and myself, rather myself and himself, as human beings. His love indeed is his life as a fellowman, but it comes to me as a gift, and apart from this gift, I know no grace of God. If the grace of God is dimly discerned among us and has been such a source of contention in the church, may it not be that we have lost sight of the gift of love, or of love as a free gift from our neighbor whom we see and without whom we do not see God? Our culture has darkened this blindness and cultivated this stupidity until now indeed it is "second nature."

c. The question arises: If we know God's power in our communion with each other, how is God's grace revealed in this communion? What reason is there for speaking of God at all? If the power of my neighbor—his love—gives me the power to love, and mine does the same to him, what necessity is there of confessing God's love? It appears that my neighbor's "personal influence" explains my good fortune, and he, rather than God, is the proper object of my gratitude and piety. The grace of God seems to be superfluous, a confused and confusing notion entertained by tradition rather than by logic. Why theology? Why is not "social psychology" enough?

I think, in answer to such questions, that it is not enough to fall back upon "revelation," or a general sense of Deity, or even the doctrine of the First Cause. I do not contend that God himself as a noumenon does not reveal himself in "man and nature" or in phenomenon. But if noumenon does not explain the phenomenal except as the transcendent, hidden First Cause, then it does not properly explain or make plain anything. There is no clear intellectual gain in speaking of a Ground of Being, or a First Cause, when we try to understand how this or that entity or event has come to be what it is. The "God" of natural theology, the First Cause behind secondary causes, can always be set aside as a logical mistake, as a being whose existence is at once doubtful and uninteresting to the mind. If men, in fact, loved one another and did not hate one another, we might explain their love biologically and in terms of social psychology. We might leave the grace of God out. It is a mistake to allow our faith in God's grace to depend upon the validity of our notion of "ultimate reality" and upon the validity of the distinction between primary and secondary causes. It is pious to acknowledge God as the First Cause of *our* love and virtue. But if we love and are virtuous, we are hardly in a position to know the power of God except as immanent in nature, and we may, in fact, identify it with the powers of nature.

As a man who violates his neighbor, I know the grace of God. It is not true that I love my neighbor as myself and therefore may refer my love to God as its first cause. It is not true that my neighbor loves me as himself and forgives my violation of him, wherefore we may refer his love and forgiveness to God. My neighbor does not receive his due as a creature from me, and I do not receive mine from him. The love in question is the acknowledgment one creature owes to another. It exists where one man, tempted to renounce his humanity—and therewith the humanity of his neighbor—nevertheless announces both and acts accordingly. It exists where men meet and are "justified," not absurdly by the claim of each that he is "righteous," but by the justice of mutual recognition as "intelligent creation." Love is faithfulness toward the creature qua creature; it is the positing of his concrete existence in communion, which is a participation in his life with its glory and misery, its hope and dread. Love is our "Yea" to our neighbor as a man and creature, in his violation of humanity, ours and his own, which is evoked by our own similar violation. It is a faithfulness from and toward forgiveness, at once received and given, for the sake of communion. In short, love is the openness of the creature to the creature, an opening that follows forgiveness; but forgiveness among violators of humanity is a miracle and not a thing of course.

Forgiveness is a miracle. Unacknowledged and therefore violated humanity is one in the throes of death. A human being lives by the acknowledgment of his neighbor. When such acknowledgment is withheld, there is murder and annihilation. And a man being murdered, unless he receives a hope of life, is hardly in a position to forgive. The living love their lives fiercely and even absolutely. Since for a human being to live is to be a fellowman, when he is rejected and ignored as one, he responds with a fury that acts as an overwhelming temptation to murder in return. It is not that he necessarily hates and will not forgive, but that he responds to murder with despair, and despair is not conducive to forgiveness. The hopeless man may resign himself to death. But such resignation, even where it is concealed as usual by good manners, is an act of suicide that relieves the pain caused by murder but cannot in the nature of the case lead to reconciliation and communion. The simulated forgiveness of violated humanity in polite society (and all societies are more or less polite) is action toward death and not toward life. The real article is a miracle and a matter of surprise. It is by God's grace.

God's grace is known in the miracle of forgiveness. Forgiveness is known as "miracle" because it appears among sinners—

violators of humanity. Our forgiveness is forgiveness by sinners, by those who forgive as those who violate their neighbors and not as those who, having forgiven, cease to violate. There is no time or occasion in which we who forgive do not need to be forgiven, and we who are forgiven do not need to forgive. Forgiveness occurs among sinners, and it does not occur among any but sinners being forgiven: being forgiven by the neighbor who is a sinner being forgiven, and forgiving as a neighbor being forgiven. There is a forgiveness of sinners that is prior to forgiveness by sinners, and it is this prior forgiveness that creates the forgiveness by sinners and makes it an occasion of communion. This is God's forgiveness in Jesus Christ.

     d. This situation becomes clear when we remember that it comes into being in the company of Jesus. We forgive and are forgiven as the sinners who are under the forgiveness of Jesus, who in the communion of saints has already forgiven us.

     In one sense, everything depends upon whether we are gathered around Christ and live in his presence and under his forgiveness. Christians are people who keep company with Jesus—with Jesus of flesh and bones who lived in Palestine many years ago and now lives among and with people wherever they may be. Where two and three are gathered together in his name, acknowledging his presence among them, there is Jesus, our brother and our Savior. He is there with his faithfulness and forgiveness, looking at us, speaking to us, communing with us as the creature and neighbor who has forgiven and forgives and will forgive us, his violators. We who will not forgive one another are present with him who forgives us and overcomes the dilemmas by which we devour one another. We who violate one another and live in the misery of violation find ourselves in the company of one who is one of us, knows our misery, and should, of course, join us in our enmity and death. But he who is one of us is not one of us in our death. He is alive as "intelligent creation," and life passes from him to us with joy. He communes with us as a human being, and his communion is by forgiveness. He acts as our fellowman and posits us as fellowmen, forgiving us who are sinners.

     Thus, our situation as Christ's company has been obscured by other "images," which are not less harmful because they are traditional and orthodox. We have come to locate Jesus primarily on the cross, with two thieves on two other crosses next to him and with an assortment of women, soldiers, officials, and spectators on the ground around him. His disciples and followers are gone, and we ourselves are away. How, then, do we think of "the work of Christ"? We think of it either in terms of a transaction between God and Christ in our behalf or in terms of Christ's "moral influences" upon us from a distance and through "Christians" now gone and especially those present with us. Moreover, we expect to receive the benefit of his "work" through "the means of grace" provided by our religious institutions. We gather together in our churches, hear sermons and receive the Sacraments, and hope for some strange blessedness. Of course, all this belongs in the Christian faith. But our traditional notions of the incarnation, the atonement, and the means of grace conspire to confuse the communion of Christ with sinners, which becomes either our private communion with him or a mediated affair in which he recedes to the background as a "spiritual reality." In either case the image of Jesus surrounded by those he loves and forgives and opens for communion is lost and in this way the gospel is nullified.

Without the love of Jesus for us, there is no love among us. We are restored for communion as "intelligent creation" by the love of a creature whose name is Jesus. The love of Jesus is not the love of a supernatural being who, by a supernatural act of "satisfaction," works "the expiation of crimes." It is the love of a creature for his fellowman: a love that every man owes to another and hopes for another, a love that posits humanity and sustains it. The miracle that has occurred among us who surround Jesus is that he has loved us and forgiven us and thus reestablished the bond of humanity among us. He who is not a sinner forgives us, and so we who are sinners forgive one another. We are at all times sinners who are loved by Jesus, and our love is the love of sinners who are loved by Jesus. We ourselves are enabled by the love of Jesus to love as loved sinners, as sinners who receive a new ability to love from Jesus; thus we love as loved sinners and not otherwise. By loving, we do not cease to be sinners. We love as sinners by Jesus' forgiveness who makes us free for communion with our fellowman. This love of Jesus is always a surprise, for it is a miracle. We know in Jesus' presence that it is neither in us nor in our neighbor to love as Jesus loves us and him. The love of Jesus is a human action, but it is his action alone. It is his action as a human being but not as any human being. Although it is a human action, it is not a general or common possibility among us who surround him. This is why we are surprised and glorify God and say that it is by the grace of God. This is why we call him the Son of

God, the Son of the Father. The mystery of this man Jesus is the mystery of the living God, who restores us to love by the love of this man Jesus, and it is also the mystery of the Spirit of God, who reveals the power of God in the weakness of man. As we marvel at the love of Jesus, we marvel at the grace of God. The grace of God is not the first cause of the love of Jesus, but its very possibility as this human love. We acknowledge the love of Jesus as an authentic act of a creature who loves us, not because he must, but because he may. But that he, in fact, does love us, we acknowledge as by the grace of God, because we know, as those who love as sinners being forgiven, that such grace is not of man but of God.

e. We may love one another as sinners, not as nonsinners or righteous people who do not need forgiveness. We may love one another as sinners in Christ's presence, as sinners who are forgiven of Christ. As bearers of this forgiveness, we may love one another, not as though we had fulfilled the law, but in our joy in Christ's presence and in our misery as sinners, joyful and sorry, able now to forgive and to ask forgiveness as *sinners*, as God's creation, alienated one from another, now in hope through Christ.

I think we should avoid the traditional fallacy that our love and forgiveness under Christ make us righteous or are evidence that we are now not among sinners but among the righteous. In Christ we become free to love as sinners and not as the righteous; and if by this freedom and love we have joy and peace one with another, it is not because we have been given, and therefore possess, the power to act as righteous men, but because of the continued act of God's mercy. We should distinguish between the freedom we receive, by God's forgiveness in Christ's presence, to love our neighbors as the sinners that we are, and that freedom, pretended freedom, to love one another not as sinners but as righteous. The first is a freedom we receive in communion with our neighbor; the second we pretend to receive by a power working in us apart from our neighbor.

This is how love and humility go together. This is also why we are continually surprised, as sinners who love one another, by the joy we receive and the joy we give, which is acknowledged as a gift. God's grace is acknowledged in this gift and this surprise. Why should we be *surprised* unless we recognize that love is not *in* us or *by* us? But why should we *be* surprised unless we recognize that we have in our communion received the forgiveness and love that give the creature joy?

The power of God is that power which forgives and saves us by the love and forgiveness of sinners. There *is* a human love that is the love of sinners. There *is* a human forgiveness that is the forgiveness of sinners. By this love and forgiveness of sinners, God loves and forgives so as to give us joy. To find the love of God in the love of man: that is faith. To hope for God's grace in the weakness and failure of man: that is hope. And to love is to love as a man, with all the anxiety and duplicity of human love, believing and hoping in God. We are not to believe in man, that is, that man can do God's work. But we are to be grateful for the affection and the goodwill of men, believing that God can and will make them occasions of joy, of the creature's consent at once to himself and to his neighbor. As Christ's company, we are to assume our ability to love our neighbor with kindness and courtesy and justice, believing that God can and will make them occasions for the joy of our neighbor. To disdain the sinner's love for us and to refuse our love to him, on the ground that such love is not "true love," is to deny the grace of God who blesses us with his own redemptive love as we love one another as human beings and sinners. Faith in God and contempt for men are incompatible one with the other.

"For if you forgive men their trespasses, your heavenly Father also will forgive you; but if you do not forgive men their trespasses, neither will your Father forgive your trespasses." (Matt. 6:14-15.) We are to forgive men their trespasses. We are not to say that we cannot forgive them their trespasses. We are not to say that if God would have us forgive, he ought privately to put it in us to do so. We are to acknowledge that we ought to forgive, that in truth we are able to forgive, that unless we forgive, we do not believe in God who forgives our trespasses by our neighbor's forgiving our trespasses. We are not able to forgive as God forgives. We are able to forgive as we may forgive, as sinners who are Christ's brothers, and unless we so forgive, we in truth do not know God's forgiveness.

In the community where we exist, our forgiveness cannot but be a response to the grace we find in it. We forgive in the church (and the church is where forgiving neighbors exist) in response to human forgiveness we have already received. We may not have been forgiven by this or that man we may have offended. Nevertheless, forgiveness does not begin with us. Human forgiveness is not and cannot be a one-way affair. Any man who poses as a forgiver among neighbors who do not and will not forgive is himself no forgiver. He is, at best, deluded and, at worst, a proud man and a pretender. I forgive only when I respond happily to forgiveness and when I acknowledge that my neighbor may and can forgive. I may forgive this neighbor, and he may forgive me. In this respect he is free and I am free, and we both are able to act as free in response to the other's freedom in Christ's presence.

Although we ourselves are able neither to love God as we ought nor to love our neighbor as ourselves, although we give up hope of peace within or among us, although we are able neither to refrain from sinning nor to rest content with our "human nature," although we appear doomed to pride, hypocrisy, and frustration in the midst of this misery in which we live with our fellows, the grace of God works mightily among us, by our ministry one toward another, to bless us and to "establish the work of our hands." Although our own affection is confused and our justice is as "filthy rags," we ourselves are amazed and joyful that we, through our affection and justice, taste of a blessing and joy that come to us as gifts, as a strange thing that we can only receive as an act of grace from the living God. Thus it is that we and our neighbor are together moved and encouraged to exercise our freedom as human beings, as these sinners, to strive that our human "love may be genuine," that we may "hate what is evil" and "hold fast to what is good," loving one another as brothers, contributing "to the needs of the saints " (Rom. 12:9, 13). Thus it is that we act as ministers of God's grace for our common blessedness as God's "intelligent creation."

The traditional doctrine of grace was that God enables us who are sinners to be righteous; he enables us who do not love to love. By grace, we were supposed to become empowered and free to love God with all our heart, soul, and strength, and our neighbors as ourselves. Doctrines of regeneration and sanctification were elaborated ad infinitum, presumably describing the process whereby grace increases in us and sin decreases. It was claimed that "the means of grace"—elaborately argued about, elaborately worked out, and perennially dispensed throughout Christendom—would produce the freedom and power in question. But Christians have continued to engage in the hostility, injustice, pride, and idolatry that beset this poor world. They have even produced "realistic" theologies that "accept" the prevalence of sin and think about our common life accordingly. But the whole thing is an embarrassment. Christian supernaturalism has been no effective antidote to man's inhumanity to man.

Surely our claims to "habitual grace" and the inhering right-eousness that goes with it are as divisive and dehumanizing as they should be embarrassing to those who live by forgiveness. Forgiveness leads to the elementary humility and decency of those who, while walking in darkness, have seen a great light, of those who, surprised by Jesus Christ, are moved to hope both to receive and to bestow forgiveness. God has revealed his grace to us in making us his people and binding us again together in the bundle of life as fellowmen. He has given us our neighbors as his *mal'ahim*, his angels or messengers. He has promised us, in Christ Jesus and in the church, that if we acknowledge this grace and receive our fellow sinners as the means of grace, we shall have peace with him and joy one with another. The very existence of the communion of saints as the body of Christ means that if we reject our fellowmen as the bearers of God's grace, there shall be no grace given to us and no freedom evoked in us. Without communion there is neither life nor power. If we despise our neighbor's communion with us, we despise the living God and his grace. There is no grace of God that is available without the ministry of our fellowmen, and to brush aside the latter is to treat God's Spirit with contempt, and is the end of life and all blessing.

Humility, said Augustine (and Calvin repeated after him), is the chief grace of a Christian. In fact, both thought that faith in God's grace is the very source of humility. That was and is still true. But, then, how is a man humble toward God when he is proud toward his neighbor? It is by the love of my sinful neighbor that God gives me life, joy, hope, and every blessing; and he does not give it unless I, who am a sinner, love and forgive my neighbor. But my neighbor comes first, and with him comes God's grace and his blessing.

In Jesus' company forgiveness and love are to be received and given as the proper response to his "steadfast love," and there can be no question of waiting around for a supernatural Power to enable us to both receive and give. There can be no question (as we are loved and received as creatures and sinners or justified) of our waiting to be sanctified and so enabled to receive and give forgiveness. The love of Christ constrains us, and we may be forgiven and forgive as the sinners in Christ's company. There is no more to the grace of God than the forgiveness and love we receive "in Christ." And the righteousness, peace, joy, and life and all blessing we receive as grace freely given are given by God in the grace and truth that we receive from Jesus. So we are given joy and hope wherewith we are opened to our neighbor and our neighbor is opened to us, and we love one another as ourselves, that is, as the creatures and the sinners that we are. Before Christ and before our neighbor we remain sinners under Jesus' forgiveness and under one another's forgiveness, and so we love one another as God's "intelligent creation."

The freedom we have under God's grace or his peculiar power, by his peculiar wisdom, is not the freedom of those who by a supernatural inward action upon the will are no longer sinners, but the freedom of sinners in communion with Jesus Christ and with their neighbors, by the forgiveness of Christ who is without sin and the forgiveness of their neighbors who are sinners under Christ's forgiveness—that is, the freedom to love and forgive as creatures, which is blessed by God, the living God, who acts by his Word and Spirit, by Christ and the church.

f. The apparent paradox that we love as sinners, loving so that we are not justified by our love or so that we, even as we love, need to be forgiven, arises from the fact that the love with which we love is at all times *a gift we receive as fellowmen, as creatures who are sinners.* We are sinners who forgive as those forgiven by sinners who forgive as forgiven by God in the forgiveness of Jesus. In communion we forgive in response to forgiveness, and we do not forgive in any other way. Our ability to forgive does not reside in us or in our wills by virtue of an act already completed. We do not, as these discrete individuals, have wills that are now able to forgive and love. We do not have, at any moment, the power or ability to love; we do not have it as these egos who are able to receive what they give. Our ability is real in the communion by which we exist, the communion in which God gives joy to those who are with Christ and one with another. There is no ability prior to and apart from this communion. Therefore, there is no will, no willing, for or against our neighbor, prior to and apart from this same communion. Hence, there is no conversion of the will already accomplished, no ability of the will already in our possession, in any act of forgiveness and love. Repentance, conversion, and sanctification are aspects of every meeting with our neighbors under Christ, and they occur as incidence of communion among us *überhaupt.* There is no will already enabled or made free to love. There is only the sinner confronted with the love of God in Jesus and his neighbor and being enabled to forgive and to love as this sinner.

There is no paradox of grace and freedom or of prevenient and cooperating grace. This paradox assumes a state of nature as corrupted or depraved and a state of the will as perverted and unable to love God and man. But nature and will have no reality outside communion, and they neither are nor are acted upon except in communion. Hence, there is no prevenient grace that operates on the will or a man's nature, and there is no prior enabling of a will or correction of a nature that is presupposed in forgiveness and love or in communion among God's people. It is inadequate to say that the will is made free to love or to enter into communion. There is no inherited will to be made free for love. The bondage of the will and the freedom of the will are known in communion and have their very reality in it. We individually are at no time free to love; we are being made free to love in the communion of saints. Our freedom is related to grace not paradoxically, so as to contradict it, but dynamically—that is, in the *dynamis* whereby our love is at all times being received and therewith exercised by us in our ultimate ontological situation as fellowmen; and this occurs, not by a prevenient grace that acts privately and irresistibly upon the will, but by an *invenient* grace or power that is from as well as for communion. The solution of the logical problem of grace and freedom, which by no means dissipates the mystery of grace, is in the replacement of the image of man as endowed with a nature and a will with the image of man as a fellowman in the company of Jesus. Take Jesus and the neighbor out of the picture and you have neither man, nor the nature of man, nor the will of man.

In short, grace is prevenient in the church by the priority of Jesus Christ and my neighbor. It is prevenient with respect, not to a will in bondage, but to the individual who is posited by communion and as a fellowman. Grace is prevenient to the individual, not as individual, but as a fellowman, in the priority of communion over the existence of the individual, in the priority of the two over the one and the many. It is indeed emphatically true that grace prevenes my love as a sinner. But this prevenience is by way of communion. Therefore, grace is not prevenient in the traditional sense as a supernatural Power acting in the individual as such. Since "prevenient grace" belongs in the context of an anthropology that is based upon a doctrine of human nature apart from communion, it is better not to use the expression in our context. We would rather speak of grace manifested in Jesus' company as invenient, as coming into the church as a society of fellowmen and into each fellowman as fellowman. Prevenient grace, which acts upon a preexistent will, is a supernatural Power incongruous with the realities of communion. Invenient grace, which creates the individual through communion, is the work of the living God by his Word and Spirit.

As for subsequent cooperating grace, it disappears with the prevenient. We may, according to the terms of this discussion, no longer speak of grace cooperating with man's power or freedom already realized by prevenient grace. If prevenient grace does not give us a power to love, there is no power in us with which divine grace might cooperate. Our power to love as creatures and sinners is at all times power we receive in communion; it is our power to respond in forgiveness and love, which is the gift we receive from our neighbor's hand in the presence of Jesus. God does not cooperate with this power we receive and exercise; he creates it, exercises it, in the communion of his people with him and one with another. In this sense God cooperates with us; he blesses our communion with his forgiveness and the joy which it creates. But he does not cooperate with us in the sense that his power, conjoined with our power (he possessing his and we possessing ours), sanctifies us or establishes our own power to love as a *habit* and therefore as a private possession with which we might face our fellowmen. In our way of thinking, cooperating grace is creating grace as seen in the presence of Jesus—which at once creates the communion of saints who are sinners and justifies it, giving the people joy under the Kingdom of God. Therefore, there is no cooperating grace supplementing a power already in us. There is only *actual grace* in the communion of sinners, and this grace is at all times active in the responses men make one to another in the company of Jesus.

The notions of prevenient and subsequent grace, of operating and cooperating grace, of habitual and actual grace, belong with a doctrine of sanctification that is oriented, not toward the communion of saints, but toward private sainthood in churches where each man is concerned and busy with his own "growth in godliness." "Sanctifying grace" presumably worked within the individual, his soul and body, to cleanse him of sin left over from baptism. It made him not only "holier" than he was before but also holier than others around him. It produced "saints" rather than communion, righteous men who no longer loved as sinners, that is, men who no longer belonged in the company of Jesus. Such men enjoyed a private supernatural Power which made them habitually righteous and able to cooperate with God's grace. In addition, they received actual grace that enabled them to excel themselves and others in Christian virtue. In the process, they came to possess minds and wills that, though not perfectly sanctified, distinguished them from sinners as saintly people or plain "saints." In the company of Jesus such a distinction between saints and sinners is out of place and so are the doctrines of sanctification and grace that have been common in Catholic and Protestant churches, in both church-type and sect-type churches.

Without prevenient and cooperating grace there is no paradox of grace in the traditional sense. There is grace as miracle and mystery, which is the grace of God. Invenient grace in the communion of saints is not a paradox. It is God himself in Jesus Christ and in the church forgiving each man in the forgiveness he receives from his neighbor and bestows upon his neighbor, not because he has the ability by a supernatural and private act of the "First Cause," but by the merit of Jesus Christ, the head of the church, who has made us fellowmen and each man his brother's keeper. In a sense, everything depends upon whether we receive our brother, who is a sinner, as the angel of God. And this, in turn, depends upon the preaching and hearing of the gospel through the Word and the Sacraments. But such preaching and hearing occurs in the communion of saints, where men receive one another as angels of God.

"The paradox of grace and freedom" is the outcome of a Christianity that has been dominated by individualism, institutionalism, and supernaturalism. Such Christianity is a state of self-contradiction that expresses itself in the perennial double-talk of Christians who feel and talk Augustinian and act Pelagian. The paradox and the contradiction can be and are removed by the living God in the communion of saints. Our duty is to think in a manner appropriate to *this* grace of God as well as we can, and this is a reasonable service for us whose very life and joy is in the same communion of saints.

Let us look back for a moment at the Augustinian Pelagian, Calvinist-Arminian, orthodox-liberal controversies. In spite of endless variations in the debates between these antagonists, we find them all working with the common assumptions about "human nature." The question has been: Does the individual man have the ability to do the will of God? The Pelagians and their successors have said yes. The Augustinians and their successors have said no. In so doing, the Pelagians have contradicted the Christian conviction that it is God who enables us to do his will. The Augustinians have contradicted the conviction that obedience is true when it is the act of the one who obeys. And there has been no way to resolve these contradictions except verbally and by sleight of tongue.

We do not pretend to have solved the problem of "grace and freedom." We have, we hope, cast some doubt upon the presuppositions that underlie it. We have argued that the will (which is supposed to be free or unfree) is an abstraction from communion, which posits it and sustains it. There is no will without communion and no freedom or bondage of the will except in communion in the responses which fellowmen make one to another. The will that is consequent upon communion is a characteristic of the responses we make one to another. It is free under love and in bondage under ignoring. It is free as sinners love and forgive one another, and it is not free in that it is being made free by Jesus and his company. The will is free and unfree, not as a matter of contradiction, but in that the individual creature is at all times being posited as a human being. This creature is free in being posited and he is unfree in that he needs to be posited. Without the grace he receives in communion he does not exist and is therefore neither free nor unfree. By the same grace he is both free and unfree in that his freedom is at all times a gift, a free gift of God in Christ's company. He is created as a human being by grace through the communion of saints, and as creation, he is free and unfree, free as creation and unfree as being created. Since the act of communion is prior to the existence of the individual, the freedom and unfreedom of the individual are subsumed under communion and are analytical statements concerning existence as it occurs by communion. In short, what we have here is not a contradiction but a living dialectic about which we can speak only in terms both of grace and of freedom and not in terms of either one or of a synthesis of the two.

Yes, but still are we not to say that invenient grace empowers our will to love our neighbors as ourselves? After all this, have we escaped the paradox of "grace and freedom"? I think we have. There is no grace of God working in us that is not the grace of God *ab extra* and *ad extra* in Christ and by the church. I am continuously posited by God, by Christ, and by the church. I have nothing I do not receive, nothing I do not have by receiving. Having is receiving, and I give as I receive. Grace in me is grace toward me, so that it is not in me except as toward me. It surely is in me, but as being toward me. I am free *by grace*, but grace is always toward me and grace toward me is the grace of God the Father of our Lord Jesus Christ by my neighbor. I *am* free by grace, but grace is always toward me from Jesus Christ by my neighbor, who by their love makes me free. Without the love of Christ and my neighbor I am not free. By their love I am free and responsible. But the grace is of God.

When we think this way, we have a mystery, the mystery of God. But we do not have the traditional "paradox of grace and freedom." What is more wonderful, we may now live by the grace of God in the church and enjoy the freedom of his children, who may love and forgive, forgive and love, and so have joy, which is from God.

6 On Hearing the Gospel

1. THE PROBLEM OF HEARING THE GOSPEL

In our theological schools we are preoccupied with the problem of preaching the gospel. We give courses in the Bible, church history, and theology to provide the future preacher with "content" for his sermons. We give him courses in homiletics to train him in the preparation and delivery of his sermons. Beyond this, there are innumerable books on preaching, books of sermons, and other material to aid the preacher in his task. All this assumes that in the communication of the gospel the serious question is, What and how must a man preach so that the people will hear the gospel? We find conscientious preachers doing their best to produce good sermons, toiling week after week rather anxiously, often discouraged and always uncertain as to what in truth "goes across."

It is right and honorable that the preachers should turn their attention to themselves and their performance. To a degree, it is wholesome that they should try in every way possible to preach better than they have done before. But since in spite of the efforts of the preacher the people appear not to hear the gospel, it may be that in our preoccupation with preaching we are neglecting the equally decisive matter of hearing the gospel.

In Scripture the chief and perennial problem—rather, stumbling block—is not the speaking but the hearing of the Word of God.

Hear, O Israel: The Lord our God is one Lord.
(Deut. 6:4)

> Hear, O my people, and I will speak,
> O Israel, I will testify against you.
> I am God, your God.
>
> (Ps. 50:7)

> Hear, O my people, while I admonish you!
> O Israel, if you would but listen to me!
>
> (Ps. 81 :8)

> And he [the Lord] said, "Go, and say to this people:
> 'Hear and hear, but do not understand;
> see and see, but do not perceive.'"
>
> (Isa. 6:9)

> Hear, you deaf;
> and look, you blind, that you may see!
> Who is blind but my servant,
> or deaf as my messenger whom I send?
>
> (Isa. 42:18-19)

> From the day that your fathers came out of the land of
> Egypt to this day, I have persistently sent all my ser-
> vants the prophets to them, day after day; yet they did
> not listen to me, or incline their ear, but stiffened their
> neck. . . . So you shall speak all these words to them,
> but they will not listen to you. You shall call to them,
> but they will not answer you.
>
> (Jer. 7:25-27)

> "Listen! A sower went out to sow. And as he sowed,
> some seed fell along the path, and the birds came and
> devoured it. Other seed fell on rocky ground, where it
> had not much soil, and immediately it sprang up . . . ;
> and when the sun rose it was scorched, and since it had
> no root it withered away. Other seed fell among thorns
> and the thorns grew up and choked it, and it yielded no
> grain. And other seeds fell into good soil and brought
> forth grain. . . ." And he said," He who has ears to hear,
> let him hear."
>
> (Mark 4:3-9)

> O Jerusalem, Jerusalem, killing the prophets and ston-
> ing those who are sent to you! How often would I have
> gathered your children together as a hen gathers her
> brood under her wings, and you would not! Behold,
> your house is forsaken. And I tell you, you will not see
> me until you say, "Blessed is he who comes in the
> name of the Lord! "
>
> (Luke 13:34-35)

The Scriptures make it plain that there is a perennial and ada-
mant resistance to the Word of God. From the exodus to the exile the
people of God refused to hear the prophets of God and disobeyed his
law with a stiffneckedness that would be surprising as well as amazing
were it not that the same obduracy is in the church today. When the Son
of Man came, as Savior as well as prophet, the words fell on rocky
ground and among thorns. The people listened to him eagerly and then
turned away, except for a few. After his resurrection, when the gospel
was preached, few that were men of wisdom or had the law, few that
were men of power and noble birth, embraced it. Many who became
Christians misunderstood the Word of God and violated the way of the
church. The triumph and expansion of Christianity was also a corruption of the Word of God in many ways, and the connection between the
church as it was gradually established and the gospel of Jesus Christ became obscured. The several reformations in the church have been followed by orthodoxies that are remarkable as the expressions of a permanent determination to turn the offense of the cross into an innocuous
piety and a manageable affair. The people want to be made happy and
secure through the good offices of the churches, but they continue to resist the Word of God, which is "like fire . . . and like a hammer which
breaks the rock in pieces" (Jer. 23 :29).

The prophet who spoke the Word of God was up against a rebellious and hardhearted people, and so is the preacher who would
preach the crucified and risen Lord of the church. The sin that provoked
Israel against the God of Abraham and Moses provokes the New Israel
against the God and Father of Jesus Christ. These two are the same
God, and the same living God demands of the people, now as then, a
repentance that they find too costly and will not offer to God even under the promise of peace and joy.

Now, it would be simple to accuse the people of folly, pride,

infidelity, stubbornness—in short, of sin—and thus to explain their not
hearing the Word of God. According to Scripture, thus it is that God
judges us and we have no self-defense against him. Certainly after the
exodus and Mt. Sinai, the people of Israel had no excuse for their idola-
tries and inhumanities; after the advent of the Word in the flesh and the
advent of the Spirit of God in the church, we certainly are without excuse if we will not hear the promises of God and live in the hope of
righteousness. So in God's sight we are judged and found guilty and are
without excuse; so we are before Jesus Christ and the Holy Spirit.

2. REASON IN NOT HEARING

Still, we who are concerned with the problem of the hearer are
not God, and the matter is not settled by saying that the people do not
hear because they are sinners. We know that the sin of not hearing God,
of turning away from him, occurs by temptation. Even while the sinner
who will not hear is responsible for his unbelief and disobedience, his
resistance to the Word of God occurs by way of temptations that are
overwhelming and irresistible. The sinner has reason on his side, not an
abstract rationality, but the concrete situation in which he exists. The
Fall in paradise was eminently rational: "So when the woman saw that
the tree was good for food, and that it was a delight to the eyes, and that
the tree was to be desired to make one wise, she took of its fruit and
ate; and she also gave some to her husband, and he ate" (Gen. 3:6). It
certainly is rational to eat of a fruit that is delightful, tasteful, and bene-
ficial. When Satan tempted Jesus in the wilderness, Satan's arguments
also were rational. Surely it is rational to turn stone into bread, to acquire power in this world, to make sure of one's faith in God. The response of Jesus to the several suggestions of the devil are surprising
and in our judgment hardly wise. The practice of mankind has been to
side with Eve and Adam rather than with Jesus.

It is therefore necessary to understand and take seriously that
the refusal of the people to hear the Word of God in Jesus Christ crucified and risen is to them eminently wise and rational. The sin of Adam
has been rightly judged as proud, rebellious, and perfidious.[1] But Adam
was no fallen archangel or ambitious superman. He did not intend to
storm God's heaven and to dethrone the Almighty. He ate of a fruit that
was presented to him as pleasant to the eye and to the taste. When Jesus
was tempted, he was not called upon to take God's place, to rebel

against him and to war against him. He was told to save his life, to acquire useful power, and to prove his faith. When Israel murmured
against God in the wilderness, they did so remembering their few pleasures and comforts in Egypt and asking only to be safe from hunger and
the sword. When people today turn a deaf ear to the preacher, to the
Word of the cross and the resurrection, they act, not as proud and rebellious foes of Jesus Christ, but as reasonable people who know that the
way of the cross is a stumbling block and a foolishness—a stumbling
block because it is contrary to "the righteousness of works" and a foolishness because it is incompatible with their way of life in this world.
Therefore, they insist, piously and quietly, but firmly and persistently,
that they be spared the offense of the gospel and be presented instead
with a religion, orthodox or modern, that will not violate their most obvious and rational interests. The preachers have to take it seriously that
the people, like Israel, have a strong and intelligent case against the
gospel of death and resurrection. The temptation to see the gospel as a
demand for self-destruction is too strong. The gospel does appear to the
mind of the flesh as a most unreasonable proposal, and the people are
determined not to act as fools.

The people wish to live, and not to die. They wish to be
strong, and not weak. They wish to be rich, or at least well off, and not
poor. They wish to be accepted and well thought of, and not rejected
and persecuted. They want to be happy, and not to suffer. Such reasonable and universal desires of men are today more reasonable than ever,
at least in the Western, free world. Science and industry, our infinity of
goods and services, our democratic institutions and way of life—all
good things available in our world today encourage the people to hope
that, given sufficient knowledge and skill, with goodwill and good
sense, we, all but the stupid and the unfortunate, shall be able to live in
comfort and pleasure, with good health and security, which are reasonable prospects in our society. The fact is that our way of life, which provides us with the solid goods produced, possessed, and enjoyed among
us, appears alien to the way of the cross and the Word of God proclaimed by Scripture.

The preacher today has to discipline himself not to take offense at the "secularism" and "materialism" of the people, not to set
himself against "the American way," not to construe the rational desires
of the people in our "age of power and plenty" as simple lusts to be de-
nounced as opposed to true spirituality. It is relatively easy to notice the

contradiction between religion and secularism and to exhort the people
to choose between them. It is not so hard to preach against selfishness
and worldliness and vaguely to recommend the "spiritual life" and altruism. A conscientious preacher today can cause much commotion by
being against this "sensate culture" and "bourgeois civilization," by de-
nouncing and exhorting and making people feel guilty.[2] But he is kick-
ing against the pricks and will end up by doing no good to himself and
to his people. It is of utmost importance to preach with the understanding that sinners are eminently reasonable and decent people and that the
way of life they follow is good and not evil. The temptation not to hear
the Word of God or the gospel is too subtle for them, and they have no
effective defense against it.

3. SIN IN NOT HEARING

On the other hand, it takes equal discipline in a preacher to
recognize that the good people before him are indeed sinners who need
to be converted. The people's pursuit of the good life in terms of the
goods available in our society, in terms of refrigerators and cars, of TV
sets and hi-fi sets, of plenty to eat and everything to wear, is not, in
fact, an innocent activity conducive to human peace. The well-
mannered folk practicing enlightened self-interest are not saints, and
their common and prevailing determination to avoid conflict does not
produce a community of human beings whose meetings fulfill their
lives. It is the business and responsibility of the leaders in the churches,
and therefore of the preacher, to know and understand that there is no
ordinary connection between the decencies of the people and the love
of the gospel and the law. It is a violation of the preacher's responsibility and a treacherous disservice to God's people to confuse enlightened
self-interest and its apparent innocence with the love of the neighbor
proposed by the Word of God.[3] We are to preach for the conversion of
sinners, which means that we are to speak to sinners, to preach the
grace of God.

A new or renewed understanding of sin and salvation is in order. The people in our churches are greatly confused on this subject.
They have been both led and allowed to identify sin with certain
wrongdoings such as cheating, stealing, adultery, murder, which they
find more in others than in themselves. Or else, they have identified sin
with pride, enmity, selfishness, not doing good, concerning which they

can readily exonerate themselves, again by a simple comparison of themselves with their neighbors. As for "the great commandment" concerning the love of God and the love of neighbor, they are able both to claim a certain obedience to it and to discuss it as hardly possible for them. It is today necessary so to understand sin that there shall be no question as to the wrongness of it and as to the people's responsibility to turn away from it. It is necessary to understand sin as a violation of truth, as an unfaithfulness that leaves the sinner without excuse and an evil that is the destruction of humanity or the very death of the sinner and of those sinned against. The subordination of faithfulness to one's neighbor to the acquisition and enjoyment of the goods in our society is a violation of Jesus Christ, and with him of God and his people. This is today, as in the days of Ezekiel, a not hearing of the Word of God, and it is the ubiquitous as well as deadly working of sin.

However, the problem before us is that when grace and judgment are preached, the people do not hear. The preacher as preacher must keep in mind his own deficiencies and work at removing them all his days. But he also must recognize that the hearing of the Word does not altogether depend upon him. Hearing is an issue between the hearer and his God. Since it is the living God alone who is able to speak his Word with power to convert, it is a first principle of preaching to commend the mind and heart of the hearers to God. It is always a joyful thing to remember that God Almighty has assumed the first responsibility for restoring his people to himself, that he has done this in the Law and the Prophets and in Jesus Christ, that he does this today in the Holy Spirit working with might in the church. It is a joyful thing to preach the Word of God by the exposition of the Scriptures, to administer the Sacraments, to maintain order and freedom in the church, knowing that the living God is in all things for all. Our God is wise and resourceful and *his* Word will not fail.

But let us not be superstitious. It is not enough to preach and to hope for the best. It is not enough for the preacher to say, "I have done my best; let God enable these people to hear." It is not enough to fall back quickly upon the double mystery of God's not speaking to some and of men's sin, which makes them deaf to the Word of God.[4] It is neither intelligent nor helpful to overlook the problem of hearing among the people. The fact is that the temptation to turn away from the gospel of Jesus Christ and from the law of God is irresistible for the people. In saying this, I deny neither their ability to hear nor their responsibility to do it. But it is still true that the temptation to choose the way of enlightened self-interest in our civilization is one that overwhelms the people in our churches. The goods, with comforts and pleasures, offered to us in our world are so real and solid that reason embraces them readily and without misgiving. There is no reason for not having treasures on earth when one can keep the moths out, and prevent rusting, and carry insurance against fire and thieving. The people know of no reason why they should not serve God and mammon too. They do not see well-being as temptation and goods as stumbling blocks. They think that they are free in the use of their possessions, and masters in the running of their machines; they are not in bondage and they need not be set free; they are not sinners and they need no forgiveness. Therefore, their bondage is settled and their sin unforgiven. When these people hear the gospel, they do not hear; they neither understand nor obey. When we consider the endless propaganda for the practice of enlightened self-interest emanating from the several "organs of mass communication" in our society, we can hardly fail to acknowledge that the people who hear the preacher are in no position to hear, and the preacher himself is up against it. The individual churchgoer, as this individual hearing the preacher, both will not and cannot hear the Word of God.

I do not pretend to know the solution to the problem of the hearer. I suspect that there is no solution that will lead to foolproof preaching. The preacher must be prepared for the disappointments that have accompanied preaching since the time of the prophets and evangelists, including the preaching of our Lord. There is no doing away with the mystery of sin and not hearing.

4. THE INDIVIDUAL IN THE CHURCH

Still, I should like to say a helpful word. As I have just said, the individual churchgoer is at a solid disadvantage in hearing the Word of God. His own mind as formed by our society and the pressures exerted upon him in it leave him helpless under the temptation to turn away from Jesus Christ crucified and risen, from the gospel and the law of God. The individual as such, without the concerted help of his fellowmen, especially his fellow Christians, is no match against the devil working behind the scenes in this age of power and abundance. It is most unlikely that the best sermons of his preacher will induce him to "seek first the kingdom of heaven." Even if he acknowledges the validity of the preacher's words and becomes concerned with his own failure to live as a Christian, even if he "repents" and worries and struggles, he will not go against the way of life around him because he knows that to do such a thing will expose him to the wrath of the great god of this world and jeopardize his good name and security and life, not only his own but those of others for whose well-being he is responsible. A man's dependence upon "the world" is such that it hardly leaves him any choice except to conform and cooperate. It is, in fact, cruel to ask a man to be in this world and not of it. The world will not tolerate such delinquency.

Even though the individual has to hear the gospel, it is futile to preach to him as an individual. I think that this is one of the chief wrongdoings in the preaching of the gospel today. On Sunday mornings what we have in our churches is a collection of individuals who worship and hear in common, in the same building, singing and listening at the same time, in the same place. But they enter and stay and go out as individuals, attending to the preacher's words, but receiving hardly any help and comfort one from another. What they do and hear, they do and hear as a "collective." They are more like a collection of money in the plate than like members of a body keeping one another alive. Members of families having a life together may worship and listen, aware one of another. But beyond that it is everybody for himself. Nobody expects much from anybody, and no man is responsible for the life and well-being of another man. Each one has his business, his problems, his troubles, his hopes and fears, which he has neither the will nor the opportunity to share with his neighbor. In fact, he does his best to conceal himself from his neighbor and would be both surprised and perplexed if a fellow churchman opened up to him with a "private matter." It is all very well to meet God together, but it would be shocking to meet one another with the soul and spirit one presumably lays bare before God. People open up one to another no more in church than they do anywhere else. They come in closed one to another, and they go out closed.

I wish to draw your attention to this closedness, to this common horror of communication or communion among churchmen as a primary source of not hearing. In this respect the churches simply reflect the alienation of man from man that is the curse of our society and our age. Humanity itself has become taboo. Men are expected to meet in their several roles and functions in our world: as scientists, teachers, workers, businessmen, as buyers and sellers, as entertainers and entertained, even as preachers and people, as white and black, rich and not so rich, Europeans and Arabs; but they are not expected to meet as human beings, because humanity, flesh and blood, the dread and hope of the creature, are at best irrelevant to the pursuit of goods and at worst confusing and detrimental to it. People may speak to each other of the weather, business, politics, and even sometimes of religion! But they may not speak to each other as human beings, in their need for the recognition of man by man as a "living soul" which is at once the essence and bond of humanity. That is not good for selling and buying. It is a diversion from the common business of our society and its institutions that are quickened, not by humanity, but by the enlightened self-interest of men, which works as though a man's life does in truth consist of the abundance of the things he possesses. Therefore, it becomes in poor taste for anyone to approach another as a human being or to expect his neighbor to approach him as one. People learn to withdraw one from another and refuse to love and to be loved as human beings. Each man turns away from his neighbor to wither and to die, guilty and accusing, building walls around himself both to shut in and to shut out. And the end of it all is misery and perishing.

The religious man is at all times apt to attend to his God by turning his back to his neighbor. When he goes to church to worship God, his mind and heart are on "God" and not on his neighbor. Indeed, he worships as one of a congregation, and his worship is a "corporate" act. He does what everybody else does. He listens to God. He sings and prays to God. He confesses his faith in God. He does all this *with* others, in the sense that he listens and sings and prays when the others around him do these things. His own worship is enhanced by the worship of the others. In short, he participates in a common practice. But, nevertheless, his business is with God and not with his neighbor. It is God he, or it, worships. It is God to whom he, or it, sings and prays. It is to God he, or it, confesses sins, and from God he hopes for forgiveness. He hears "the Word of God" and not the word of man. There is in his mind no logical connection between the two things. On the contrary, he is quite ready and able to attend to God without attending to his neighbor, quite in the same way that a man might attend to John and not to James. In fact, he shuts off his neighbor in order to attend to God. Thus it is that in church, people remain closed to the word of man, and the "communion of saints" is turned into a collective worship.

5. THE WORD OF GOD AND THE
WORD OF THE SINNER

There is no hearing the Word of God without hearing the word of man. This is obvious in Biblical prophecy and in preaching in our churches. It is established by the Word become flesh. God of the Christian faith is God who speaks, and he speaks by the mouth of his servants. "And how are they to hear without a preacher?" (Rom. 10:14.) But we need to go farther. Unless the people hear the Word of God in "the congregation of believers" or "the communion of saints," how are they to hear it? There is neither preaching nor hearing without the church, and the church is a people responsive and responsible one to another.[5] The Word of God, the gospel and the law, are addressed to "two or three . . . gathered together" under Jesus Christ. These two or three are not peas in a pod. They are human beings whose very life is a communion with God and one with another. There is no individual man outside of a fellowship of people, and no man can hear God unless he hears his neighbor. No man has eyes to see, ears to hear, a mind to understand without having been seen, heard, understood by his neighbor, without seeing, hearing, understanding his neighbor. God in the beginning created two "intelligent" beings, and since then it has taken two to make "intelligent creation." For our very existence as human beings we are dependent not only upon God who made us but also upon our neighbor whom God made to be our fellowman. It follows that the problem of hearing the Word of God is inseparable from hearing the word of man.

Now, what is meant by hearing the word of man? The word of man is the word our neighbor addresses to us as a creature who is a sinner. It is the word of the living soul in his need for acknowledgment as a creature who, being intelligent, exists in his need and hope.[6] A man is a creature who lives and keeps alive by the love that makes him a fellowman, and his word is the demand he makes upon his neighbor as a responsive and responsible creature, responsive to love and responsible for love, love being the bond of union between two creatures who exist by their mutual recognition as "God's intelligent creation." By the word of man we know ourselves and our neighbors as finite beings whose living is a dying and for whom love is life as it overcomes the power of death.[7] We who are creatures know ourselves as creatures by the word of our neighbor and in this knowledge we are and live as human beings.

Accompanying all our intercourse as human beings, in our way of life and institutions, there is this word of man that calls upon us to recognize our neighbor as a living soul or to love him as ourselves. In all our businesses one with another, in the family, the school, the marketplace, the city hall, the church, our fellowmen approach us as human beings and rejoice or lament according as they are or are not known as the creatures that they are by the will of God. In all the words that they speak to us and hear from us, whatever the business on hand, they speak and hope to hear the word of man that is the encounter of human beings in their restiveness and need of love. They may speak of the weather or the political situation. They may persuade us to buy or to sell. They may gossip about a neighbor or discuss a matter of policy. Whatever they do and hope we shall do, they do with the hope and concern of the living for life, which is the love of their fellowman. In this concern and hope they speak as human beings and communicate a word that is the human substance of all that they say and hope earnestly to hear from us. The word of man is the word in all our words and acts that evokes our humanity and binds man to man in the bundle of life for joy and peace and every blessing.

How, then, is this word heard? It is heard by love. In this case, hearing and loving are inseparable one from the other. As with the Word of God, hearing, understanding, obeying, go together, so with the word of man also, hearing, understanding, and responding in love go together. To see a human being is to love him. If a man does not love, he also does not see, and if he does not see, he also does not respond, or understand, or love. Alas, in this matter we must speak in negatives. Not to hear the word of man is to be separated from our neighbor, to be indifferent to him, to neglect him and reject him, to be unfaithful to him, to violate him, and to destroy him. There is no injustice, no perfidy, no oppression that equals the shutting off of the neighbor, the denial of the love due to him. There is no humiliation and failure and savor of death that equals the misery that goes with creature's turning away from the creature. Thus it is that the anxiety and despair celebrated by modern existentialism are quickened in the isolated soul, and meaning gives way to madness and suicide follows murder.[8] The word of man is heard by love, and where love is not, there is only silence and nothing. And the creature exists toward death as sinner.

The word of man is the word of the creature and sinner, of the creature in sin under the power of death and wrath and the flesh and the devil. We speak one to another as sinners and hear one another as sinners. The commandment, the law of humanity, is: "Thou shalt love thy neighbor as thyself." We know that the commandment is true and right, not an imposition of the impossible but a declaration of our very being.[9] We live and act as human beings only as we love our neighbor as ourselves, as ourselves who are creatures existing by love. The commandment is the way of life, and obedience to it is life itself. And yet, with us it is confused and, in fact, disobeyed. We know we neither love nor are loved as the commandment requires. We know this as we approach one another and as we leave one another, and our knowledge fills both us and our neighbor with bitterness. Each man is at once guilty and an accuser and as both he shuts the door on his neighbor. This is the first enmity and the exercise of that false humanity which subsists by lust and war.[10]

How, then, do we hear the word of man? Surely we do it by hearing the Word of God in Christ Jesus crucified, risen, and reigning; by hearing the words, "Your sins are forgiven; go and sin no more." Once there was a man who loved to forgive and forgave to love. This man was the Son of God, who dwelt among us full of grace and truth, and by his obedience God reconciled the world to himself.[11] This is the good news the preacher is called to preach, the Word that is the source and life of the church, the very possibility of our communion as human beings. We are to hear the word of man, we are enabled to hear the word of man, by the speaking of God in the sermon and Sacraments. This is our faith, and there is no need to say more about it at this time.

6. HEARING GOD'S WORD AND MAN'S WORD

The purpose of this chapter is to establish that the Word of God is heard by hearing the word of man, not as though the latter came first ("By grace you have been saved"), but in that if a man does not attend to the word of man, he does not hear the Word of God. How do we know the love of God and the forgiveness of God unless we approach our neighbor with zeal and hope: with zeal to love and forgive and with hope of being loved and forgiven? We do not know the love and forgiveness of God, we do not know "the living God," in separation from our neighbor. If, *per impossibile*, we were not fellowmen, we would not be men; if we were not men, we would not know God. But we are fellowmen only in our responsibility for love and in the hope of forgiveness, in love toward our neighbor and forgiveness from our neighbor. When we hope for a forgiveness that is not in us and a forgiveness that is not in our neighbor, hoping by the promise in the forgiveness of Jesus, we hope in God. And when we hope in God, we hope by the promise for forgiveness received and given. So it is that the Word of God and the word of man are not separable one from the other, and hearing the one is united with hearing the other. The gospel of God is, first, that God in Christ has reconciled us to himself, to ourselves, to our neighbor. The same gospel secondly, but not separably from the first, is that in this reconciliation we and our neighbor, by the working of the Spirit of God, are ministers of God through whom, as creatures and sinners, God restores us to himself, to ourselves, and to one another.

It is the Christian faith, by the Word of promise from God in Jesus, that salvation is in the congregation of believers, by the agency of sinful men gathered together, two or three, in the name of Jesus. For hearing the Word it is required that we accept our brother as we accept Jesus and God himself. It is required that we approach with hope this creature and sinner as the means of grace as truly by God's appointment as preaching and the Sacraments, yea as truly and indispensably as Jesus Christ himself. If we approach our brother saying, "I will not love him as myself and he will not love me as himself; he will not forgive me and I will not forgive him; I cannot and he cannot," then we shut ourselves to the Word of God and will not hear it. We do not believe in God. We do not believe in Jesus Christ. We do not believe the Holy Spirit and we withdraw from the communion of saints. Hearing is by faith and hope and love. If we have no hope, neither do we have faith or love, because we both believe and love by hope, by hope in God, by the hope that we shall love and be loved, shall forgive and be forgiven. If we say our neighbor will neither forgive nor love, we do not believe in God. Neither do we know him. If we say, "I cannot and will not forgive and love," we are equally guilty for repudiating the promise of God and scorning the Holy Spirit. (Cf. Mark 3 :28-30.)

Scripture and tradition have put first things first, and clearly and once for all upheld the sovereignty of God in the redemption of man.[12] We may in no way alter or confuse this tradition. On the other hand, the time has come, and none too soon, for taking to mind and heart the truth that God in his grace and sovereignty has bound our love to him with our love one for another and insists that we receive our neighbor as the living means of his grace both for judgment and for mercy.[13] The freedom of the living God is known in two surprises: one, in our redemption through the offense of the cross, two, in reconciliation through men who are at enmity toward us as we are at enmity toward them. The sovereignty, the omnipotence, of the same God is known in that we may live in the hope of righteousness, hoping and expecting that we shall love and forgive our enemies and that they shall love and forgive us who have rejected and condemned them. To believe in God is to believe in miracle, and there is no miracle worth the joy of a human being, apart from forgiveness and love given and received in the communion of saints, which is hearing the Word of God.

7. PREACHING WITH HOPE

The openness of man to man considered in this discussion is not too evident in our churches. Our churchly habits as well as our culture are against the communion of sinners one with another. Inertia in this matter is so great as to unnerve us. Many find it easy to approach God, but they find it very hard to approach man. They find it easy to ask God's forgiveness, but they find it very hard to surrender to men as sinners. They think they love God with some zeal, but they will not love their neighbor as themselves. They will trust God, but they would rather perish than put themselves at the disposal of their neighbor. The wall between man and man is too high and too thick for the "people of God" to live together in the fruition of the creature's communion with creature. So in our churches men will not hear the word of man, and therefore they will not hear the Word of God.

But this last statement is too presumptuous. We are not to judge our fellowmen and we are not to question the sovereignty of God. Preachers are to trust God and live in hope, for themselves and for others. They are to mind their business and preach the Word of God. Only, they are to preach intelligently. Preaching must be a studied and steady struggle to proclaim the Word of God to sinners who resist the Word of God because they resist the word of man; to a people who turn away from God because they will not trust God's working in their neighbor. If the preacher would understand that all worship and prayer are confused and even counterfeit unless they open man to man in love, unless through them men receive the courage and hope to approach one another in the hope of righteousness, it would greatly help the people. Preaching toward such courage and such hope, inspired by the promises of God in Christ Jesus and Scripture, is integral to the Word of God. To preach, to minister, to counsel, to do all things, hoping, in practical ways, that "the new man" in the church will open up as a redeemed sinner to his neighbor and in truth will receive and give love—this is to preach in faith. It is to preach by faith in the sovereignty of God, hoping that God will give us the grace to love one another. With God, who spoke to his people in the faithfulness of Jesus Christ, all things are possible. The miracle of Jesus who forgave sinners is the promise of forgiving of sins among his people, rather, the promise that sinners may forgive one another. Since Christ in truth justified sinners, it is illogical not to believe that sinners may justify one another and commune one with another for the unveiling of their common dignity as fellow creatures. The mighty arm of God has once for all been revealed in Christ Jesus. In Christ, by Christ, God has made his sinning people his ministers one to another. Such is his sovereignty, which is the substance of preaching. Preaching is the proclamation of this sovereignty or of the possibility of justification among sinners, of the power by which the people, under all the temptations peculiar to our age and time, may love their neighbors as flesh and blood, as themselves, for their common peace. So it is that to preach is to proclaim the gospel with hope.

The preacher's own hope is sustained, first of all, by Jesus Christ by whom in truth sinners were justified. It is sustained by the preacher's cleaving to "the fact of Christ." There is no failure and failing in the church that can logically and in fact annihilate Christ himself and his gospel. In the freedom of the Christian by the very existence of Christ, the first thing a preacher may do is to hold fast to Jesus Christ. But this holding fast to Christ is by the working of the Spirit of God in the church. There is no holding fast to the person of Christ without holding fast to his work. But his work is the forgiveness of sins in the church. It is not possible for a man, the preacher, to believe in Christ and not believe in his work; it is not possible for him to believe in his work and not believe in his people who are his work. To believe in his people is indeed to believe in the Spirit of God, who is the power of forgiveness in the church. But how is one to believe in the Spirit unless he believes in the people, rather, in the work of Christ by which the people are free to forgive one another? Holding on to Christ, holding on to the Spirit of God, holding on to the people of God, are aspects of one and the same holding on to God that is the substance of hope and preaching with hope, that is, preaching.

It is hard for the preacher to believe in the people, for the people, as he sees them, will not hear. For this reason he is tempted to believe in God, to cleave to Christ, but not to believe in the people and not to cleave to them. But this is, as we have tried to show, illogical. Besides, it makes preaching to become nonpreaching. The preacher as the preacher must believe in the people, because where there is no faith, there is no hope, and where there is no hope, there is no preaching. He must believe in the people as sinners who are in Jesus' company, as his own fellow sinners in Jesus' company. Preaching is done in the church. It is done by a man in the church. It is done by a man who exists by the forgiveness of sins, therefore, by the hope of being forgiven by his neighbor. Without this hope, he does not preach. With it, he preaches with hope that the Word of God may be heard among the people. What is possible for him is possible for his hearers. In this there is no difference between the preacher and the hearer. Both live by the Word of God and the Spirit of God in the church. In short, the preacher may hope to be heard insofar as he may hope to hear the Word of God. As he hopes to hear, he may hope to be heard in the communion of saints.

It is indeed impossible for individuals in isolation, deprived of the counsel and comfort of their fellowmen, to resist the temptations of this world. This we all know. But we also know that nothing is impossible for the Spirit of God who does his mighty work in the communion of saints by the ministry of men toward one another. When two or three are gathered together in Jesus' name, knowing their peril in our society, and, being responsive to the Word of God, are responsible one to another, loving one another and encouraging one another and fortifying one another with proper intelligence and hope in the face of all the temptations of this "Power Age"—then God himself will bless their communication and bring victory to his church. God has spoken his Word with power through the word of Man spoken to man. Thus he has promised that he will speak to us and save us. We may hear this promise in approaching one another in hope and in loving one another by hope. When we do this, we shall hear the Word of God and win as brothers against every temptation and taste of the Kingdom of God.

At least one more word needs to be said. The communion of saints is not a thing apart from the common life we have one with another. There is no hearing the word of man apart from attending to the needs of men in our society. We meet one another as fellowmen, to love one another, as we meet one another to be just one to another. The communion of saints occurs in transactions of daily life in families, shops, and city halls, as we are occupied with food, shelter, security, with buying and selling, acquiring, possessing, and enjoying. We commune one with another as fellowmen as we do whatever we need to do in order to allow our fellowmen to participate in the satisfactions available in our world. Thus it is that we treat them justly and in so doing we show forth our love or humanity. Thus it is that we and they forgive and have peace one with another. Forgiving, loving, doing justly, so go together that any one of these three may be a sign of another. Let us not despise matters of justice and mercy nor forget to attend to them for faithfulness toward one another. They belong in the communion of saints for the creature's joy and the joy of God in the creature. By justice in our transactions we hear the Word of God and the word of man and enter the Kingdom of God.

PART THREE—LOVE IN THE COMMON LIFE

7 *The Problem
of Love*

1. LOVE AND AGAPĒ

Before the second decade of this century, there was no problem of love as envisaged in this chapter except that of expressing it in goodwill and justice. The imperfections of human love and the difficulties in its way were recognized. It was known that love involves suffering and sacrifice and that it is commonly mixed with selfishness, which makes it come short of the ideal of unselfish love. Men even recognized, especially as against "humanism," that faith in God and a sense of our need of his help are necessary for maximum exercise of love. So the problem of love was one of faith and effort, of enlightenment and a willingness to pay the price: a problem that could be solved more or less successfully, depending upon the conjunction of divine grace and human virtue in the strivings for the ideal as presented by Jesus. The preacher appealed to the goodwill and the good sense of his hearers and left to them the task of making decisions more or less in conformity with the standard of unselfish and beneficent love.

One facet of this view was the acknowledgment of the value of love as the basis of community and of "the brotherhood it brings."[1] Love was recognized not only as practical but also as conducive to the making of a good and just society. It was understood and commonly believed that where there are affection, sympathy, goodwill, there is the proper motive for justice and an adequate basis for a community of brothers.[2]

Another facet of this view of love was the belief that it would spread out from limited circles of the family and the neighborhood to larger circles of the city, the nation, and the world; from personal relations to political and economic relations—until it would become universalized, so that people would come to love all men without regard to color or creed, class or kind. If love were an attitude and affection, there seemed to be no prohibitive impediment to its expansion through enlightenment and effort, especially with God's help and the good influences already present in the community.

Thirdly, there was the conviction that there is a congruity between the ideal and "man's deepest strivings."[3] It was held that love is at once an expression of God's and of man's natures. It was, of course, well known that human nature is marred by selfishness and that ill will has created a grave problem for love. The facts of human cruelty and injustice were too obvious and deeply felt not to raise questions about the nature of man. But it appeared evident that we must nevertheless believe in man and hold as true that his "deepest strivings" are from love and for love. It was a matter of logic and hope. Once you deny that love is the ideal of man and that he is striving for it, even if weakly and confusedly, there is no hope for a better society, and without hope all is lost. Therefore, it was believed that love, with God's help, is a human possibility.

The above view of love was never proved to be wrong. It was attacked with more or less logic and great persuasiveness because world events after the First World War produced, not progress toward the ideal community of love, but terrifying outbursts of inhumanities and miseries. Instead of a decrease in human woe and peril, there was an increase. Neither faith in man nor faith in enlightenment could withstand the onslaught of facts that uncovered massive cruelties and stupidities in our world. Affection and goodwill were not getting us very far, and reason was at large overwhelmed by unreason. Something was deeply wrong, and men began to think in radically new ways. "Realism" dictated that human love is inadequate for the need of the present, and theologians turned to God, not as the bearer of love's ideal, but as the revelation of another love beside which man's love was seen as sentimental and hypocritical and his righteousness as "filthy rags."

Thus, the First World War and its aftermath of troubles and frustrations led to strong reactions to the "idealism" of the first decades of the nineteenth century. Neoorthodox writers accused "liberalism" of

idealism, romanti- cism, evolutionism, monism, humanism, rationalism, and even suggested that liberals had been stupid. They set out to
rediscover the Bible, the gospel, and the "Reformation theology." They
inveighed against the pride and complacency of modern religion. They
spoke vehemently of revelation and redemption. They rediscovered the
depravity of man and the hypocrisy of his ways. And with a newly acquired realism, some insisted that love is not a human and historical
possibility. Others were content to contrast God's love with man's,
agapē with *erōs*, hoping that once the distinction was properly made
and Christians came to know it, somehow the church would come to its
own.

In our present situation it would hardly be helpful to compare
liberal "idealism," and neoorthodox Biblicism and realism, as contra-
dictory doctrines. Liberal theology was a response to a human situation
in which the dignity of man was jeopardized by ideas derived from science and economic life. The interpretations of love in terms of affection, sympathy, goodwill, mutuality, had to be understood over against
the indignities, privations, miseries that human beings suffered in the
industrial societies of the times. When people spoke of respect for personality and of the infinite value of personality, they were using language intended, not to inflame the pride of men, but to induce them to
treat one another with the justice and decency due to human beings. It
goes without saying that the liberals were right and are still right. Respect for personality is never out of date.

When the neoorthodox attacked the liberal position they also
were responding to a human situation. There is today something futile
in saying "love and goodwill and respect for personality": not that we
do not need these things, but it seems impossible to have enough of
them for our present need. It does not seem to be in us to love as the
times require, and the love we do have seems irrelevant as well as insufficient. It is no wonder that we have had Christian thinkers who have
sought to remind us of another love which might be what this age needs
for its peace. It is natural that they should have opposed the love we
know with another love and should have insisted upon the disparity between the two. It is no wonder that they have turned our attention to
God, who alone, they say, makes love possible. Every note struck by
the new orthodoxy on the subject of love is to be understood as a criticism of opposing notes that seem no longer to serve the purpose of
peace.

On the other hand, the new expositions of love are not obviously relevant to our situation or promising for our future. Affection, goodwill, sympathy, humanity, had the advantage of at least being within human reach. They appeared relevant and needful; they made some kind of sense, and man could be induced to take them seriously. People could see and understand that love is the bond of humanity and the way to peace and joy in the community. They may have been too romantic and sentimental in thinking that they loved as needful or that they could love if they would. They may not have been properly Biblical and realistic, but the love they were talking about was relevant and they assumed the responsibility to practice it.

The new love, *agape*, may be relevant as an impossible possibility, but it is no way for human life in this world. Nobody lives it. Nobody intends to live it. Nobody who has any sense of responsibility toward his neighbor can live it. And perhaps the notion that it is necessary for the realization of the mutual love and decency that we do need and must practice is not valid. One can understand the *agapē* of neoorthodoxy as a criticism of sentimentalized and hypocritical humanity, but as a positive way of life in this world it appears futile.

According to its expositors, Christian love, or *agapē*, is a spontaneous, unmotivated love that is "indifferent to value" and utterly alien to prudence.[4] From Jesus' love for "sinners" and "enemies," Dr. Nygren deduces that God's love is directed toward creatures who in no sense are in a position to move him to love them. Men have no value before God, and he loves them, not because they are worth loving, but because he loves them. In loving those who are worthless he endows them with worth and value.

Barth has spoken of God's love in similar terms: "This love of God is his grace. It is love in the form of deepest condescension. It occurs even where there is no question of claim or merit on the part of the other. It is love which is overflowing, free, unconstrained, unconditioned. And we must add at once: It is love which is merciful, making this movement, this act of condescension, in such a way that, in taking this other to itself, it identifies itself with its need, and meets its plight with its own concern."[5]

Emil Brunner has written in a similar vein: "'And what is worthy to be loved can be an object of friendship,' says Aristotle, in so many words. But love asks no questions about the nature of that which is to be loved. That is precisely the miracle of the love of God, who loves not only the man who is worthy to be loved, but also the unworthy. It is always love all-the-same, never love because. It is loving born simply of the will to love, not of the nature of the beloved. It is not a love which judges worth but a love which bestows worth. Neither Aristotle nor any other pagan knew this love; it is identical with the message of Scripture."[6]

Dr. Brunner refers to Nygren's *Agape and Eros* as "the authoritative work on this subject."[7]

Coming to our own country, Dr. Nels Ferré has characterized *agapē* as follows: "Agape is, first of all, always God-centered. God alone is the Source, Standard, Authority and Dynamic of Agape. . . . Agape is therefore not rational in the sense that it is dependent upon community. . . .

"Agape is also completely universal in its creative and redemptive concern. No wall or barrier can shut out relation to God who is Agape. Agape is, furthermore, unconditional love. Agape is never dependent upon the response of its object for its motivation. In Nygren's terms in his *Agape and Eros*, Agape is unconditional, uncaused, unmotivated, groundless, uncalculating, spontaneous love, creative of fellowship. . . .[Agape is] completely outgoing and selfgiving, as witnessed by God's going to death on the Cross, not for friends, but for sinners. . . . Such is the heart of biblical faith." [8]

The consequences of such a view for the Christian life have been drawn properly by Paul Ramsey: "Not anything in the neighbor, not anything in the agent himself nor any treaty of peace between them but the controlling love of Christ reverses natural self-love into neighbor love and, at the same time, requires of a person infinite willingness to be himself. . . .In short, he ought to love himself for the purpose of loving his neighbor as he naturally loves himself."[9]

"Christian love in its nature gives some good, it is not primarily concerned to seek good. It is deontologically, as a matter of obedience, related to the neighbor as such; it is not teleologically, as a matter of desire, related to some norm."[10]

Reinhold Niebuhr has made further deductions from the nature of *agapē*. The self-sacrificing *agapē* of Christ is a non-prudential love that "transcends all particular norms of justice and mutuality in history."[11] As a love "which seeketh not its own," it "is not able to maintain itself in historical society,"[12] and is bound to end in tragedy. It is, therefore, not a "simple possibility." Men cannot practice it without destroying the structures of mutual obligation and power that are essential for social existence.

"Sacrificial love thus represents a tangent towards 'eternity' in the field of historical ethics. It is nevertheless the support of all historical ethics; for the self cannot achieve relations of mutual and reciprocal affection with others if its actions are dominated by fear that they may not be reciprocated. . . . Sacrificial love is thus paradoxically related to mutual love, and this relation is an ethical counterpart of the general relation of super-history to history."[13]

We do not wish to deny the validity of the above conceptions of *agapē* as criticisms of varieties of cheap love to which we all are too readily subject. Selfish, sentimental, calculating, dominating loves are recognizably bad, and we cannot be too often warned against them. Loves that lack spontaneity, unselfishness, creativity, and even "self-sacrifice" are counterfeits and a disgrace to humanity. But the definition of love in negatives as "unconditional, uncaused, unmotivated, groundless, uncalculating"; as selfgiving, self-denying, self-crucifying, simply outgoing; as unprudential, unevaluating, unteleological, etc., leave us with a "love" that is not only impossible for human beings, regenerate or unregenerate, but also of doubtful Biblical and theological validity. "Liberal sentimentalism" is sobriety itself compared with the neoorthodox *agapē* that violates divine and human nature alike.

I agree with Reinhold Niebuhr that the love of which he speaks is an impossibility for human beings and I deduce from that that no man lives by it, or is obliged to live by it, or can be expected to live by it.

The problem is that while theologians extol the excellence of their *agapē*, and preachers propose it from their pulpits, the people are turned away from the gospel and the law alike. It is, and cannot but be, confusing, frustrating, and conducive to a "neurotic personality" that a man cannot be a Christian and live as one unless he is engaged in "self-sacrifice," in a groundless and unmotivated love that sets no value upon its object and *does not even hope to be loved back*. The notion that mutual and teleological love, love in which human beings seek a common good, is sub-Christian and calculating as well as selfish and sentimental does not make sense and is practically intolerable. No matter what goes on in his mind, in his relations with others, no man stands for it. The relationship between Christian love ("sacrificial love") and mutual human love cannot be "paradoxical." Either Christian love is mutual love or it is a violation of humanity. Either sacrificial love expresses mutual love or it is misunderstanding and a stumbling block. In this day and age when we are likely to perish for want of mutual love, it is no service to humanity that Christians should come out with a groundless, unmotivated, self-abnegating love as their contribution to the peace of the world. The problem is to state properly the love in mutuality and not to find another, unmutual love that admittedly is beyond us.

2. THE LOVE OF JESUS

The common doctrine of the agapists is that Jesus loved with a love that flowed out of him as water from a spring: spontaneous, outgoing, and unmindful of any reciprocation. In the orthodox fashion, when these writers consider Jesus they can only see one who loved sinners and died for them. The primary image in their minds is the One hanging down upon a cross. They interpret the cross as "sacrificial love" and interpret the whole life of Jesus in his dealings with his fellowmen in terms of selfless, outgoing love toward "sinners" who in no sense and way evoked the love with which Jesus loved them. So we are given a picture of Jesus going about and loving sinners unworthy of love and going his way to love some more, until, on the cross, he crowns his love with his self-denying death.

Now, I do not deny that the Gospels, especially John's Gospel, say much, especially about the cross, that seems to justify this version of Jesus' dealings with those around him. But another view of Jesus' ways is available from the Gospels. It is true that Jesus seems to have a special solicitude toward "sinners." But perhaps they were people who aroused, as the people they were, affection and friendliness in him. May it not be that he preferred them to the "righteous" because he saw in them a grace that was lacking in the latter? Some of these people were "publicans and harlots"; some may have been thieves and other shady characters. But it is not self-evident that they were unlovable. Many were "common people," "people of the land," Jews who were not "righteous" because of their failure to be good according to standards of the synagogues. They were guilty, confused, lost people who were supposed to have incurred God's displeasure and been more or less forsaken by him as they were by "the righteous."

Jesus was on the side of the sinners and presented God as with them and as their Father. He loved these people who were sinners because he saw in them a humanity that escapes the righteous and is, in fact, repudiated by them. Sinners, like the adulteress at Simon the Pharisee's house or Zacchaeus the publican, for all their sins and wrongdoings, showed a sensibility that is the love one creature hopes for from another and owes another. Jesus loved Peter, in spite of all his impetuosity and inconsistency, because Peter was a compassionate human being. He loved the young aristocrat who asked him what he might do "to inherit eternal life," in spite of all his double-mindedness and attachment to his wealth, because he had the grace to realize that his goodness fell short of the love that gives men joy and peace one with another. Maybe "because" is too causal a word to use in such situations. There need not have been any conscious evaluation of these sinners as a basis of Jesus' love. But surely it is not self-evident that Jesus was not responding to these people as creatures who were sinners. A centurion, a Mary, a Zacchaeus, a Peter, a Matthew, were not to Jesus simply sinners, *for there is no such being*; they were bewildered and "lost" creatures of God who in their bewilderment and lostness, already despised and rejected by the righteous, sinned against God and their neighbors. They indeed put forth no claim to Jesus' love because they did not have any as sinners. But it does not follow that Jesus did not acknowledge them as "flesh and blood." They were, in fact, human beings who were sinners, whose sin at once alienated them from polite society and made them eager for the love of Jesus. In this they were lovable, and Jesus, as against "the righteous," loved them, recognized them as human beings, and drew them to himself and one to another, thus making community (Mark 10:17f.; Luke 7:36f.).

At this point, something should be said about man as the creature. Christians have traditionally thought of the creature as a finite being and of man as creature as a finite being who is endowed with reason and freedom, which distinguish him from other creatures or finite beings. It has been noted that man is a finite being in that he is born and dies and has finite powers of mind and body, which limit him in all his ways.

The truth of the above statements is undeniable. But by themselves they are profoundly misleading. Man is not only a finite being but also a being who knows he is finite. He experiences finitude and is

anxious about his life. This experience of finitude goes with his ability
to objectify himself to himself and to say "I" and "me." But this self-
consciousness, this ability to say "I," is a consequence of his life as a
fellowman, of his speaking and hearing, of his responding to his response to others who address him and propose to act in a given way at a
given time and place. The rationality that distinguishes man from other
animals is a function of speech and so is "the sense of creatureliness,"
which is peculiarly human. Man knows himself as a creature because
he is a fellowman and as a fellowman. His finitude is not only that of
an organism but also that of a fellowman. He at once exists and is limited as a fellowman. And thus it is that he knows himself as a creature.

When a man recognizes himself and his fellowmen as creatures, as limited in lifetime and power, it is himself and his fellowmen
that he recognizes as finite or as creatures. He is bound by his speaking
and hearing to his fellowmen who are creatures, both as organisms and
as fellowmen. He is bound for life and for death as a human being, so
that it is not possible for him to love his life or to love himself as a
creature without loving his neighbor as himself. It is absurd that he
should as a creature love himself but not his neighbor, to love himself
with one love and his neighbor with another, or to love himself and
hate his neighbor. As a creature whose life is from, by, and for his communion with his neighbor, he may love his neighbor as himself; this
means that he may love himself as a fellowman and creature, as he
loves his neighbor. In love among fellowmen the contradiction between
self-love and the love of neighbor or enemy is meaningless. It is not
possible to love oneself and not one's neighbor. The "love" of self as
against the love of the neighbor is a falling away from humanity or the
life of a creature who is a fellowman.

The love of Jesus for the sinners was love for fellowmen who
with all their sin responded as creatures to a creature. Let it be that their
response was by God's grace and did not mean that they deserved the
love of Jesus. Neither Jesus nor the sinners saw their response to him as
meritorious. Merit is irrelevant to the situation. Still, Jesus loved the
sinners as fellowmen and creatures, and they loved him and began to
love one another as such. And in this they were lovable; therefore Jesus
loved them. There were those who did not respond as creatures, and Jesus was not happy with them.

Agapē is commonly described as not seeking but offering
love. We must agree that Jesus' love was not self-seeking, utilitarian,

calculating, etc. Jesus was not buttering his bread or feathering his bed. But does it follow that he was indifferent to the response of these people to him? Any man who loves but does not care whether he is loved back or not is a monster. Imagine a man going around and "loving" people and doing them "good" without giving a fig what they think of him and how they feel toward him. The "love" of such a man is counterfeit and the good he does is evil. Any man who does not have the grace to hunger for the love of his fellows, who does not feel empty when they do not love him and full when they do, has removed himself from human society and already destroyed the bond of humanity. He is a sinner beside whom publicans and harlots are, unless they are like him, very models of humanity. There is no love of a creature for a creature that is not evoked by the one loved and that does not rejoice in the love of the one loved. Whether the one loved is righteous or sinner is irrelevant. Righteous or sinner, a man is a creature, and one owes him the love of a creature and from him he must hope for the love of a creature.[14]

The agapists who deny or soft-pedal Jesus' involvement in mutual love, which alone has validity in human relations, deny the humanity of Jesus. Such denial has been common among the orthodox but is nonetheless heretical and a repudiation of the gospel of God.[15] They derive their doctrine from the Gospels by distorting and overlooking much that goes contrary to it. Jesus not only loved but was also loved in return by the sinners. It is true that he did not love so that he might be loved in return. But it does not follow that he did not care whether he was loved or not. It does not even follow that he did not love people because he found them lovable as his fellow creatures. Nothing but theological prejudice and confusion, accumulated through the centuries by distorted interpretations of the cross, would lead a man reading the accounts of Jesus' encounter with people to judge that his love was a one-way affair.[16]

If a man engages in "sacrificial love" toward another whose love for him is a matter of indifference, his sacrifice even if he gives his body to be burned, is an affront to the creature and a damning act. Such sacrifice is neither human nor divine; it is the doing of a diseased mind, at best a waste and at worst a murder of humanity. Sacrifice presupposes the love of the creature, and such love seeks to be loved. I do not say that one loves in order to be loved; but I do say that one loves as a man who depends upon the love of others for his joy as a creature.[17] One sacrifices oneself, if one does, for those he loves, for people whose love for him is not a matter of indifference but a matter of a most wonderful hope. Any sacrifice, any self-denial and self-sacrifice, is authenticated by a love that gives because it has already received. Sacrifice on the part of a man is an act of justice:[18] a response meant to be according to the due of the loved one; of a person and a community, which are recognized as worthy of the sacrifice of one's time, goods, or any other good, and even of life itself.

Jesus judged the "natural" love of people for their own kind and kin, for those who pleased them either by beneficence or by some common love and interest, as insufficient and even as inauthentic (Matt. 5:43 ff.; 6:25 f.; Luke 14:25 ff.). But it does not follow that he substituted for it this other love described by the agapists. He practiced and advocated a love that binds man to man as a "living soul," as a being who is by creation bound to another as fellow man, as a *Mitmensch*, as a human being without whom he himself neither exists as a human being nor has joy as a human being. This creaturely love, suffused with the anxiety and hope of the creature, both experienced in the communion of human beings, is the valid presupposition of self-denial and sacrifice.[19] It is that love without which the love of kin and kind becomes a constant source of alienation and conflict in the human society. It also is the love that legitimizes "the partial loves" that the agapists deride, and rightly, as sources of idolatry and injustice.

3. LOVE OF GOD THE CREATOR

I think that Jesus loved the sinners around him without raising the issue as to whether they did or did not deserve to be loved. Or maybe he recognized that the sinners were loved of God in their state of sin and, therefore, without deserving God's love. But it does not follow that Jesus saw in these sinners nothing but offenders or that he loved them absolutely, without regard to their humanity or their misery as creatures who lived as though God were not with them. I think his love was one that recognized the sinners as creatures and in this recognition bound them to God and to their neighbor, he being in the forefront of the new community to which they entered by his love. These people deserved his love as God's creation, as his good creation. They deserved his love because God deserved it. God the Creator deserves the creature's love as God who has created the creature whose existence as such is good.

God is to be loved because he is good and his mercy endures forever. And this goodness of God is acknowledged when a man confesses that the existence he has as a fellowman is good, when he acknowledges that the existence of his fellowman is good, good in the same way as his own existence. God's goodness is acknowledged when a man confesses that his fellow creature deserves to exist as God's good creation, and to be loved as such; loved in his anxiety and his sin as the object of God's judgment and mercy, which position and life he shares with the one who loves him.

The love of Jesus may well be seen as compassion (as a love in which the very bowels were agitated together with the soul) for the people who were "like sheep without a shepherd." These lost people still were people; they were flesh and blood; they were flesh of Jesus' flesh and blood of his blood; they were human beings who were Jews or Gentiles—creatures, there for him to see and understand and to recognize as fellowmen, whose very lostness pointed to the bond of creation with which they were bound to him.

I think there is something pathetic about our troubles with the love of Jesus. The Christian tradition has been perennially confusing in this respect. Even though we have had elaborate doctrines of creation, and even more elaborate doctrines of sin and salvation, we have thought that we could discuss the creature apart from the sinner and, what is more relevant here, the sinner apart from the creature. This is where the agapists, submitting without proper criticism to a longtime practice, have made their crucial and consequential mistakes.[20] They say, with the Augustinian tradition, that man is a fallen and sinful being who deserves or merits no pleasure from God. The rest of the fantasy about God's and Jesus' "unmotivated" love follows. For surely the sinner is without merit and in him as sinner there is no ground for God's love. But the sinner is a creature, and as a creature he is an object of God's love: the love that created him and preserves him. The creature exists by God's creation. He is creation while he is creature, and so there is no creature except by creation. On the other hand, creation posits the creature as an object of God's love, so that God at once creates by love and loves what he creates. The sinful creature exists by God's love, both as creation by grace alone and as a creature who is the object of God's love. What God creates freely he loves as his creature worthy of his love. The worth of the creature is indeed bestowed upon him by free grace, as is his being. But since the creature exists, God loves him as this existent creature who is neither God nor nothing, but a human being responsible to God.[21]

God is not a man that he should forget the creature because of sin. That is the way of man the sinner who is tempted at all times to annihilate his neighbor because of the enmity between them. It is we and not God who pretend that our fellowmen are sinners and not human beings; it is we who overlook, under the stress of anxiety and enmity, both ourselves and our neighbors as creatures. Men alienated from themselves and one from another can see only the sinner or the enemy, and attribute to God the same blindness. They can see only themselves as violated and their neighbors as violators, themselves as rejected and their neighbors as the rejectors. In the fury that goes with the injury they receive, they will the annihilation of their neighbor and express it by denying that the sinner is a creature. This denial justifies them in their enmity toward their neighbor, because a sinner who is not a creature, to whom one is not "bound in the bundle of life," is justly hated and destroyed.

It is illogical and impossible to forgive and to embrace a sinner who is not acknowledged as a creature. Enmity is destructive. My enemy is out to annihilate me. But annihilation by an act of a responsible being is absolutely evil, and in the nature of the case is not to be forgiven. Insofar as men see one another as wrongdoers, as violators and murderers, they can "forgive" only by calculation, by fear and prudence, which is no forgiveness. The enmity remains and continues in its career of injustice and murder. Not even the celebrated "self-sacrifice" of Christ, praised all over Christendom for its saving power, has kept those who "believe in" it from hostilities and persecutions that give the lie to the "new being in Christ Jesus." For instance the insistence of Christians that the Jews are "deicide," rather than creatures is part and parcel of the inhumanities they have perpetuated against them through the centuries to the shame and confusion of the church. Not even "saints" can and will forgive malefactors, or presumed malefactors, whose excellency as creation is repudiated. The forgiveness of the sinner qua sinner is impossible. No wonder, therefore, that the forgiveness of Jesus, his love for sinners, has been construed as an irrational, supernatural, groundless, unteleological act by which we are presumably saved, yet so that love for us remains an "impossible possibility." The self-sacrificing love of God in Jesus Christ, as understood by orthodoxy and neoorthodoxy alike, is a misunderstanding and utterly unassimilaassimilable to our lives with our fellowmen. It is unintelligible; therefore it is neither practiced nor practicable. This to me is the deepest irrationality in traditional Christianity and the source of pretensions and frustrations and neuroses that attend being an orthodox and neoorthodox "Christian." It turns love into an insoluble prob- lem as well as a source of living—rather, dying—confusion.

4. LOVE OF MAN THE CREATURE:
THE SECOND COMMANDMENT

Protestants, repulsed by the Catholic love for heaven, with its immutability and perfection, have preferred to discourse on the love of God for man as against man's love for God.[22] Such a recovery of the gospel and the consequent recovery of faith in the loving God was the crown of the Reformers' glory and it remains the justification of Protestant Christianity. The gospel is the celebration of the love of God for sinners; when it is confused or replaced by a celebration of man's love for the transcendent, faith is turned into superstition, hope into wish, and love into vanity.

Nevertheless, the love of God is the possibility of our love for him. The creature restored to his integrity in Christ is no pipe or channel of God's love. It is not proper to celebrate the love of God without heeding the commandment that we love him with all our heart, soul, and strength. There is no gospel without commandment, because man is a creature, not an outlet.[23] God loves as Creator and Redeemer; we are to love as creatures being redeemed. God loves as one who forgives; we are to love as sinners being forgiven; he loves as Reconciler, we are to love as being reconciled. God loves us as creatures who have sinned against him; we are to love our neighbors as creatures being reconciled to God, as human beings who are our fellowmen by God's creation and redemption. But such love for our neighbor presupposes freedom from bondage to sin and death, and the love of God for the praise of God. In the creative and redeeming work of God, in the Word and the work of the Spirit, the creature is posited as creature, as being who glorifies God by his consent to himself, as a responsive and responsible being who receives with the gospel of God's grace God's commandment: "Thou shalt love the Lord thy God. . . ." What do freedom, reconciliation, restoration, mean if not the hearing of the commandment with joy and hope? The love of God in Christ is for the creature's love to

God in the same Christ: a love expressed in the consent of the mind, the confidence of the living soul, and the exercise of one's powers as God's intelligent creation. Since we are human beings, we do not know the love of God for us except in a freedom to know and love him as our Creator, to consent to "being in general," to love his handiwork both in ourselves and in our neighbor.[24]

We are to love God as Creator; we as creatures are to love him who is our Creator. But how can we love God unless we love ourselves?[25] There is no love of God without a love of the creature, as there is no knowledge of God without the knowledge of his works. The living God is known in his acts; his acts reveal him in his glory *as God*; and we love him as we glorify him, as we thank him for the life he has given us among our neighbors and for the light that enables us to reflect his glory by our intelligence and consent to "being in general." Consent to our being and destiny as God's intelligent creation, in our relatedness to universal being, in our rightful place in creation as beings with our fellow beings, is inseparable from love to God. Such consent is a proper love of ourselves without which we love neither God nor our neighbor.[26]

The traditional and endlessly repeated doctrine that selflove is incompatible with the love of God and the neighbor is due to misunderstandings that have become deeply rooted in the Christian mind. Otherworldly Christianity distinguished the love of self from the love of God by making the former a natural love of one's mundane good and the latter the love of a supernatural good. So self-love was affirmed as a legitimate but inferior love, whereas the love of God was proposed as the highest and best love open to man. The love of self was interpreted as the love of the temporal, and the love of God was attributed to the soul with its yearning for the eternal. So those who were spiritual and concerned with the eternal sought to ascend from the love of self to the love of God.[27] Although self-love was deemed natural for the common people, the truly spiritual preferred the love of God. But this love of God was bound up with man's desire to transcend his creaturely existence in this world, and the love of self worked as the love of goods without the love of the creature.

The thesis that man's self-love is corrupted by sin or his alienation from God into egocentrism and injustice was the grand affirmation of the Protestants,[28] and it does not need apology. But that Christian love is a selfless love is a confused and confusing proposition that has done deadly harm in the church. It is not true that God's own love is selfless, nonteleological, undemanding, a love that finds its last end in the forgiveness of the sinner. God who loves, also saves; God who saves, also commands. He loves toward the liberation of the creature from bondage to sin and death, and this liberation finds its proper expression in the creature's consent to God's creation. As God illumines the mind of the creature, the last end of the creature's existence is the glory of God. There is a divine integrity which demands that the glory of God be the chief end of man and, therewith, the enjoyment of God's glory by the creature. We are saved and made free as we acknowledge God's glory to be the last end of creation. Hence, God has created us, saved us from sin and death, and through all, loved us for his glory as Creator. To make God's love undemanding, to see the creature as its last end, is a subtle and confounding misrepresentation of the proper relationship between the Creator and the creature, and a temptation to egocentrism in its most deadly form. A man who says "God loves me, period, and no questions asked," has succumbed to the devil's last argument and repudiated himself as a creature who exists by the light of intelligence and in the knowledge of the glory of his Creator.

God loves as God, man loves as man; God as Creator, and man as one who knows and glorifies his Creator: glorifies him by his consent to his own nature and destiny as a creature. If sin is rebellion against God, and if the source of this rebellion is the anxiety, despair, self-repudiation of the creature as creature, then righteousness is not contempt for life and the world; it is not the repudiation of the living, thinking, loving, hoping, individual human being who must not only affirm himself as a creature but must also distinguish himself from his neighbor as *this* creation and a fellow creature to his neighbor. It is simply impossible to affirm the existence of the neighbor *as a creature* without affirming one's own as such. A man and his neighbor are the two foci of an ellipse, and without both the foci there is no neighbor to be loved. Self-denying love is a contradiction in terms. There is no knowledge of the neighbor as creature and love of the neighbor as oneself without one's loving oneself as a creature, without glorifying God in consent to one's life as a creature.

The notion of a selfless love is not peculiarly Christian. It arises out of a natural revulsion against selfishness, which is universally abhorred in others. All men occasionally, moved by particular attachments, lapse into unselfish love and act for the good of the neighbor without hope of reward. They may not do so as often as they think they do it. But they do do it, even without reconciliation and freedom in Christ Jesus. Such love is conducive to peace among men, and one is grateful for it. It is a gift of God bestowed upon men universally, even though universally corrupted by man's prevailing anxiety and alienation from "being in general."

But to confuse this selfless love with the creature's consent to his life and his openness to his fellow creature is to misconstrue the whole meaning of Jesus Christ. Jesus Christ brought into the world an "unselfishness" that means the conversion of the rebellious spirit and his reconciliation to his Creator. What is realized is not self-repudiation but the restoration of man to his original dignity and integrity as a creature. Jesus reconciled man with God by giving him the freedom to consent to himself as a creature. He posited once again God's intelligent creation, who by his very willingness to be the individual human being God made him is enabled to love his neighbor as himself. To be a human being, to be *this* person, is to be a neighbor, a fellow creature. To know one's neighbor is to love him as a fellow creature, to love in the knowledge of him as a creature, and this goes with self-knowledge and gratitude and love to God as a creature. So it is that we are commanded to love our neighbor as ourselves.

The real issue is not self-love as against the love of the neighbor. It is the faithfulness of the creature to the end for which he is created, and therewith, faithfulness to himself and his neighbor. No man can love his neighbor unless he consents to his own being as a creature, unless he lives in the love and praise of God as his Creator. Love is a faithfulness that presupposes a man's peace with God as his Maker and the love of God's creation which goes with that peace. It is absurd to love one's neighbor while one ignores one's own life. It is absurd to be unselfish through self-denial, to be generous through indifference to good and goods. A man cannot seek the good of his neighbor while he will not receive thankfully God's gifts to himself. Indifference to one's own good is not a sign of unselfishness but of alienation from God the Creator, and its real fruits are not love and justice but enmity and tyranny disguised as self-sacrifice. Such indifference is more poisonous than the selfishness of the man who prefers his good to that of his neighbor. The latter may be prudent, but the former can be only a hypocrite.

Men have sought to remove selfishness by unworldliness, by ceasing to desire wealth, power, comfort, and the sundry sources of pleasure within man's reach. Selfishness has been opposed to unselfishness, and "self-denial" has been set up as a cardinal virtue. What drastic measures have been taken by Buddhists and Jains, Stoics and ascetics, and Christians, to break the power of cupidity and to exercise freedom from greed! What self-repudiations, contempt for men and the world, what tyrannies and cruelties, in short, what inhumanities have been practiced by "unselfish souls" who have escaped every evil but pride and despair!

In the meantime, multitudes have followed their self-love and loved themselves more than their neighbors, living in uneasy peace in societies where the common life has been constantly poisoned by their impregnable if ill-concealed selfishness. Community has been confused by men's "innocent" self-love; and strife, with injustice and oppression, has contaminated human life everywhere, making peace a delusion and happiness a mirage.

There is a common notion that unselfishness is impossible under the best of circumstances. Hence, our realists speak of it as a "transcendent ideal" and hope that it will mitigate more or less the primitive selfishness of men. It is, it has been and remains, a matter of doubt and debate as to whether men can be unselfish. The realists accuse the believers in unselfishness of sentimentalism, and the latter accuse the realists of cynicism and despair. Meanwhile, there is confusion both of mind and of life.

This whole discussion, which is as old as Christianity, is not carried out on the basis of adequate premises. It fails to take seriously man's nature as a creature. The first duty of man is not to deny himself, but to know himself and his neighbor as creatures; it is not to mortify the flesh, but to consent to his nature and destiny as spirit, to glorify God as his intelligent creation. It is to cleave to God as the creature that man is by virtue of his knowledge of his neighbor as creature who with him has his peace and fruition by faith. It is the proper exercise of human intelligence to acknowledge that a man is himself only as he is neighbor to his fellowmen. There is here no question of self-repudiation or the repudiation of the neighbor, of selfishness or unselfishness, of seeking one's own good or the good of his neighbor. It is a matter of faithfulness, of truth, of justice, of acting toward oneself and toward one's neighbor in the love and fear of God. Love is the communion of spirit with spirit, the recognition of creature by creature, the respect and justice of the creature toward the creature. This recognition and respect are of the essence of love and the love in all love, prior to love of family and friends, of neighbors and enemies. It is the love that is the salt of all love between man and woman, between parent and child, between nations, races, and tongues. It is the love without which no man has friends and no nation has peace. It is the love every man needs for his life and every man owes to his fellowmen. It is the very root as well as flower of faith. It is the origin and end of hope. It is the glory of God reflected in the creature and the creature's own fruition and foretaste of eternal life. It is the grace of our Lord Jesus Christ; it is the essential gift of the Spirit; it is the knowledge of God as Father and the knowledge of men as brothers. It is the Kingdom of God among us.

What bedevils human life is not that men seek their own good. If this were so, God would be the devil who has made us so that we must have power with life, and goods and health and comfort and pleasure and friends and all the things men seek after. What bedevils human life first of all is the creature's alienation from God and his fellowman, his refusal and inability to meet his neighbor as a creature. That is what embitters man against man and drives each one mad for hostility. A man is a creature and wants above all to be recognized as such. He is not first of all rich or poor, male or female, black or white, capitalist or communist. He is a creature and he is either respected as a creature or not respected as one. When he is so respected, the ground is laid for a common life of fruition. When he is not so respected, there is only bitterness and strife. No man really wants to be the beneficiary of another's unselfishness; but every man lives in the community of creatures and will die when he is excluded from it. The love of would-be self-sacrificers is poison compared to the love of man for man as man, and the just and generous impulses that flow from it.

What the community needs is not self-sacrifice but the creature's justice to the creature. Love is nothing else than such justice. Justice is defined as giving every man his due. But what is first of all due to every man except faithfulness to him as a creature, and what is love but such faithfulness? It is a misunderstanding of the Christian faith and a confusion of thought to argue that love is higher and more difficult than justice.

Love defined as self-sacrifice, and justice defined as giving men their due (except as creatures), confuses the problem of the good life. Men who define love as God's love for sinners have a rather dim view of love between the sexes, the love of friends, and all the decencies that make life sweet. *Agapē* is contrasted with *erōs* and *philia* to the discredit of the latter as deficient or even false love; and ordinary *justice* is looked down upon as a poor substitute for the transcendent, self-giving, and uncalculating love. Since self-love enters into the commonality of love and justice as practiced by men, Christian poets look at these as inferior virtues to be superseded by *agapē* in the world to come. So we have once again a spirituality that contains elements of alienation from the life of the creature as creature. All this may make a man critical and uneasy, but it does little toward the redemption of our common life.

In the Bible the word "love" is used with a positive appreciation of *erōs* and *philia*. It is taken for granted that a man's love of his being and good; his love of wife, family, and friends; his love of his people and tongue—all are unqualifiedly and without reservation real love. A man's affection for his fellowmen, his love of beauty and goodness, his kindly and generous impulses, cannot be brushed aside as inferior and short of the glory of God. How, in fact, is true love, the love of the creature as creature, to be expressed except in human love and justice as exercised in daily intercourse at home, in the marketplace, and among one's neighbors? What does the practice of Christianity consist of if not in the quiet and small decencies that are the very vehicles of "true love"? How does a man practice *agape* if not in his faithfulness to his neighbor, in his sensitivity to the needs and hopes of his fellowmen, in his understanding and patience and doing what he can for the fruition of his neighbor? How does one love if not by his thoughtfulness and by giving a man his due as the occasion arises? In short, the concrete decencies that men owe one another and expect from one another in affection, with justice and faithfulness, are inseparable from the love that is the creature's regard for the creature.

It is as we acknowledge our responsibility day by day in this matter and that, in this form or that, to treat our fellowmen according to obvious rules of justice, that we come to grips with the ultimate questions of life and meet our God and his creation. It is in the give-and-take of "the concrete problems of ethics" that we actually come to know the grace of God and the judgment of God, the meanings of justice and love, of repentance, faith, hope, and the whole mystery of the

Kingdom of God. There is no existence of the creature as creature except in the exercise of his powers as a human being; and he exercises these powers in his intercourse with his fellowmen and the responsibilities that emerge from it. Love among sinners is the vehicle of the Creator's love; and by our exercise of such love or justice, the living God redeems our common life for the creature's peace in our common life together.

8 The Prospect of Love

1. THE BASIS OF HOPE IN THE LOVE OF JESUS

When love is defined as self-giving—as spontaneous, unmotivated, unevaluating, self-emptying—the prospect of love is dim indeed. It is dim because God the Creator, who put us in this world to enjoy him in his creation, in ourselves, in our neighbors, in the opportunities and fulfillments this world affords—will not bless a love that does not grow out of respect for creation and does not tend toward a fulfillment of the creature. And man is no more favorable to self-sacrifice than God. Even while he is alienated from creation and seeks a good beyond it, he still has sense enough to love his life and seek after goods, friendship, security, power, and the like, which are the contents of his self-love and essential to his commerce with his fellowmen. He may engage in self-sacrifice. But he does it, not spontaneously, without motivation, but because and when he cannot live as a human being, in his integrity and love, without choosing the loss of some good and even of life itself. The prospect of love becomes other than sheer failure and frustration when, as the mutual recognition of creatures as creatures in their common anxiety for life and hope of fulfillment, it is acknowledged as the very possibility of life and its fruition in humanity. If love is to have a decent chance in this world, men must consent to it with all their mind as well as with all their heart. It must be clear that love is humanity, the way of man that is eminently rational or intelligent, as well as the law of God. If Christian love were not human love, the love that is the substance of human existence as the bond between man and man, it would be an alien principle, a *faux pas*, which would be condemned to eventual disqualification as the way of life. Therefore it is of utmost importance for the future of love that it be thought of not as a transcending but as a fulfilling of humanity.

The agapist notion that love is a divine and not a human possibility needs to be qualified with a recognition that it was, in fact, exercised by a human being whose name was Jesus, a man who lived in Palestine "under Pontius Pilate." The Christian faith stands or falls, the possibility of love is established or removed, we have hope or do not have hope, according as we do or do not take seriously and consider joyfully that a man, flesh of our flesh, bone of our bone, did in truth love God with all his mind, soul, and strength, and did in truth love his neighbor as himself. Jesus loved as a man; with the powers of a man; with the spirit of a man; with the will and affections of a man; tempted as a man; and with the faith and hope of a man in God. His freedom to love was the freedom of a man in whom the power of anxiety and despair worked with its common virulence and was overcome through the same faith and hope energized by love. In short, a man loved as a man, consenting with joy at once to the Creator and to creation. It is this fact which gives love a prospect of fulfillment. It is because Jesus loved that sinners were saved, and without his love as a man there is no salvation. The good news is that a man has loved and still loves. The gospel of the resurrection and ascension without the gospel of the love of the man Jesus is incongruous with the Christian life.

A Christology in which the humanity of Jesus Christ, the Son of God, is stated clearly and without double-talk is indispensable for the establishment of love as the ethos of the Christian church. Any view of Christ that obscures this humanity, whether by subtly denying it or by idealizing it beyond the reach of ordinary people, in its orthodox, liberal, or neoorthodox forms, darkens the prospect of love. The neoorthodox Christology, as implied in Nygren's view of *agapē*, and stated by other well-known proponents such as Brunner and Barth, is in line with the orthodox doctrine of Christ according to which the person of Christ, as it were, in the core of his being is the divine Logos and not a human being.[1] When Nygren identifies the love of Jesus with the love of God, he identifies Jesus as God and not as man, and this not only goes against the evidence of the Gospels but also confuses the prospect of love. If Jesus' love was the love of God and not the love of a man, it is not a love for men or a love that is at once required of man and possible for men. But if it is not required of us and possible for us, it is none of our affair. The whole point of Jesus' humanity in relation to us is that his love is a presentation to us both of the necessity and the possibility of it.

The Sonship of Jesus in this connection means that God was in Christ restoring love to its own as the bond of community. Were there no God, there would be no Son of God, no humanity of Jesus, and no saving love creating the love of Jesus among us. If God were not for us and had not saved us from the bondage of sin and death by his Son, we would know no Son, no Jesus, no realization of love, no promise, and no hope. Without the love of God, there would have been no love of Jesus. This we know because our own love is a gift through Jesus. The gospel is the gospel of God, of the love and omnipotence of God. In this, the orthodox and the neoorthodox are right in expressing the mind of the church.

But the doctrine that the divine Logos is the "Person of Christ" is still untenable. Even though the possibility of the love of the Son of God was and is from God, the love of the Son is the love of a man, a love that goes with the faithfulness of a man and the hope that grows from it. In this matter, the power and acting of God are no simple substitutes for the power and acting of a man. It is the peculiarity of the acting of God the Creator that it realizes rather than annihilates the acting of man. The power of God is contradistinguished from the power of the creature in that the exercise of it establishes the power of the creature, so that when by God's creation and redeeming act the creature acts as creature, by God's omnipotence the creature's act—*his* faith, hope, and love—becomes "the means of God's grace." Such is the working of the living God who both creates and saves by his Word and Spirit. When God acts as God and man acts as man—God speaking as God, man hearing as man—the Spirit of God brings to pass the love that is humanity.[2]

But the point of this paragraph is that if we may live in the hope of love, it is because we were first loved by the man of Nazareth. The promise of love can only be in its actuality. Love is neither first of all a human ideal nor an *Eigenschaft*, a private and incommunicable property of the Deity. It is what has been accomplished among us (Luke 1:1). It is the love of Jesus for us creatures who are sinners; the love that has made us free to love our neighbor as ourselves; the love of Jesus, crucified and risen, which is the possibility and prospect of love among us.

We are not to forget "the suffering servant" who reconciled us to God and to one another by his death and resurrection. But it is a grievous error to see self-sacrificing love in Jesus without remembering that what makes the self-giving of Jesus saving and joysome is the love that restores men to the joy of humanity by the recognition of man by man. Jesus' self-giving, with the suffering it entailed in his living and dying, was a necessity laid upon him by the very joy of his being with his neighbor, which overcame sin, death, the devil, and all evil. The spontaneous and undemanding creative love of Jesus was, nevertheless, the outcome of a faith, a faithfulness to God and man that goes with faithfulness to one's own being as God's creation. The self-giving love of Jesus was grounded in his love for his *neighbor as himself*. It is because he loved as himself that he gave himself. It is by his love as himself that the sinners were "saved," regained their dignity and joy as human beings. Jesus saved the sinners into humanity by re-creating community between them and himself. And doing this, he loved them as himself.

It is a great pity that the connection between Jesus' fulfillment of the law of God in his conforming to the great commandment and his death in obedience to the will of God has been commonly overlooked by Christian thinkers. Orthodox theologians have been anxious to present the cross as a supernatural exchange in which Christ's punishment and suffering was accepted by God in the place of the punishment and suffering deserved by sinful humanity. They have habitually ignored the continuity between the life and the death of Jesus, or between his obedience to the great commandment and "the obedience of the cross." There were not two obediences, but one. Jesus' love of God with his whole heart and soul and strength was the very love by which he laid down his life with the hope of the coming of God's Kingdom. The love of Jesus for sinners, which was the practice of his obedience to the second commandment ("Thou shalt love thy neighbor as thyself"), was continued and fulfilled and exhibited in "the substitution," which has been rather mystifyingly recognized as integral to his saving "work."

We might say negatively that had Jesus not loved his neighbor as himself, and showed it forth in the love of sinners, there would have been no "substitution" for us on the cross. Positively, is there not a certain "substitution" in the love of neighbor as oneself? If the love of Jesus was the love of a fellowman toward fellowmen who were sinners, a self-presentation of himself to them as a fellow creature, this love or self-presentation was a love as himself. He was a creature who loved his neighbor as himself. But love as oneself is an act of substitution, or substitution is love as oneself. The love of Jesus was more than the meeting or dialogue of two creatures; it was a meeting that was his taking the place of the sinner. He did not only meet the sinners, or acknowledge them, or feel with them in their guilt and misery. His communion with them was not only an act of body, mind, or feeling. It was his act as a fellowman that was a taking of their place. He so took their guilt and misery on himself that he displaced them as sinners. He was their fellowman who had the grace to be their neighbor, to know himself as one with them. His love for them as a fellowman was thus an act of substitution: not a substitution in which they were annihilated as his neighbor, but one in which they came to their own as his fellowmen. In this substitution he was at once righteous and sinner—righteous by his turning to them and sinner by his taking their place, which he did, not as an angel, but as one who was subject to the temptation that overcame them. However, if he took their place as a sinner, it was because he was their fellow creature, so that he took their place as their fellowman. Had he not been the sinners' fellowman, there would have been no substitution and no vicarious atonement. In short, he who loved the sinners as himself was their fellowman, and his atoning work was accomplished by his loving them as himself. But this appears as such on the cross, so that the orthodox are right in saying that the cross is the place of reconciliation.

Had Jesus not loved sinners as his fellowmen, he would not have died for them on the cross. Had he not loved them as a fellow creature, as himself, he would not have taken their place, either in life or in death. The substitution on the cross was the act of the fellowman, and it is as such that it was possible, valid, and "satisfactory." God accepted Jesus' payment of the sinner's debt, not by a legal fiction or an arbitrary bargain with the Son, but as a fulfillment of the law of humanity by which God commands a fellowman to love his neighbor as himself. The substitution of the cross was integral to this fulfillment; or, the law was fulfilled by substitution both in Jesus' love of sinners and in his death on the cross, which was one piece with his love of sinners.

The justice of God, which is fulfilled by such substitution, is the law of communion that subsists by a "turning toward" on the part of fellowmen, and it is satisfied by their presence one to another. By this justice it is God who is satisfied, and the fellowmen are satisfied with him in their presence before him and before one another. It is God and fellowmen who are satisfied, and not the law of equity in general. Hence, the substitution here considered is neither legal nor physical. The law of God is not satisfied by the punishment of one in another's place, and it does not require that there be a legal substitution of one for another. And it certainly does not require the impossibility of a man's becoming someone else rather than himself. The law of God requires that a fellowman love his neighbor as himself so that he be present to him as a fellow creature. The substitution required here is by and for such a presence, and it is a substitution that overcomes the turning away of one man from the other. It is the substitution which overcomes the sin that alienates fellowmen one from another and unites them in faithfulness and hope. By this substitution, fellowmen love their enemies and pray for those who destroy them. By it, in short, they know themselves as fellowmen and bear one another's burdens, and each makes his brother's burden light. It is the substitution by which a fellowman is other than an organism and will lay down his life for the communion of fellowmen. Substitution is the miracle of the existence of fellowmen as determined by the cross of Christ, who loved his neighbor as himself. Without it, the traditional statements of "the marvelous exchange" are mythical; and worse, they corrupt the faith that is in Christ Jesus.

2. THE FOUNDING OF THE CHURCH

There has been much discussion as to whether Jesus founded the church. If by the church we understand churches with their ministries, Sacraments, governments, none but an anxious ecclesiastic would be sure that Jesus founded them. The matter is doubtful. But if by the church we are to understand an association of human beings saved by Jesus, then there is no doubt that Jesus founded it. When Jesus revealed himself as the sinners' neighbor and persuaded them to be neighbors in faithfulness one to another's humanity, he restored community and in that very doing, he founded the church. When a man by the love of Jesus loves his neighbor, there is the church, and nowhere else is the church except in a state of negation and corruption. The church is the right association of creatures created by God. It is an association of sinners who have met Jesus Christ and in joy have met a man who loves

them with the love every man owes to his fellowman, but will not give
to him. It is a company of people who have eaten with Jesus, and drunk
with him, and laughed with him with that laughter which comes from
the exercise of humanity. The church is the people who have followed
Jesus around and seen his mighty works, none mightier than their own
salvation, and glorified the Father in heaven. The church came with Jesus and it will remain with Jesus.

The church exists where Jesus is received with joy, where this
creature (Jesus), open to his neighbor, opens a man to his own neighbor. Since the saving work of Jesus is the opening up of men one to another, there is a living connection between gospel and good works,
Christ and the church. People have asked for ages, "What connection is
there between God's loving us and our loving one another?" We have
been told that because God loved us, we ought to love one another, that
since God gave his Son for us, we ought also to give ourselves one to
another. But Christians usually find it easier and less demanding to love
God who loved them than to love others who do not love them; because
it is one thing to love one who loves us, and quite another to love one
who does not love us. And the "ought" uttered by reason has dubious
validity. It simply does not seem to us that we ought to love men because God loves us. Reason and affection alike dictate that we ought to
love one who loves us; but they do not dictate that because one loves
us, we should love another.

But such arguing has nothing to do with love in the church.
The love of Jesus is not a *virtue* we *imitate*, but a *power* that makes us
free for love. The love of Jesus is his openness toward us that opens us
to him as this person who loves us, and so, to our neighbor. By the love
of Jesus we enter into community, and the church is founded and established. It is not possible to love Jesus and not to love someone else, because it is not a goodness peculiar to Jesus we are to love, but him as a
human being who by his humanity has made us free to be human, that
is, to love all men as human beings. This love is a power that overcomes sin and opens up the shut-up and self-destroying soul to men as
men. Jesus made sinners free for love, and in so doing, he enabled them
to love their neighbor as themselves. The bond between Jesus' love for
us and our love for our neighbor is first of all not an "ought" but a freedom with joy from the power of sin, death, the devil, the world, wrath,
and hell, a freedom whose proper exercise is the love of man for him-

self, his God, and his neighbor, without confusion and without separation.

We should not confuse the "thou shalt" of the divine commandment with the "ought" and the "therefore," the imperative and the rationale, of the individual conscience responding to "the superego," to society and its coercions. The "ought" pronounced by institutions, including the ecclesiastical, has indeed a confused grounding in love. "God has loved us, therefore, we ought to love one another" is, without its grounding in the love of Jesus for the sinners, a pseudological statement and carries a coercive undertone. It is incongruous with the love of the neighbor as ourselves, which is an act of obedience having for its context the church, not as an institution, but as an association rooted in Jesus' love for sinners, in the meeting of man and man through him. It is one thing to be constrained by the love of Jesus and quite another to be coerced by the threats and promises of an institution, even if it is called the church. The former makes us free; the latter makes us conform. The former puts us in a position to love; the latter draws out submission. Love belongs with association, not with membership in an institution.

The love of Jesus is at all times a love of sinners, and as such, it cannot but be a freeing forgiveness. Here we are to be careful not to confuse forgiveness as offered by an institution with that which we are offered by Jesus, in association with him. An institution does not know sin. It only knows crime against society. A crime is an act against an institution in a society, recognized by the public through the law as disruptive or destructive of that society. Society is concerned with the non-recurrence of the crime. To this end it may punish; it may exact some satisfaction, or even "forgive" when it feels safe, by softening or even omitting a punishment due the criminal. It demands and encourages "repentance" only insofar as a criminal sorry for his deeds of crime is likely not to repeat them.[3]

A society cannot legalize love. It cannot make it a crime that a man does not love his neighbor. It cannot punish enmity except as expressed in a criminal act, and it cannot forgive enmity because it is not concerned with it. Its acquittal of a criminal, insofar as it is an institutional act, has no quality of forgiveness in it, except as the judge sets aside his role as a judge and meets the criminal as a human being.

The forgiveness of Jesus is directed toward sinners and not toward criminals, even though thieves may be recognized as criminals as well as sinners. Jesus saw people, not as individuals in "society," but as people among people. He recognized, not crimes against society, but sin against God and fellowmen. This is why publicans, thieves, harlots, who are criminals, received from him a recognition and forgiveness that are beyond the mores of society and the practice of its institutions. He was not concerned with their position as criminals, and the forgiveness he offered them was not an acquittal of criminals, but a restoration of their humanity. The miracle of Jesus, which gave joy to sinners, is that he was able to see criminals as sinners, and therefore as human beings; he was free and able to see them as sinful men. This very seeing and knowing was his act of forgiveness for which the people glorified God because they knew that such understanding is a gift. The miracle of Jesus was a faithfulness, which is forgiveness in the love of sinners as creatures.

We must observe that forgiveness comes under faithfulness. It is the faithful man who forgives, and unless he is faithful, he does not forgive. Prudent men may forgive others for the sake of avoiding dangerous conflict, or for the sake of some benefit they expect by not pressing for the payment of debts owed them. Society may remit lawbreaking for the good of its institutions, and it may even seek the reformation of criminals for their own as well as the public good. However, the forgiveness of prudent men or of an enlightened society is on a different plane from the forgiveness practiced among fellowmen as they keep faith with their fellow creatures. Fellowmen forgive or do not demand retributive justice, not for the sake of some private or public good in their common life, but for the sake of communion by which they love their neighbor as themselves. Forgiveness is an act of faithfulness among fellowmen and is conjoined with the love of enemies. It is enemies that fellowmen forgive, and they forgive them as their fellow creatures. The recognition of the enemy, of one who has turned away from the one who may forgive him, as a fellowman is integral to forgiveness on the plane of communion. To forgive is to turn toward one who has turned away. It is possible only as an act of faithfulness, and its sole end is reconciliation or the redemption of "life together." The forgiveness of the sinner is the forgiveness of him who has turned away and thus broken the bond of humanity. Its reality and meaning are the communion of fellowmen. It is from faith and to faith, and faith is the substance of it.

Sin occurs in a "vicious circle." We sin because we are sinned against, and we are sinned against because we sin. We are indifferent because we meet indifference, and we meet indifference because we are indifferent. Love refused breeds the refusal of love; enmity breeds enmity. And deep and devastating is the offense of enmity. When we are not loved, we are murdered and retaliate even as we die with murder, which is sin. And our misery becomes immovable because we see our sin as a just response rather than the provocation. The only way we know to hold on to ourselves is to protest our own justness in the matter, which only establishes both our fury and the fury of our neighbor, our fury of violated innocence and his fury at our infinite injustice. The only thing institutions do or can do in this state of human misery is to provide us with the law that coerces a way of life that makes for "peace" and order without giving us joy. For this reason we meet "good" people in our churches as well as in our other institutions, but we meet too little joy.

The miracle of Jesus is that in him the vicious circle is broken. Here was a man free from the fury of violated humanity, a man who in his faithfulness was able to destroy this fury and to meet the sinner as a man meeting man. Something unheard of was here: a man who would not allow the wrath of the sinner to blind him to the creature who cried from the depths for recognition as creature by his neighbor, a man whom neither death nor the devil were able to coerce into rejecting the sinful creature. This is how (and mystery it is) death and the devil were vanquished, and with them the sinner's fury; and the people praised God. Once the miracle occurred, the circle of sin was broken into and humanity was dug out from under a mountain of offenses, and there was a "new creature." When this one man loved his neighbor as a creature, as himself, and freed him from his despair and fury, man was opened for man, and justification entered the world as the glory of the Christian church.

The church exists by "the forgiveness of sins," which is by Jesus' meeting the people. This is another miracle, another mystery. In the church, Jesus, crucified and risen, meets the people, in his humanity, to recognize them as sinners who are his neighbors. The risen Christ is still the man Jesus, and it is as the man Jesus that he forgives our sins, restores us to God, ourselves, and our neighbor.[4] This is the miracle that is the work of the Spirit of God. When we meet our neighbor, this man and that, this sinner and the other, we meet Jesus; rather, Jesus meets us with the love and faithfulness of God. Every man presents Jesus to us, and Jesus speaks by him and forgives by him. Not a ghostly Jesus, not our idea of Jesus, not a Jesus we can objectify and dispose of, but the living and reigning Jesus who overcomes our sin and by whose meeting us God creates a "new man" or us in our humanity. When Christians associate one with another, they associate in Jesus' company. He is in the midst of them, as he was in the midst of those who ate and walked with him nineteen hundred years ago. Thus the church is gathered around Jesus by the power of God's Spirit, each man speaking to his neighbor in Christ's behalf because Christ in the Spirit speaks by his "brother."

3. FORGIVENESS IN THE CHURCH

I am not Jesus, and my neighbor is not Jesus, I am a sinner before Christ, and so is my neighbor a sinner before Christ. I am forgiven by Christ, and so is my neighbor forgiven by him. Nevertheless, as Christ forgives us, we are to forgive one another. Christ's forgiveness makes us free, and we act in our freedom when we forgive one another. We cannot associate except to love, and we love to forgive and to be forgiven; ourselves to forgive our neighbor and ourselves to be forgiven by our neighbor. If we despise the love and therefore the forgiveness of our neighbor, we have no neighbor and we reject the love of Jesus. If we do not receive our fellowman in the name of Jesus, if we do not rejoice in *his* love and forgiveness, we reject the love of God and blaspheme against his Spirit. If we do not meet our neighbor, in all simplicity, as those who have sinned against him and need his forgiveness for our very existence as human beings, we have not met Jesus and we do not know the power of God. Unless our neighbor be our minister and we our neighbor's minister, there is no church, and if no church, neither ministry, nor the Word and the Sacraments.

Ecclesiastical institutions tell us that each man sins against God, that he sins by transgressing the law, which is most insistent in matters like theft, adultery, and murder, which are crimes against society. They tell us that Jesus Christ has atoned for our crimes by his death and provided "the means of grace" available through the institution for our acquittal and restoration to God's favor, which shall ensue in a happy life in this world and in the next. They offer us God's forgiveness, provided we repent of our crimes and promise not to commit them again. But they are well aware that we are not reliable. Therefore, they also impress upon us the dire consequences of sin, which are excommunication of a sort in this world and hell in the next. The whole system is shot through with appeal to fear of punishment, which is an institution's ultimate device for producing conformity. Institutions provide for "godly and lawful" behavior compatible with a "righteousness" which neither forgives nor asks for forgiveness. It is, in fact, understood that it is a beastly business to need men's forgiveness and that nobody can blame a man if he will not forgive those who offend him. Thus it is that unforgiving men not only exist in our churches but also thrive in them, if they contribute palpably to the work of the institution. Forgiveness is not essential to the existence and prosperity of any institution— including the church.

This is not so in "the body of Christ." The members of this body live by the love of their neighbors. Forgiveness is the way to life and the way of life among them. With Jesus Christ in their midst as the head of the body, they live one to another, building one another up with the love of Christ that makes them free from the power of sin and death, free to quicken one another and to give one another joy. With them it is not a matter of law, crime, fear, and the like, but of faithfulness, repentance, prayer, hope, always blessed by the grace of Jesus Christ and the miracle of love. "The body of Christ" is no institution, with its claims upon men's "loyalty" because of services rendered, but a company of people gathered around Jesus, joyful with him and one with another, hearing his words laden with God's grace and happily breaking bread together in thankfulness. Indeed, they know the wrath in sin and the bitterness of death in it. Publicans, harlots, thieves, murderers, cry out for mercy. But so do all the loveless who, having committed no crimes, have turned away from their neighbors in the misery of despair. Not that they do not know the difference between a thief and an honest man, or an adulterer and a lover. But in Christ's company, they are equal. They are human beings forgiven of their sin and made free to love one another as themselves. The honest man breaks bread with the thief and the adulteress with the faithful housewife. Indeed, it does matter that some people commit crimes and that others are good citizens. But in this company it does not matter as it matters that they all are with Jesus and one with another, forgiven, forgiving, hoping to be forgiven and to forgive. They know one law: that they are to love one another. They know one evil: that they have been unfaithful one to another. They know one guilt, which is incurred by denying that they are neighbors; and one fear: that they will be separated from their neighbor. These people know that their business is with God and their neighbor, and not with an institution. Of course, they have to behave themselves and play their roles in the institution. This is necessary "for order and decency." But when it comes to worshiping God, confessing their sins, hoping for salvation, they have to do, not with law, institution, organization, but with souls and people, with flesh and blood, with human sensibility. They know that joy and misery occur, not in organizations and playing of roles, but among persons who alone are competent to give joy with their love and to induce misery with their indifference. In the world where men despair of love, people pretend that what is good for the institution is good for human beings. But in the church where Jesus creates the hope of love, people know that it is their neighbor who makes the difference between joy and sorrow. In the world where sinners despair of their neighbors, people pretend that every good is from the institutions. So they do their duty and wait for their reward. But in the church where Jesus creates hope among neighbors, people dare even to expose themselves to their neighbors, knowing that only thus shall they be and keep alive.

4. FOR A NEW FAITH IN MAN

Of course, it is contemptuous for men to say that love is a "simple human possibility"; it is contemptuous of God, of his Son, and his Spirit. But it is equally contemptuous of the triune God to say that it is not possible for a man to love his neighbor as himself. If love be impossible, God has no power, and there is no God. But God is and is able, for Jesus lived and loved and saved sinners. Since Jesus loved, and Jesus was a man, love is possible among men; and with love, the church also is possible. If this were not so, faith and hope also would not be possible, and it would be as though Jesus had not lived. But Jesus did live. He did found the church. Therefore, we live in hope.

Christians hope, not as solitary heroes, but as they are prayed for, helped, encouraged, suffered and rejoiced with, in short, builded up by the body of Christ, by Jesus himself, by the members of his body. Christians build one another up as they hear the Word of God and participate in Baptism and the Lord's Supper and accept the discipline of the church.[5] These institutions *in* the church are "the means of grace" provided by the living God, and without them the Christians have no life to share. But they are institutions *in* the church, institutions that presuppose, and therefore, by God's power, create and sustain the church. They are not the church, or a substitute for the ethos of the associated community. Unless there is grace in the church, there are no means of grace in it. There is no love and forgiveness of God without the love and forgiveness of Jesus, and there is no love and forgiveness of Jesus where "Christians" have no hope of loving and forgiving one another. The mission of the church today requires that we insist upon this point and put it at the center of our believing that the church exists as the body of Christ.[6]

The prospects of love in our day are bright insofar as God in Christ Jesus creates and sustains the church by his Spirit, who creates and sustains love and forgiveness among us, the love in question being the love wherewith we are loved of God in the love and forgiveness of Jesus. But this love we receive by the love of God working in our neighbor, by the grace of God working in us and opening us up to his judgment and mercy that we know in our commerce with our neighbor, who is being saved for the exercise of love and forgiveness even as we are. It is a pity to regard this love either as impossible or as already possessed, because in either case we are tempted to reject the gospel of God.

It is not that if we understand love better and approach the practice of it with hope, we shall readily forgive and love, and the golden age will be here. There is no sure and painless prescription for success in this matter. My duty is to point out that the communion of saints is, together with preaching and the Sacraments, an indispensable "means of grace"; and that when we receive our neighbor as God's minister for us, we have the promise of God in the church that we shall enjoy a peace and joy that shall make for the peace and joy of God's world, to his own glory with joy, which is the last end for which he created the world and sustains it.[7]

What I am pleading for is faith in man, in any man; rather, I am pleading for faith in God, whose love and forgiveness are promised in the communion of saints. There was a time when people believed in man and said they believed in God. They construed their own goodwill and sundry kindnesses as expressions of the love of God and Jesus. I do not say that these "liberals" did not love the creature. But I do say that faith in man was understood as the conviction that men are "good," possessing kindness and justice, and therefore to be trusted to love and to do good. What was obscured and even forgotten is that good men are sinners and need the forgiveness of God and their neighbor. With this obscuring and forgetting went a failure to recognize the human being as a creature in bondage, a failure of the kind of love that is the ethos of the communion of saints. Therefore, "Thou shalt love thy neighbor as thyself," which belongs properly in the church or among creatures under the power of Jesus' love, became unintelligible and was construed as a counsel of perfection. In short, insofar as faith in man was not faith in man the creature in sin, it was a faith that despoiled the gospel and misunderstood both Jesus and the church. God was understood, not as a Creator and Redeemer, but as the ground and perfection of human love as exercised by the believers in man. Such faith made superfluous the church as the means of grace and blocked the very grace of God among his people.

But the recent protests against such faith in man have led to a revival of the traditional absurdity of faith in God as against faith in man. Of course, Augustinianism, as against Pelagianism, is valid. Without the grace of God, man is without the power of both being and loving. Without the Creator, there is no creature, and without the Redeemer, there is only the bondage of the creature to sin and enmity. In this matter, and so far, the neoorthodox have made their point, which belongs at the center of the Christian faith. But unless we go farther, we turn this same faith into superstition. The grace of God, which creates a "new being," does not operate as a private power by the action of God upon the individual sinner apart from the church. Faith in God that denies the means of grace is a supernaturalism which itself is a denial not only of the incarnation and the atonement but also of the whole self-revelation of God as understood through the Scriptures.[8] Moreover, faith in God that limits the means of grace to the cult of the Christian institutions, to Baptism and the Lord's Supper, even when it adds to these preaching and discipline, is bound to end either in sentimentalism or in despair. The truth seems to be that any faith in God that omits faith in the grace of God working in the communion of sinners acting as priests toward one another is an idolatrous superstition and leads, not to the upbuilding of the church, but to its corruption into a cluster of religious institutions lacking the grace of God. If faith in man does not create love, neither does faith in God, unless it is exercised in the communion of saints or the church.

The miracle of love occurred by the grace of God through the love of Jesus. Our faith in God is inseparable from our faith in Jesus by whose love we are saved for love. We are saved by the power of God working by his love, not by the power of Jesus' love. So we have faith in God. But without the human love of Jesus, the love of the creature with the power of the creature, we do not receive or know the power of God's love. Therefore faith in God and faith in the man Jesus are bound together, so to have faith in the one and not in the other is not to have faith. But faith in God is not faith in man, and faith in man is not faith in God. These two are distinct as well as inseparable.

Are we, then, to believe in Jesus the creature as the bearer of God's grace and not in our neighbor the sinner as the bearer of the same grace? Are we to say that God loves in and through the just but not through the unjust? And who is it that ties God's hands? Besides, God in Jesus called to himself a people to be his servants and the means of his grace among themselves for the upbuilding of the church. If Jesus by his love founded the church for their life and strength as members of one body, then it is blasphemous and deadly not to believe in man, that is, not to believe that the creature and sinner who is one's neighbor is in truth the means of grace ordained by God and enabled by Jesus to fulfill his vocation. There is no faith in God without faith in man the sinner, who is being quickened and strengthened for his life and vocation in the communion of saints, whether the sinner be oneself or one's neighbor, since by God's grace I who am this sinner am as this sinner the means of my neighbor's faith in God. I am to have faith in myself, or I am to believe that by God's power the love and forgiveness of this sinner and creature which I am mark the salvation of my neighbor. By this miracle, and under it, we are to believe in God and in man: in God who is Creator and Holy; and in man who is creature and sinner. For by the peculiar omnipotence of the living God, the sinner's love and forgiveness, under grace the love and forgiveness of the creature, are the means of God's grace and blessing to the joy of his saints.

Faith in man the creature and sinner cannot be limited to the church as those who live under the Christian institutions and participate in them. Whereas it is easy to distinguish between the baptized and the not baptized, between churchgoers and not churchgoers, it is not equally easy to separate the servants of God from those who are not his servants. To have faith in a Protestant but not in a Catholic, in a Catholic but not in a Jew, in a Jew but not in a Buddhist, in this man one meets but not in that other, is not to have faith in God. If having faith in God is believing his promise of love in Christ Jesus, then to think that he will not and cannot fulfill this promise through a man we meet because this man is not a "Christian" is to deny God's freedom and providence. To meet any man with the fixed notion that he is not an angel of God, a means of grace, an occasion for the working of God's judgment and mercy, is to deny God. To despise the love and forgiveness of any man because he does not confess the Messiah and his cross is to act in a pride that can end only in shutting off God who is the Lord of all men and will do with them as he will do with them. The freedom and sovereignty of God in his dealings with us can mean no less than that we are to love and forgive any man, and are to expect him to love and forgive us; and God's arm is not shortened, so that he may not bless him and me because of the sin in us. We are to believe in all men, provided we approach them as creatures and sinners under God's grace. No man is excluded from the service of God; therefore we are to believe in anyone we meet as our neighbor. We are to be grateful to God for him and to rejoice in his love by the hope in us. Christians are to love all men; therefore they may hope in all men. One-way love is no love for human beings.[9]

The habit of not expecting grace in the hands of people who are not "good Christians" reveals a hardness of heart and a radical misunderstanding of the Second Commandment. When we insist that the good man alone shall be an example and influence for good to us, we are speaking, not of love among creatures, but of the love of the good; not of the love of neighbor as ourselves, but of the love of a quality in our neighbors. Such an insistence is a sign that we have become blind to ourselves and to our neighbors as fellowmen who exist as creatures and sinners, and the very category of humanity is obscured. So also the grace of Jesus Christ and the grace of God are obscured. The grace that is among the neighbors, the good alone, is not the grace that is in the church, and the love among those alone who are good is not the love of fellowmen. The love among men who know one another as good is the love of the Good. The love among sinners is the love of the creature, who is a fellowman. The issue is whether we are or are not able to recognize one another as human beings who exist by forgiveness that is from communion to communion. There is no one who may not be our neighbor; who may not love us as himself and whom we are not to love as ourselves, who are his fellow creatures.

5. LOVE IN DAILY LIFE

The agapists have had a dim view of the prospects of love in our common life as citizens engaged in economic and political activity. They have countered the "sentimentalism" of the past with a "realism" that delivers our public life to the operations of legal justice and power. Their "sacrificial love" is so incongruous with business and politics that the men engaged in public pursuits have been left with "enlightened self-interest" as the working ethos of their activities. The agapists hope that love is not altogether irrelevant to justice and common well-being in society at large, national or international. They have insisted that *agapē* is needed for a proper execution of justice in a harmony of interests in our world. But self-sacrifice remains inassimilable to economic relations and to our political life. The "practical man" does not live by *agapē*, and indeed can make neither head nor tail of it. We are in the embarrassing situation of being Christians who talk of *agapē* and live by "self-interest," more or less enlightened, more or less qualified by regard for the interests, economic and political, of others.

I think we have to allow that in the daily and continuing life of the people engaged in the pursuit of goods, status, security, power in our "age of power and abundance," self-sacrifice is neither offered nor expected among us. In our way of life and in our institutions we do not ask or expect that men shall sacrifice their interest for our own; we do not intend to and are not expected to sacrifice our interests for those of others. Producers and buyers, managers and workers, businessmen, technicians, professionals, teachers, and preachers—in short, all who make a living in our society and seek the goods available in it are expected to receive as well as give, to live in a mutuality without which there would be no common life. In international, interracial, and sundry more or less global relations, the several contending entities are expected to pursue their own interests, but to do so intelligently and with a minimum of peril to themselves in the context of the one world being forged by "the age of science." Nobody expects another to sacrifice his interests for another, and nobody expects to do the same. Self-sacrifice is out of the question. *Agapē* as policy is absurd. It remains, with its cross exhibited in churches, a cultic symbol, a verbal as well as material symbol that identifies the churches as institutions, but it does not characterize our way of life. As much is admitted by thinkers who hope that *agapē* somehow makes for an increase of justice. This hope is not altogether a dream. Justice, regard for others' interests, is likely to exist more among people who love one another than among strangers and enemies. In fact, without love, justice is likely to turn into a scramble for goods and may utterly disappear. This is too obvious to require elaborate discussion and proof.

But the question remains as to what the love is that makes for justice, and even becomes a bond of humanity among seekers of partial goods, especially their own. Is it an unmotivated, self-denying, self-sacrificing love that enables us to live in peace, and even affection, with people who may well be our rivals? Hardly! What makes for peace and joy among men engaged in the businesses of our common life is not *agapē*, but the creature's regard for his fellow creature, even while they are engaged in a given business, each for his benefit. What the people of any race, color, or creed, of whatever status and power, hope for when they meet others in the several businesses that bring them together is not only a private or public benefit but also a "look" that will be one of reconciliation and love. We can stand and accept various degrees of self-love and self-seeking and we can have joy, provided we meet a "neighbor" who recognizes us as the restive creatures that we are and stays before us, open to give and to receive love. When our business with others is blessed with the union of man with man, then it is successful with the authentic profit of humanity. When it lacks this union, there is no profit that will make up for it, or will not leave us empty. The grave and infuriating injustice in public life is not "selfishness," as the justice in it is not *agapē*. It is, rather, the ignoring and virtual annihilation of human beings. It is the identification of them with roles, the definition of them by their classification in the public life, the denial to them of their dignity as "intelligent creation." Primal justice is humanity, and humanity is the love of the neighbor as oneself, and without it, public life lacks the meaning that alone makes every man's life a *bonum solidum*. Without it, no unselfishness, no unprudential and self-sacrificing love, is of avail for the making of peace. With it, politics and business become occasions for the fruition of the creature.

Therefore, it would be better for the health of the church in the world if love were recognized as a mutual concern of God's creatures made at once real and possible by the Word of God the Creator and Redeemer, and not a supernatural, self-annihilating altruism which avails only to confuse and paralyze the people called Christians. Love may and will give itself, as indeed did Jesus. But self-giving as such is not love; it is a corruption of it. What the age needs is men who love and hope for the love of their neighbors, and not self-immolating martyrs praised by institutional propagandists to the permanent confounding of the church and the continued and perilous virulence of inhumanity in our world. If we are serious about the gospel, let us stop "talking big" to the people about a Christian love that is as inhuman as it is impossible and futile and let us become witnesses to Jesus Christ, who came to enable us to love our neighbor as ourselves, that is, to love men and to hope for their love, as befits creatures who exist under the grace of God.

In short, what the sinner received from Jesus, and the creature expects from the creature, is the fellowman's turning toward fellowman in the recognition of him as "intelligent creation" who exists by his presence to him and transactions with him. By the presence of God, who is "in Christ reconciling the world to himself," and by his Spirit, who opens fellowmen one to another, such turning is an enduring possibility in our common life, so that, while we pursue our self-interest in our several institutions, we may love our neighbor as ourselves. No one will deny the temptation of our civilization, the temptation under which we exist and perchance groan daily, to turn aside from our fellowmen in our common pursuit of goods. It is true that love is not a "simple possibility" for us who are sinners engaged in the works of self-love. Nonetheless, we live and act, not by our simple possibilities, but by the grace of God and the love of Christ, which accompany us in all the things we do among ourselves. By this grace and love we exist as fellowmen; and we have our neighbor with us. We do exist as fellowmen. Therefore, we may love our neighbor as ourselves. Such love is not only possible but also actual. Otherwise, we would not be alive, or there would be no humanity. On the other hand, we are so alive that we are called upon to keep alive, and this is the human enterprise.

9 *Freedom and Liberty*

1. THE LAW OF NATURE VS. THE LAW OF GOD

a. The Law of Nature

Men like to believe that they are intelligent, or that they behave rationally. They may tolerate being told that they, at least on occasion, do evil, but they cannot tolerate being told that they are stupid and act contrary to reason. Even men who are manifestly evildoers justify their actions on the grounds that they follow natural law and the law of reason. They persistently argue that their conduct is in some important way or ways good, and that what they are doing is according to human nature and issues in some clear benefit to themselves and perchance to others. In some such way, everyone imagines himself as following the way of truth and right, or the law of nature.

There was a time when people identified nature with reason and the law of nature with moral law as known to conscience.[1] Having defined man as a rational animal, they regarded truth and justice as at once natural and moral, and the conditions of a good life. They assumed that the happy man is the just man, or the man who follows truth in his life with his fellowmen. They identified the rational-moral law of justice as the law of God, and they found true virtue in obedience to this law. They saw the body, or the physical organism, as a source of unreason, and agreed among themselves that the wise and good man holds his body and its affections under the control of reason. To them, physical law as seen in the impulses and habits of the organism was included in natural law insofar as reason was able to control organic process and to direct it toward a good that was regarded as the fulfillment of moral law.[2]

In the modern world, this order, with its subsumption of physical law under the moral and rational, has been inverted. It now appears that the one law that governs human conduct is natural or physical. Man is defined as a physical organism rather than as a rational animal.[3] It is assumed that reason and morals serve the ends of the organism, with its impulses for food, drink, shelter, security, and the like, which serve in turn the end of the preservation of the species. When men speak of natural law as the law that governs human behavior, what they mean is that man is a being who lives by eating and drinking and a complex of sophisticated satisfactions and pleasures that fulfill impulse and satisfy organic need. It appears that "justice, mercy, and peace" are instrumental to the organism's quest for life, liberty, and pursuit of goods.

In the case of naturalism, man is classified as a highly complicated and sophisticated animal and as continuous with and included within the realm of "organic life." Together with other animals, he is built in a certain way and functions in certain ways. He eats and assimilates food; he breathes and moves around. He gets hungry and tired. He feels pain and pleasure, is afraid and fights, and is happy when satisfied. When he meets difficulties and problems, he tries to overcome them; and to this end, he uses his intelligence. He forms habits, sets up institutions and mores, and learns to distinguish between good and evil, right and wrong. He uses tools, engages in speech, and produces civilization and culture. However, he remains an animal among animals, and remains occupied with his impulses and instincts, his needs and their satisfactions. As rational, he is nonetheless an animal, and under natural law together with other animals.

At first sight, there appears to be a radical difference between the premodern image of man as a rational animal and the latter-day image of him as a physical organism. However, this has not been always true in practice. The notion that the emotions are to be under rational control, and the notion that reason is instrumental to the satisfaction of the organism, may amount and commonly have amounted to the same use of the mind for the direction of impulse toward harmony and a happy life as realized by it. Here the ancients and the moderns agree. A man may think of reason as master of the body, or he may think of it as instrumental to harmony among the impulses of the body. But in either case, he seeks harmony among his impulses and satisfactions, and uses his mind or reason to that end. He recognizes mind and body as constitutive of his nature and he understands natural law as that which governs his behavior in his quest for happiness in satisfying experiences. The transition from the notion of natural law as rational to the notion of it as physical is not as abrupt as one may think at first sight. What is more to the point here is that in either case natural law is seen as one, so that man is seen either as a rational animal or as a physical organism. In either case, no radical conflict is envisaged between the mind and the body. On the contrary, it is recognized that among wise or intelligent people, the one serves the other and lives in peace with the other, included in one nature and under one "natural law." The Western mind before Darwinism saw the body as domesticated by the mind. After Darwin, it saw the organism as domesticated by the intelligence. But in both cases, man has been seen as a unitary entity, existing under one law, called the law of nature.

Both rationalism and naturalism are committed to the notion that man is to be included in a "system of nature." Man is a microcosmos who reflects in his mind the rational order of or in the universe. Since man is able to think, or rather contemplate, the cosmic order, he is included in it and coordinated with it. Man is continuous with the cosmos in its intelligibility, and the same law and order are valid for both man and the cosmos.

In both rationalism and naturalism, the law of nature is the law of human life. It is the law that comes naturally to man; the law that he regards as rational, to which his own intelligence subscribes, which his conscience accepts as right and salutary. Any conflict between man and law, except through ignorance and stupidity, and perhaps illness, is unthinkable. Man, like the animal, lives by the law of his being, and under it he prospers, provided he lives intelligently. What a man needs is knowledge of the law and its operations, and behavior according to such knowledge. In short, natural law is the law of his nature. It is the law of good and right. Hence, he conforms to it as water runs downhill.

b. The Law of God

Such a conception of law in relation to man is in rather sharp contrast to the behavior of Israel under the law of God. It appears that from the very moment when the law was delivered to Moses and the people accepted it with much enthusiastic trembling, Israel transgressed the law and remained perennially restive under it. They acted as though they were subjected to a most onerous imposition, and behaved themselves so as to provoke a constant controversy between the Lord and his spokesmen, on the one hand, and themselves, on the other. Prophet after prophet came forth crying out against the transgressions of Judah and Israel "because they have rejected the law of the Lord, and have not kept his statutes " (Amos 2:4). A man like Hosea had to break forth with:

> Set the trumpet to your lips,
>   for a vulture is over the house of the Lord,
> because they have broken my covenant,
>   and transgressed my law.
>   (Hos. 8:1.)

There is hardly a prophet, after as well as before the exile, who did not speak to the same effect. The men of God appealed to the great goodness of the Lord toward the nation, in their election, deliverance from bondage, and their very existence in a rich and wonderful land. They recounted the mercies of the Lord toward them, his wars in their behalf, his unmerited providence in their preservation and prosperity. They appealed to their presumable gratitude. They set before them, in the name of the Lord, "life and good, death and evil," and invited them to "choose life, that you and your descendants may live, loving the Lord your God, obeying his voice, and cleaving to him" (Deut. 30:15,19-20). But the people would not obey the law of God, and they would not hear his voice.

We remind the reader of this situation, not inviting him to judge the people of God to whose company he belongs, but by way of pointing out that the law of God, which is summed up in the Ten Commandments and the great commandment, has perennially been an offense to "the natural man." It is and has been hard for Israel and the church to accept the law of God as the law of nature that reason might accept as good and conducive to good. If natural law is law that the human mind will spontaneously and readily hear and obey, then the people of God have not received the law of God as natural law. Not unlike the apostle Paul, they have found in their "members another law at war" with the law of God; a law that resists, as it were, to the death the commandment that they love the Lord and cleave to him and that, therewith, they love their neighbor as themselves. Even while with their heart or in their "inmost self" they have acknowledged the law of God as good, and the way of life and peace, they have acted as though it were an alien law, an imposition at once unnatural and irrational. If natural law is what men spontaneously live by, then the natural law of human life has been and still is self-love as it operates in self-preservation and the satisfactions that are compatible with it and conducive to it. In this sense, the law of God has not been regarded by God's people, before and after Christ, as natural. This is why prophets of Israel spoke of a new heart and a new spirit as needful for the people's hearing and obeying the law of God. (Ezek. 36:26 f.) This is why Jesus Christ was hailed by Paul and the early church as the fulfillment of the law.

It must be of paramount importance that our obedience to the law became possible by the death of Christ—the death, not as against his life and resurrection, but as essential for our understanding of the nature of his own obedience. The death of Christ was nothing if not an act of obedience, and that to the eternal law of God.[4] It occurred by the operation of the law and in response to it. It was according to the law and in proclamation of it once for all. Christ revealed the "soul" of the law (Calvin) by fulfilling it not only with his words but also by his life-death-resurrection.

The death of Christ was the ultimate judgment upon the law of life as it prevails among us—the law out of which comes the injustice prohibited by the law of God and condemned by his prophets. It was the final declaration that absolute love of one's life is not the law of human life, that it is, rather, the corruption of humanity and all of man's works. Christ was crucified for political reasons that were justified ultimately by the law of self-preservation. The innocent was sacrificed for the public good, and public good was the maintenance of public life. Christ himself died voluntarily because he knew something beyond self-preserva- tion, which is the love of man for his neighbor. By his death, Christ fulfilled the law of an authentically human life, which is faith working by love.

Why have men killed, stolen, lied, maligned, been unfaithful, and coveted, with oppressions and cruelties? They have done such things for money, food, power, security, etc. But in and through it all they have been propelled by an impulse deep in their beings: the law of their lives, by which they have cleaved to life itself as the ultimate good. And why, in spite of the law of God and of all his prophets, did

God's own people, age after age, in prosperity or adversity, bring upon themselves unanimous condemnation by continued inhumanities in which they broke every commandment of the law? Surely it was because they yielded to a law of their lives that was nonetheless a radical violation of their humanity.

There has been no inhumanity of man to man that has not been exonerated—if not openly, at least tacitly by common consent—on the ground that it followed the law of life, which is a desperate cleaving to life as the absolute good.

Not everything men do is intended for bare preservation; but self-preservation, insofar as we exist under the threat of death, is a decisive and pervasive factor in our behavior, so much so that without the law of self-preservation, the basic pattern of human behavior as inspired by self-love makes no sense. Men indeed seek goods, security, power, reputation, pleasure, friendship, and so on; their concrete pursuits can be readily recognized as deriving from such motives, which make for an endless plurality of objectives. Still, if we remove the law of self-preservation or the vehement impulses of the living to live, it is as though we had taken the starch out of human activity.[5]

I wish to emphasize that this law of our lives is expressed in its full force in our social relationships, in what man does, in fact, do to man, as he seeks the goods acknowledged as such by mankind in general. In personal relationships, with their limited scope and frequent distance from "the struggle for existence," the impulse for self-preservation is relaxed, and this basic law of life is not too evident. Therefore, those who reserve the province of ethics to personal relations are not too impressed with the virulence of inhumanity. But when we keep our eye on social life, as the Old Testament enjoins, the depth and extent of man's disobedience to the law of God becomes manifest.[6]

The law of God is the law of human life as revealed in Christ Jesus and as we find it in Scripture, in both the Old and the New Testament. It is a law that stands in grand and awesome opposition to the law by which men seek life as an absolute good and thus fill the world with oppressions and misery. The law of Moses, as interpreted by the prophets and fulfilled by Jesus Christ, is a law that has always stood over against the way in which people conduct their lives. That is why the prevailing tenor of Biblical prophecy (until the exile!) is one of judgment against the people. Justice, kindness, mercy—in short, love, especially in political life—are constantly overwhelmed and undone by man's deep obsession with the precariousness of his life. As men cling to life as the absolute good, truth, right, friendship, justice, begin to fly out of the window or are constantly shoved under the rug. Integrity and love, on the one hand, and man's perennial and decisive anxiety for his life do not mix. A man can be a just man or he can be an anxious man, but he cannot be both at the same time. But since man's life is pervaded and formed by his anxiety, and so his humanity is both vitiated and overcome, God chose himself a people and gave them his law toward the restoration of mankind to its humanity, to its freedom to exist by truth and justice.

The law of God is given as a set of commandments and statutes. It is the law of God and not the law of man or the law that, in fact, governs human life. But it is not merely a rule for living. It is, in fact, a mirror of man's true nature and destiny. It is the law that calls man to be free and faithful to his humanity. Justice and love are exercises of freedom; they are the very expressions of it. No man can be just without being free—free from anxiety for his life and free to love his neighbor as himself. Actually what the law of God enjoins is that men be free and live as creatures whose proper destiny is freedom, a freedom whose proper expression is that love which acts according to the neighbor's own freedom.

What is freedom from "the law, the devil, sin, death, the world, and wrath" basically but freedom from anxiety and its works of death? How could the devil tempt us if we were not anxious for our lives? What is the power of death but anxiety, and the power of sin but cleaving to life more than the truth? Surely we would not corrupt the law of God and turn it into an occasion of pride and injustice were it not that we would wield power over our own lives; and sin would not be so strong in us and wrath so terrible if it were not that we tremble daily for the breath of our flesh.[7]

But since the Bible brands anxiety itself as guilty, we have to go farther for an understanding of freedom. Injustice grows out of anxiety, but anxiety itself grows out of sin. Anxiety in man is not a natural outcome of the love of life; and the love of life absolutely is a corruption of humanity.[8] There is a primary freedom that makes anxiety a violation of our nature. There is a sense in which we share with all living beings a certain aversion to death. But what makes us human is the freedom to love our neighbors. The crown of the glory of men is love, the freedom to love, even though we would not know the glory of love without the power of death in our lives. This is the primary freedom which is obedience to the law of God, from which flow faith, love, faithfulness, justice, kindliness, patience, forgiveness, and all that makes our lives human according to Christ Jesus. Behind the freedom from anxiety which is definitive of freedom in a negative sense, there is the positive freedom of the human spirit to love God and all his creatures according to the excellencies with which he has endowed them. This is an intelligent freedom which is adumbrated in the thesis that "man is a rational animal."

However, I wish to point out that a solid apprehension of the freedom for love is by faith; more precisely, by the illumination and persuasion by the Spirit of God that Jesus is the bearer of man's "original righteousness." Our own spontaneous understanding presents our anxiety as an all too natural and even inevitable consequence of expected nonexistence. Are we not animals or living beings endowed not only with the will to live but also with memory and imagination? What could be more natural than that death should fill our lives with anxiety, with its effects of introversion, indifference toward our neighbors, and even fear and cruelty toward them? There is a common "psychological" interpretation of selfishness and inhumanity in terms of despair and frustration that presents our misery of lovelessness as, at worst, a corruption of a natural self-love by anxiety, which is all too understandable if we consider "human nature" and the perils that surround us. Some such interpretation of our troubles is what we contemplate by the unaided working of our own minds. In this way, what we called "the primary freedom " is set aside, and even denied and repudiated as not only fanciful but also vicious. For how can we deal with anxiety and its ill effects if we attribute it, not to a known and manageable cause, but to an act of freedom that seems to be as obscure as it is hidden? We have, in fact, neither the competence nor the inclination to take a clear and obvious view of our freedom as human beings. We are offended by our very birthmark as "intelligent creation," and know neither our freedom nor our humanity.

Hence, God's greatest gift to us is Christ, who by his life, death, and resurrection has once again confronted us with our freedom. But God who was in Christ has given us not only an exemplar of freedom but also his Spirit who works freedom in us, or restores us to our freedom. He makes us free, and our new freedom is expressed in the confession that not to love is to sin. So begins our Christian life with repentance and hope for the freedom that works by love and is known by faith as the ground of love and justice and all the elements of a good society.

It is necessary to remember that man's true freedom is represented by the Bible as expressed in obedience, and that the converse also is true. Obedience before God is an act of freedom, for to obey is to acknowledge and love "the Lord God," which are acts of freedom. This would be more than a paradox. It would be nonsense were it not that the working of the Spirit of God is unique as God's working and in a manner beyond our imagination. God's acting is the ground of our freedom, or that which he makes is free. The Spirit alone makes us free, free for love. He alone removes our anxiety by the Word of God made flesh and addressed to us. So he makes us free by uniting us with Christ and restoring us to himself. In all this, as he created us without our help, so he redeems us who need his help. As our freedom as human beings is an act of God alone, so our recovery of this freedom is an act of spontaneous grace. We say this, not to revive the threadbare controversy against Pelagianism, but to emphasize that human freedom as we have it in Christ Jesus is the decisive locus of our existence as creatures. To be free is to live and die so that anxiety is overruled by faith. But we do not, in fact, so live and die. Therefore, our life is "hid with Christ in God." If our life is so hid, so also is our freedom, for our freedom is our life as human beings.

2. FREEDOM AND LIBERTY

Now, it would be quite false and unedifying to disregard the simple and common doctrines of freedom as the absence of external, illegitimate, and coercive constraint upon human beings.[9] We are obviously free when no impediment is put in our way to our pursuit of happiness. We are free when we are able to follow our desires, reason, and imagination in accomplishing some good or acquiring some goods. We are "higher animals" and have our needs for food, shelter, comfort, security, and the goodwill and respect of our fellowmen. There are, in fact, organic or vital urges that drive us, with the aid of imagination and under the sundry stimuli of our social environment, to seek after the means of prosperity. In the pursuit of good and goods, we do exercise self-love and appreciate our own well-being better than that of our neighbors. So we follow our several ways and engage in economic and political enterprise with a keen eye on our own interests. And we want to be free as we try to make a living and enjoy life, in the sense that we want social life so arranged as to help us rather than hinder us in pursuit of well-being. This is the kind of freedom we desire and are constantly interested in. We want to be free to compete and acquire what good we can. So we speak of political freedom and economic opportunity (or freedom) as obvious goods worth fighting and even dying for, since without these we would be deeply wounded and, in a real sense, even destroyed.

Freedom in the above sense might better be called liberty. It is made necessary by the constitution of man as a deliberating and imaginative animal. And since man is in fact such an animal, it is intelligent and rational that he have liberty. Liberty as described above is grounded in nature and reason. Even autocratic states, ancient and modern, insofar as they have had laws and enforced them, have recognized liberty as a form of human existence. Where there have been rights of citizens, however limited and fragile, there has been liberty. Where there have been institutions and mores, insofar as these have been upheld and maintained, there have been rights and liberty. The more civilized a society, the more dependent a community upon accepted ways in its common life, the more consistently liberty and rights are honored; and the better they are honored, the more there is peace and well-being in such a society and community. And the value of liberty as providing the individual a space in a given society has been widely recognized in our world. It is today desired fiercely in many lands and among many people: by Christians, Muslims, Buddhists, and "irreligious" people. It takes no special revelation for people to know it and no special grace for them to pursue it. Where liberty is curtailed or denied, some special and high-sounding or even "scientific" reason must be provided to justify its diminution or absence. In short, the pursuit of liberty is natural to man as man, and when it is repudiated, there is violence done to his nature. The pursuit of liberty is rooted, not in what we have called man's freedom, but in his animality as illumined by his reason and imagination.

Moreover, we should not deny that even love as a sense of kinship and justice as mutuality are related to the animal we call man; they are natural in that he desires them and feels responsible to exercise them.[10] Hatred, injustice, oppression, lies, exploitation, and the like are evil; and a man need only be rational and imaginative, and in a sense true to himself, not only to admit but also to affirm that they are evils. The fact that the world has been full of these evils by no means proves that mankind has been bereft of the sense of truth, the impulse for love, or the knowledge of justice. Given the human organism and mind, "liberty and justice for all" is an authentic and spontaneous cry of "the rational animal." So it is absurd to say that the love of liberty and justice are limited to a fraction of mankind blessed with a special revelation in the matter. In short, the thesis that liberty and justice are exclusively Christian ideas is permanently debatable and appears patently false.

It has been pointed out repeatedly and well that liberty, as we know it in Western civilization, and justice and equality in our political life, are products not only of Christianity but also of the Greek and Roman societies. The advocates of democracy as we know it were not always orthodox Christians, and they often received their inspiration, not from the study of Christian doctrines, but from reason wrestling with the social life. If they followed "natural religion," many of their ardent followers since the eighteenth century have been no theists at all. In any case, the history of Western democracy is much too complex to justify the conviction of good Christians that the idea of liberty, and even zeal for it, is Biblical and only Biblical. It cannot even be shown that any theology or philosophy is necessary as a basis for "the pursuit of life, liberty and happiness" for all.[11]

But the Bible itself is witness that rapine and oppressions with wanton cruelties and bloodletting have been much too common to make liberty with justice in the world impressive. Tyrants have stalked the earth from the beginning, and power, rather than truth or justice, has settled matters among men. Even while truth and justice are natural to man as a rational being, it has been his second and operative nature to lie and wrong and play the devil with peace.

If our understanding of freedom as the ability to prefer faithfulness to life itself is correct, we must acknowledge that it is necessary for liberty. Although political liberty is a dictate of intelligent and rational self-love in principle, actually it does not flourish without a wisdom rooted in the freedom of the human spirit in relation to the will to live. The same will to live that, united with reason, inspires political liberty does, in fact, confuse and vitiate our practice of it because of the bondage of the same will to death and the anxiety and irrationality that go with such bondage. Without freedom, liberty withers and in spite of reason it is sacrificed to the will to live turned into a lust for life, a lust that has the savor of death.

To put the matter another way, there is a radical difference between justice implied in liberty and the justice we may practice by freedom. Justice in liberty is the work of reason in the exercise of self-love. Such justice demands that we render each man his due in the common life where we are together in the pursuit of "enlightened self-interest." It is a matter at once of prudence and consistency in the common pursuit of goods, and it is exercised insofar as it is compatible with prudence. Justice is pursued with zeal when the interests of people coincide. When they do not coincide, justice is sacrificed to self-interest, and reason loses its power to enforce consistency. The liberty of another is subordinated to one's own, and a man refuses to give another his due. Hence, it is always necessary that one be able to defend one's recognized rights with force.[12] It has always been difficult, if not impossible, to maintain justice in the context of even enlightened self-interest without the coercive power of the state. In short, insofar as justice is a demand made by intelligence in the service of "vital impulse," it must give way to self-interest where interests conflict. The more serious the conflict, as in political life, the more precarious is the practice of justice or the Golden Rule.

For this reason, the confidence of the civilized man in the Golden Rule ("Do unto others as you would have them do unto you") as practiced under enlightened self-interest is misplaced. The history of God's people under the law points to the fact that the anxiety of man for his life does not permit him to practice justice when it conflicts with self-interest involving "good and evil" and "life and death." Justice under law and for liberty requires "law enforcement" agencies, or the state with its coercive capabilities. Although the state enforces the Golden Rule, everybody, as it were, knows that conflicts of interest are overcome not by reason but by force. Thus justice becomes not a rational but a coercive principle. But coerced justice is a contradiction in terms, and "the rational animal" chafes under it. It is a logical impossibility to maintain justice for liberty on the basis of "the enlightened self-interest" of the organism engaged in self-preservation. Conflict of interest combined with the stirrings of anxiety for life makes consistency in justice impossible. But inconsistent justice is a constant source of frustration and bitterness in "the body politic" and may well end in madness and turmoil. A society that recognizes primarily, if not solely, justice as practiced by men of "enlightened self-interest" is less than a human society and contains the seed of its own self-destruction.

For this reason, the pursuit of liberty common to civilized men, for the sake of the acquisition and enjoyment of the goods available in their institutions, must involve power conflicts that not only jeopardize "civil rights" but also dehumanize people and threaten their common life. Justice as demanded by the law of God is indispensable for human existence. This justice, which we have called "justice in freedom," is the expression of an intelligence and a rationality that are the practice of humanity itself. It is called justice because it demands that we render men their due. But what is due to men now appears as nothing less than the love of the neighbor as oneself, which may not fall short of the love of the enemy.[13] Whereas justice for liberty is an anxious man's ideal, justice in freedom is the life of a fellowman who exists by the Word of God and man no less than by food and breathing. It is the justice of a man who recognizes his neighbor, in their common pursuit of self-interest, as "flesh" with himself, and subordinates his pursuit of liberty to the exercise of freedom by which he fulfills the law of God in love. This is the justice that works by mercy (Lev. 19:9f., 17f., 23f., 33f.). But the heart of mercy is to give each man his due "as God's intelligent creation," who lives by the communion of his fellowmen, hoping in it, rejoicing in it.

It is hard to know what could be more dangerous to human existence in civilized society than the confusion of these two kinds of justice one with the other, and the use of the word "justice" in one sense and not in the other. Insofar as in our civilization justice for liberty is recognized, but not the justice of communion, there is among us a misunderstanding that is today the misery of us and may tomorrow be the death of us. Insofar as our reason concedes justice for liberty but not the justice of mercy, we have become irrational; and a society in which such irrationality prevails is condemned to live by a lie. But when men lie about themselves, to themselves, they are hardly fit to live.

It is necessary to distinguish between freedom and liberty, because otherwise the necessity of freedom for liberty is obscured, and, in the failure to make this distinction, we lose liberty with freedom. Anxiety for life cripples reason and justice. A man who is anxious about his "life space" (*Lebenstaum*) is in no position to cooperate with his neighbor who must have his own life space. He seeks to provide for himself, to make his life space secure, by acquiring an advantage over his neighbor in power. The practice of justice or the Golden Rule requires that a man be free to love his neighbor as himself, for without this love, or unless a man acknowledges love as having priority over life itself, anxiety for life must enervate justice and turn our common life into a struggle in which mutuality is subordinate to self-love. In a sense, the commandment of God is: "Thou shalt be free, free from anxiety and the lust that goes with it, free for faithfulness and justice. Thou shalt be free; for it is only by freedom that thou shalt make liberty for thy neighbor as thou wouldst for thyself."

The law of freedom by which a man loves his neighbor as himself is no less "natural" for fellowmen than is the law of liberty by which he practices self-love. Nevertheless, the law of God or the law of freedom is commonly in conflict with the law of liberty that works by self-love. Hence, we find that there is a continued "controversy" between God and his people, and the law of God is an occasion in which the "natural" operation of self-love among us is under the judgment and condemnation of God. Thus, the law of self-love, the law of "the flesh," "the law of sin and death," are experienced by us as one "natural law" that is against the law of Christ, the law of Moses, the law of the Spirit, the law of fellowmanhood, which are experienced by us as the one law of God.

The law of God, the law of Moses, the law of freedom, are acknowledged in the Christian community as "the law of Christ." The law of Christ is the fulfillment of the law of Moses, the law of God, the law of freedom. It is Jesus the Christ himself, in his freedom from the anxiety in self-love, by which freedom he loved his neighbor as himself and laid his life down in preferring love to life itself. The transvaluation of values demanded by the law of Moses, which is the law of fellowmanhood, was once for all accomplished in his person as he lived and even dared to die in the love of God and his fellowmen; thus breaking the hold of sin and death upon his fellow creatures and restoring among them the covenant of human life that is our life itself. What appeared in this way was not a collection of organisms but a community of fellowmen who are the people of Jesus Christ and live in his presence and by his "grace and truth." Thus the hope of Israel by the Word of God and the law of God was fulfilled, and the Spirit of God promised by the prophets of God was poured upon his people.

But we know that the law of God and the law of the flesh are in strife among us. We who are fellowmen exist by the law of God; however, we exist in hope, and not as though we were free and the law were fulfilled among us. The Spirit strives in the church, and we our-selves strive, with hope that is by faith and love. Thus we taste "the freedom of the Christian man." Even while we are surprised by free-dom and know it as gift, we also know that it occurs by the priesthood of believers as they acknowledge the power of the Word among them; as they become responsible for love; as they testify to God's forgive-ness; as they repent and forgive. So emerges freedom, and lust is turned into love. So it is that man's natural quest for liberty is purified of lust, and reason's demand for justice is satisfied by love or faithfulness.

In short, political liberty is a rational principle; that is why rea-son has played a decisive role in its definition. But its vigor and stabili-ty require that freedom which is essential to humanity, freedom to love and to be faithful. But this freedom in the church is the gift of God in Christ Jesus and by the working of his Spirit. It is a gift not alien to our humanity, but one that restores us to our true nature; one that opens our eyes once again to the mystery of the human spirit as it lives by the creative and redemptive act of God. Our thesis is that freedom for faith-fulness is the work of God the Redeemer, by the Word and the Spirit, and that freedom is necessary for the vigor and stability of political lib-erty.

Now, we need to look into the working of the Spirit of God. Even while the Old Testament draws our attention to individuals as bearers of the Spirit, and the same is true in the Gospels where Jesus re-ceives the Spirit for the fulfillment of his mission, the New Testament makes it clear that after the resurrection of Christ, the Spirit moved among, as well as in, the people of God.[14] In short, the Spirit creates free men in the community of believers or the church. This is a matter of capital importance. The special charismatic endowment of the ser-vants of God whose task it was to do God's will for his people must not obscure the fact that the Spirit works *among* the believers, in their com-mon life and in their intercourse one with another or others Even while freedom from anxiety and for love is an individual affair, it, in fact, transpires in the association of human beings called the church. The Spirit of God neither recognizes nor in-dwells individuals as abstracted from society. His common mode of action requires a living and respon-sible interaction of people, so much so that there is no working of the Spirit apart from the social life of the church.

Obviously, men are quite capable of loving liberty and practic-ing democracy without the benefit of the church. But without the love

of fellowmen, which makes for integrity both in the love of liberty and
the practice of democracy, the former is absorbed by the lust for power
and the latter suffers a diminution of justice. Where there is not an association by consent to God's law, and men are not quickened in freedom
to obey it, liberty and democracy alike are in constant jeopardy, as well
as perpetually in a state of corruption. Although the law of liberty de-
velops from animal impulse and does not depend upon the law of God,
or the gospel of God, yet it is inseparable from the love of the neighbor
as oneself. It cannot subsist on the self-love of an anxious animal alone,
however enlightened and farsighted. Unless self-love becomes integral
to the communion by which men exist as fellowmen and becomes an
occasion of obedience to the law of God, humanity itself is violated and
the self-love of the organism works toward the disintegration of human
life. In short, the human organism is a fellowman, and as fellowman it
is an organism. When the organism's love of liberty takes precedence
over the fellowmen's communion and the love that goes with it, society
suffers a radical disorder, and liberty is turned into exploitation of man
by man, which has the savor of death for liberty and democracy alike. It
is the church's business with God and the world to live by communion
and its law of freedom. The church exists insofar as there is in it the
freedom that in part makes for the vigor of political liberty and the economic health of God's people.

It should be acknowledged as one of the signs of the integrity
of the church that Christians should be free to care for liberty and prefer
it to goods, comfort, security, and all that may well cover their anxiety.
Christians, of all people, need to be impressed with the peril to liberty
in our impulse to save our skins. They need to see the conflict between
the law of God and the law of the flesh, and to seek to purify the quest
for liberty with their freedom in Christ, And this cannot be done apart
from "social education and action," apart from persistent participation
in the social struggle for liberty. Since the political and economic life,
in which men seek their security and power, is the primary setting for
the working of the power of sin and death, there it is that freedom is to
be practiced and tested, and exercised toward increase and vigor.

The practice of political liberty is not only a sign of freedom
but also a necessary occasion for it. A nonpolitical Christianity is almost certainly a counterfeit, or a church whose members do not pray
and labor for liberty can hardly be said to believe, or hope, or love. For
without such praying and laboring, the freedom of the Christian man is

once again turned to bondage. The energy in love is generated by the
struggle for freedom from anxiety for life. Anxiety for life operates
with its peculiar power in the struggle for existence or self-preservation
in our economic and political life, where our quest for goods is turned
into lust and "power politics." Therefore, insofar as the struggle for
freedom occurs in our common life and its several institutions, there it
is that we have to experience both our freedom and our faith. Even
while liberty, which is a political matter, needs freedom for its flourish-
ing, freedom is denatured without the zeal for liberty. The church is not
"of" the world, in that freedom is not the same thing as liberty. But the
church is in the world, in that freedom is exercised in the quest for liberty. Christ came to make us free from the law of sin and death. The
law of sin and death works by anxiety for life, and anxiety for life occurs in our common life. It is, therefore, in our common life that we are
made free: and that by "justice, mercy, and peace," which are the signs
of freedom as well as the elements of liberty.

CONCLUSION.
THEOLOGY OF COMMUNION:
PROPOSALS FOR INQUIRY

1. THEOLOGY IN RETROSPECT

This last chapter is a look ahead to theological work that might be done in the light of the foregoing discussions.

First, it is necessary to take a backward look at the history of theology. As we have repeatedly suggested, the main line of Western theology has been dominated by the Augustinian doctrine of grace. This doctrine, in turn, has been based upon conceptions of grace and nature which presuppose the church as a grace-dispensing institution. Theology in the Western churches has been at the service of the organized churches as the means of grace, and this fact has been a primary factor in the making of the theologies in our historical background. There is no doctrine in orthodox Christian theology that is not in line with the purposes and interests of the ecclesiastical establishments called churches. These establishments have been "the arks of salvation," or places outside of which there is no salvation. Hence, not only the doctrine of salvation but also the other doctrines have been so stated and elaborated as to function in the rationale of these establishments and their practices.

Given the religious institutions, it has been both logical and inevitable that God should have been experienced and acknowledged as supernatural Power made available by these same institutions for salvation from evil. If the church institutions are the means of grace, or Power, then this Power is beyond the grasp of the people, or superhuman and supernatural. Although it is ignorant and wrong to say that religious institutions have fabricated a supernatural power in justification of their existence and power in the community, it is clear that it is their reason for being that they mediate such Power to their membership. It is certainly in line with their function in society to contrast the power of God with man's weakness, his blessedness with man's misery, his infinity with man's finitude, and his eternity with man's brief span of life.

It is convenient for religious institutions to teach the sinfulness of man (the fall of man and original sin); to insist that man is saved by the grace of God alone; to tie up firmly salvation with participation in the cultus of the institution. Church theologians have, of course, been aware that it is not enough to justify the institution as the means of grace. The people must also be impressed with their responsibility to support it and to do their duty with regard to its demands and teachings. Hence, it has always been necessary to insist *both* on grace and on accountability or "free will"; and there has been, to this day, no end to the attempts at doing both without self-contradiction. Once again, even while the depravity of man and his accountability may be quite real apart from institutional ideologies, it is nevertheless true that discussions of this "paradox" cannot be separated from church membership. People who receive salvation from religious institutions must believe that they need these institutions and that they are accountable as their beneficiaries. It has been the theologians' responsibility to state the situation with as good logic as possible; and it cannot be said that they have shirked it, even though their accomplishments have been inconclusive.

Again, one does not have to overlook the mysteries of Christology to recognize that the perennial preference of the orthodox churches for the "divine nature" of Christ as against his "human nature" is quite in line with their institutional interests. If Christ, no less than God, is mediated to the people by the religious institutions, he is no less supernatural than God. If he is present and available to the people through the preaching of the Word and the administration of the Sacraments, or if certain practices of the churches are the signs of his presence as Savior, it is logical that he should be supernatural or divine in his "Person," rather than human or natural. If he were, at the core of his being, human like the church people, the need for the churches as mediators of his presence and especially salvation would be obscured, if it would not become invisible altogether. It is true that the churches have not denied, in their official or orthodox theologies, the "human nature" of Christ. The "theories of the atonement," since Anselm, have recognized the obedience of Christ as essential to his saving work. The Bible and Christian common sense alike have made docetism out of the ques-

tion. The Son of God, who "suffered under Pontius Pilate, was crucified, dead, and buried," was, to the Christian mind and piety alike, endowed with "human nature." The worship of the churches has always
been directed to a Savior who is "very man" as well as "very God."
However, the "hypostatic union" of Divine Power with human frailty in
the Person of Christ has always been an embarrassment to the mind;
and the mind, in its embarrassment, has traditionally upheld the institutionally formed piety of the people, who have subordinated the humanity of Christ to his deity. When all is said and done, such piety lives on
supernatural Power. Therefore, its Christ has been "really" God and not
a man.

Like God and Christ, the Holy Spirit has been identified as
Power, immanent in the religious institution. The doctrine of the ubiq-
uity of the Spirit has not impressed the ordinary believer who has
turned to the institution as the means of grace. The Spirit has been lo-
calized in the cultus of the churches. The Christian life, analyzed and
elaborated in terms of justification and mainly as the inner life of the individual and his lawful conduct, has been credited to the Holy Spirit or
the supernatural power, channeled to the people by the preaching and
the Sacraments of the churches. Still, the Christians have been led to
believe that heaven is for the good and that the wicked go to hell. A
purgatory has been provided for countless souls who have not been
good enough for heaven or bad enough for hell.

When the Enlightenment, rationalism, secularism, and lesser
acids of modernity turned away many people—"the modern man"—
from belief in supernatural Power, there was also a corresponding turning away from the churches and from "the faith of the Christian
church." The churches had become the custodians of supernatural Power. When people came to disbelieve in such Power, they lost their zeal
for the churches. When they lost their zeal for the churches, their
"faith" lost its hold upon them, and many became atheists. The embarrassing thing was that the unbelievers claimed they were none the
worse for it, and it could not be shown that they were wrong.

Of course, the churches as institutions of long standing have
had no inclination to disappear. Their theologians, intelligent and resourceful men, worked out neoorthodoxies that, for all their critical attitude toward the churches and serious heretical tendencies within them,
gave new life to the theologies of the institutions and appeared to have
provided them with convincing apologetics. The neoorthodox theolo-

gians have criticized traditional supernaturalism, ecclesiasticism, other-worldliness, and the like, and they have tried to avoid every semblance of being ignorant of and impervious to the "situation of the modern man." They have brought together theology and ethics in new and commanding ways and have bound private piety and public life together with bonds of iron. Their work is nothing less than a call for a new reformation of the churches.

Still, they have neither cared nor dared to touch the orthodox doctrines of the means of grace. This means that their criticisms of traditional supernaturalism have been less than theoretically adequate and practically fruitful. Being good Protestants, they have, whether a Barth or a Bultmann, singled out the preaching of the Word as the primary, if not the only, means of grace. Therefore, in spite of their, especially Barth's, insistence upon the church as the believing multitude of Christians, their neoorthodoxy has functioned as a new apology for the churches as institutions dispensing grace through the sermon. Barth has deliberately made theology into a critique of preaching; Bultmann has, rather, identified the gospel with the Word as preached. Of course, both have had fresh and profound things to say about the Christian life as the hearing and doing of the Word. But still, the traditional doctrine that the grace of God is brought to the people by the ministry of the officials of the institutional churches has been left intact; and in this respect, so has traditional supernaturalism. This being so, for all its criticisms of the churches and its ethical and political zeal, neoorthodox theology has been a massive and highly sophisticated apology for ecclesiasticism.

Theological schools, which provide the churches with their ministers, have embraced neoorthodoxy and taught it to their students, who have gone into the churches with a new conviction of the power of preaching. It is perhaps true that neoorthodox ministers have preached the grace of God in Christ Jesus with much zeal and that they have been listened to with considerable interest. However, there has also been much frustration on the part of the preacher and deafness on the part of his hearers. It can hardly be said that the preaching of the Word, "theological preaching," has produced the results one might expect from the grace of God, which is said to be sovereign and omnipotent. It apparently takes more than preaching (good or best) and the administration of the Sacraments to realize "the freedom of the Christian man" to hear the Word of God and to do it.

2. TOWARD A THEOLOGY OF COMMUNION

We have said much about "the communion of saints"as a means of grace and we need not weary the reader once again with it. However, it appears to us that the next task in theology is to engage in a disciplined and fruitful statement of it. We need to work out a theology of the means of grace that will do equal justice to *sola gratia* and to *sola fide*. We have to learn to avoid both the traditional denial or neglect of the Christians' life together as a means of grace and the "humanistic" denial or neglect of the grace of the triune God. It will take much doing to state this matter as correctly as possible, so that we shall not be caught again with pitting God against the church, or the church against God, as the source of grace.

a. The Doctrine of God

Such a theological enterprise may well lead to radical revision of the doctrines of God. We need to explore the significance of the insight that in Christian theology we have to do with God as he is known among his people. The context of our knowledge of God is our life together as Christ's people. It is in this context that we confess God as Creator, Providence, and Redeemer. Here it is that we come to speak of his transcendence and immanence; of his goodness, wisdom, and power; of him as "infinite, eternal, and unchangeable"; in short, of him as God. It will require much discipline and dialectic, and sustained effort on the part of many, to make the kind of restatements of the doctrine of God that will do justice to the coherence of our knowing God and living together under the Word of God. Whether we speak of the eternity or of the providence of God, we shall have to learn to speak of him as God in and over the church. So it will have to be with regard to his power or wisdom or goodness. We here propose the principle that to say anything whatever about God in a manner irrelevant to his covenant with his people is to say what is defective, and as such untrue."God" is the shorter form of "God in Christ over Christ's people." The doctrine of the Trinity may not mean anything less than that we confess God who was in Christ reconciling his people to himself. We shall need much theologizing to state adequately how this God is the God of "universal being"; how he is the Lord God in and over nature or the physical world, from stars to atoms. However, one thing appears clear to the writer: there is no God but the God of his people; or, God of all being is God the Father, Son, and Holy Spirit.

The orthodox scheme of natural and revealed theology will no longer do. The two ways of knowing God, by reason and by faith, belong in the life together of God's people."The light of nature" shines in the society of fellowmen, and revelation occurs among them. The mind of the individual person has its *sensus divinitatis* in his communications with his fellowmen and hears the Word of God in hearing the words of his fellowmen. He lives and knows in the physical world as a fellowman and he believes in "revealed doctrine" as a fellowman. The exercise of reason and the exercise of faith are functions of fellowmanhood, and both "nature" and "supernature" are disclosed in men's life together. Faith and reason, nature and supernature, are analytical concepts and belong in the logic of communion. There is no faith without faithfulness and no reason without communication; and both faithfulness and communication have their reality in communion. Hence, faith is not an addition to reason, and reason is not transcended by faith. Natural theology does not precede revealed theology as a human possibility, and revealed theology does not supersede natural theology as a divine possibility. Such traditional contrasts between the two types of theology, with the corresponding contrasts between faith and reason, are off focus in theology that does justice to the logical priority of communion to both faith and reason and sees them as inseparable one from the other in the life of "intelligent creation." Here also there is rethinking to be done.

b. Christology

In this book we have no chapter formally given to a consideration of Christology, even though there is hardly a chapter that does not turn again and again to it. However, it is clear that in a theology of communion there is the possibility of fresh thinking on the subject. We may be able to move aside from the traditional dilemma of having to choose between the deity and the humanity of Christ. It is no secret that in spite of the catholic churches' assertion of "the two natures" of Christ, they have found it necessary to insist, in one way or another, that the Person constituted by the two natures is the Word, or the Logos, or the Son of God, or God the Son, or the Lord, etc.; in short, God and not man. If God alone is Savior, and if Christ is the Savior, Christ can be none other than God. On the other hand, the Western theories of the atonement since Anselm require that Jesus Christ be a human being, with no "ifs and buts." If the individual person who "suffered under Pontius Pilate, was crucified, dead, and buried," and "descended into hell," had not been a human being, his work would not have been "fitting," and he would not have been the head of the church. Christian instinct, as it were, has never tolerated "gnosticism," and the gnostics, for all their acumen, have been declared heretical. Christian reason and piety alike have repudiated the notion that Jesus Christ was a God and not a man. And yet the theologians, of the church from Athanasius to Barth, determined to uphold the gospel as good news from God to man, have insisted that Jesus Christ is "Jehovah."

The question of Christ's "person"—as to whether the "person" constituted of his two natures was Deity or a man—hardly belongs, in its traditional forms, in a theology of communion. We have argued that the nature of a person is a characterization of him in the process of communion. There was no Jesus Christ without his communication with God and his fellowmen. He was the person that he was in and by this communication. The communion of God with him and the communion of his fellowman with him, and his communion with them, constituted his "person." He existed by double and reciprocal communion, rather than by the hypostatic union of the two natures. Jesus Christ was the person engaged in communion and was a person by virtue of it. It appears to us a "categorial confusion" to inquire whether this person was God or man. Our contention is that Christ, as a communing person, was the Son of God by virtue of that communion by which God was in him "reconciling the world to himself." But he was Son of God and Savior as a fellowman, that is, in his communion with his fellowmen outside of whose company and apart from whose word to him he neither existed nor was the Savior and Son of God. In short, when we recognize that a person is constituted, not by his nature, but as a locus of communion, it is hardly to the point to ask whether he is endowed with divine or human personhood. We might well say that communion creates a nature, or that beings in communion have a certain nature. However, this personhood consists in their communing and not in their "natures." Christ's saving communion, rather than the union of the two natures, constitutes his "person." Considering the fixed embarrassments of traditional Christology, such an approach to it may be worth examination. Jesus Christ is mystery; but he need not be the nemesis of theology.

c. Sin and Temptation

A theology of communion may also help us with the doctrine of sin. The total effect of traditional theology has been the doctrine that sin consists, on the one hand, in certain attitudes such as pride, ambition, selfishness, etc., or on the other hand, in disobedience to "the laws of God," especially as contained in the moral commandments of the Decalogue. We have spoken of "man the sinner" and of sinful acts. We have located sin in attitude and in deeds. There have been pietistic-subjectivistic views of sin and those which we call moralistic. But in any case, we have seen the individual as the locus and agent of sin and fixed our attention upon him both for understanding the nature of sin and for finding the antidote or antidotes to it. The outcome of our cogitations on the subject has been theoretically mystification and practically frustration. Sin appears to be positive and negative, real and unreal, freely done and inevitable, guilty and not guilty. Its origin is obscure, its nature is vague, and its importance in human life uncertain. Its universality, if it is universal, is passing comprehension. It is said to be imputed to all mankind. It is said to be inherited. It is said that all men have a weakness for it.

In our judgment, it takes two and more to make sin. Sin occurs by communion, and it is the failure of communion. Pride and ambition, hate and selfishness, lawlessness and deeds against the law, the inward and outward aspects of sin alike, are signs rather than the reality of sin, which is a breaking of the bond of communion, which is the death of fellowmen. Sin is a state of affairs among fellowmen in which men sin in response to sin and evoke in others the response of sin in turning away one from another; and by this turning away they destroy one another. Since men exist by communion, sin is the deadly thing among them; and if they will not take it seriously, they declare themselves fools by virtue of sin. There is hardly another failure among the teachers of the church that is more confounding than the failure to explain to the people that sin is the death of man because sin is the breaking up of communion by which men exist and live and have peace. Pietism and moralism alike, which have formed the traditional doctrines of sin, have trivialized sin and ended up with turning it into an "ugly word," which is as boring as it is unilluminating.

Sin is a refusal of communion, and it occurs by way of temptation in our life together. It is amazing how little our theologians have done with temptation, even though both Adam and Christ are presented to us by the Scriptures as having been tempted to sin. The reason for this oversight is not far to seek. Assuming "original sin" as a second nature to man, somehow inherited like the color of one's skin and working in the individual as a virulent infection, temptation could not have been taken seriously as the occasion of sinning. When " original sin " was denied, or declared washed away, and man's free will was proposed as the presupposition of his humanity, temptation, as we find it in the stories about Adam and Christ, was both minimized and set aside as theologically irrelevant. But the truth is that men do evil in thinking that they do good, and they do it in communion. They sin or turn aside from Christ and God and their fellowmen believing that in so doing they achieve power and become masters over their own lives. Power may achieve more than security of life, but it must achieve that. Thus for life's sake men prefer power to love in which they are dependent for life. So it is that they are tempted and sin and lose life and good alike. In a sense, sin is inevitable because men will save their lives. But it is also a failure of intelligence because anyone who "would save his life" by overcoming the dependence that is in communion will lose it—and that for the reason that communion is the life of a fellowman. In this respect, Adam was a fool and author of folly; Christ was a wise man and author of wisdom, without which there is no salvation.

The devil has been credited with having single-handedly tempted both Adam and Christ. We do not deny that without him there would have been neither temptation nor fall. However, Eve tempted Adam. Christ was tempted with power and authority that belong in a world of fellowmen. It is fellowmen who tempt one another to exercise mastery by knowledge and power. One man turns away from another and in so doing tempts the other, who in turn turns away from him and in so doing turns away from another, who turns away from the second man and tempts a fourth man; thus men turn away from men and tempt one another, and there is a *massa corruptionis*. This is a "chain reaction" that began with human society, Adam and Eve, and is apparently coextensive with it. Indeed, original sin is due to "the flesh." But the flesh in question are fellowmen in their anxiety for life, which is a peculiarly human trait and occurs in the communion of fellowmen. If anxiety tempts for sin, sin makes for anxiety and tempts for sin, and sin makes for lust and lawlessness. Of course, the flesh who sins is an organism, and the organism's "love of life" makes for anxiety and sin. In a sense, animal impulse is a temptation, by way of anxiety, to sin. Nevertheless, sin is a human and not an animal thing. It occurs among fellowmen and is apparently coextensive with the race of mankind. The above may not explain sin and its pervasiveness in society. But it at least gives us a way of approaching the subject that is alternative both to the theory of physical propagation and to the theory of "bad example"; the former, the orthodox or Augustinian theory, turns sin into a physical defect, which is awkward if not absurd; the latter, the heretical and Pelagian theory, makes sin into an act of the individual will, and this is too myopic to be true. Both theories obscure our existence as fellowmen, and to do this is bad theology and bad ethics. The context of sin is communion. We should begin there and proceed from there as we are able, according to the word of Christ, by the Spirit, in the church.

d. Salvation: The Crucial Issue

The subject of sin leads to the subject of salvation, which was not formally discussed in the foregoing chapters. Here in a sense we are at the nub of the matter and should be able to distinguish between the wisdom of God and the wisdom of man, or between the wisdom of Christ and our wisdom. What the flesh is concerned about is salvation from evil and weakness in the presence of evil. What exacerbates the heart of man is his helplessness before powers, human and physical, that threaten him with death and all evil that exudes the savor of death. Hence, what he cries for is safety from nature and man, and man and nature. He cries for a supernatural and superhuman Power that will save him from the perils that surround him, the miseries that invade him, and the *nihilum* that annihilates him. He wants to move from this world to another, from the temporal to the Eternal, from the evil to the Good, from the unreal to the Real, from the unsafe to the Safe. He will try magic and ecstasy. He will try bribery and payment. He will try good thoughts and good deeds. He will try religion and science, art and technique, piety and politics. Whether "highbrow" or "lowbrow," philosopher or meatcutter, he will be saved from his finitude and enjoy the utopia of the Infinite. He will create institutions and submit to their authority. He will believe as he must and behave as he must, hoping to be free of nature and man alike. He knows what he wants to be saved from; and if he does not know too well what he will be saved to, he nevertheless will seek after it with all his might. Finitude is what troubles his spirit, and from finitude he will be saved. We should not deny that the will to escape our finitude has worked with power and much consequence in the Christian doctrines of salvation. There have ever been theories of deification and angelification. Heaven has been described as free from suffering and death, and immortality as painless and peaceful."God, freedom, and immortality" has been said to sum up the Christian religion as well as any other, and disbelief in "life after death" has appeared as even more pitiful than disbelief in God, not to mention freedom. Recently there has been much uncertain sound made about "resurrection," and it appears that one can hardly be saved without saying "eschatology." One can hardly understand the orthodox passion for revealed theology, authority and tradition, "high" Christology and high churchism, without keeping in mind that in the main line of Christianity the gospel has been understood as God's answer to the universal human quest for salvation from evil. *Pondus animae*, said Augustine, is the love of the Good; and everybody has, as it were, known that the Good is beyond evil and that to find it is also to find life beyond death. In short, there has been a steady conviction in the Christian churches that Christianity is the way of salvation from hell, which is foreshadowed in the evils and miseries of this world. This conviction has been expressed in notions that have been more or less spiritual and sophisticated. But it has been both pervasive of and powerful in the Christian mind, and neither the cults nor the theologies of the Christian tradition can be understood without it.

The truth appears to be that there has been an over whelming temptation in the churches to seek salvation from evil rather than to cleave to the communion of saints. The flesh of the Christians has cried out for the Good rather than to the living God of his people; and it has found its Good in the hope of escape from death and all evil, rather than in the love of God and neighbor. It has believed in its anxiety, rather than exercised truth and mercy in its freedom. Hence, it has sought salvation by believing rather than by turning to God and neighbor. Justice, mercy, and peace have been taken as the requirements of salvation, rather than as the enjoyment of it; and love itself has been subordinated escape from evil. In short, faith has not meant faithfulness, and the church has not been communion; and God's covenant with his people has been replaced by the claim of religious institutions that they possess and provide the people with "the medicine of immortality." Thus the churches have become gatherings of anxious flesh seeking to save their hide. This is why men observe little freedom and little joy in the churches, and the light shining out from them is dim; so much so that "You are the light of the world" makes rather a hollow sound.

A theology of communion must be clearly critical of theologies that function to pacify the flesh and its anxiety rather than to quicken freedom in the communion of saints. It is the business of theology to help the people understand that communion is the last end for which God created man, and that there is no salvation for fellowmen other than reconciliation and communion. New birth is by and for the peace of God's people in their life together. It is by election, adoption, and call for communion; and all three are acts of communion. Justification is turning among sinners for communion, and sanctification is the process and progress of the same. And adoption, justification, sanctification, are salvation because they are aspects of our being made free and making free for life, which is communion among fellowmen.

"Man's chief end is to glorify God, and to enjoy him forever." But God is the living God of his people, and it is absurd to seek to glorify God and enjoy him forever apart from the communion of saints. When the pious enjoy God and not his people, and glorify him but not in his people, and hope for "forever" more than they hope for life with God in his Kingdom, they are of the flesh and its anxiety rather than of the Spirit and his freedom. And both their piety and their hope are stumbling blocks.

As we argued in the Introduction, what is at stake in theology is, in a sense, man's self-understanding. Our business is indeed with God; but it is with the living God of his people, who exist as fellowmen. Christian theology is critical reflection upon the doctrine of the living God. Therefore, it is a critical reflection upon the doctrine of men as a people who exist by the Word of God and exist together by their words among themselves, speaking about everything as fellowmen and making good and evil as fellowmen. The thing to understand, according to a theology of communion, is that communion is not one good among other goods a man might enjoy. It is not a moral principle, a duty imposed upon men who might be otherwise occupied. It is not for the enrichment and the enhancement of pleasure in life. In short, it is not an addition to the life of the existing individual, who might prefer other ways of self-fulfillment. There is no substitute for communion as a good thing; no virtue, or accomplishment, or satisfaction. Communion is the existing individual's life, the very process of his existence, and as such, his very being. He exists by communion, and this is what we mean by saying that he is a fellowman. In a way peculiar to fellowmanhood, communion is at once given as a gift and required as a responsibility. Here there is a peculiar conjunction of *is* and *ought* that signifies the fellowman and determines his good and evil as a fellowman. Such is the mystery of humanity, which is the mystery of freedom, and to live with this mystery, in "fear and trembling," but also in joy and hope, is to exist as a human being by the works of justice, mercy, and peace. A theology of communion is thus also an ethics of communion. This matter also needs to be worked out.

But there may be no such thing as a politics of communion. Politics is our way, "the art of the possible," in our common life. It is the way a society works for common goals. It consists, not of communion, but of common enterprise. It is necessary, both in theory and in practice, to distinguish between communion and politics. Otherwise communion is turned into the practice of "enlightened self-interest," and our very humanity is corroded; politics is turned into a pretense of altruism, and justice in our common life is corrupted by sentimentality. Politics is the occasion of communion, and communion is the humanization of politics. There is no communion without politics, and politics without communion is no longer an activity of fellowmen. Still, it is necessary for both communion and politics that they be kept distinct, for it takes both for human existence.

e. At the Lord's Table

Moreover, it is to be hoped that a theology of communion will be of help in putting new life into the Protestant "Communion service." It is only reasonable that "the communion of saints" should be celebrated at the Lord's Supper, or that the Lord's Supper should be a lively celebration of the communion of saints. The churches have traditionally insisted that the Lord himself is present at his Table, and that there the people partake of his body and blood. There has been much controversy as to whether the eating and drinking at the Lord's Table is "real" or "spiritual," as to whether the elements should be regarded as providing grace or signifying it. Many have regarded the doctrine in such controversies as much too "magical" and have turned the Lord's Table into a service in memory of the death of Jesus. The total effect of such approaches to the Lord's Table has been a weakening, if not a disappearance, of the Supper as the celebration of Christ's communion with his people. The traditional disputes about this central act of worship in the church have served, above all, to establish the churches as the loci of grace. The Lord's Supper, as one of the two primary means of grace, if not the only one, has become a cultic act rather than a festival of God's people, and it has been characterized, not so much by the joy of communion, as by mystic awe induced by holy institutions and the actions of their "ordained" personnel. The people have taken and eaten, and drunk, but they have hardly been in communion. If they have communed with the saints in heaven, they have hardly rejoiced in the company of the sinners on earth and around them. In short, Jesus' Table for the sinners has been turned into a religious cult, and Christians have not so much enjoyed his company as relished "the supernatural food " provided by the churches.

According to a theology of communion, the Lord's Supper would be a celebration of the Christian life as the communion of God with his people, of the people with their God and one with another: God being Father, Son, and Holy Spirit; the people being the company of sinners reconciled by Jesus Christ to their God and to one another. Any "Eucharist " that is less than, or other than, the joy of reconciled and reunited fellowmen is a travesty of the Lord's Supper. Any eating and drinking at the Lord's Table that is altogether different from Jesus' eating and drinking with sinners, and the working of his grace among them as they eat and drink with him, may be a theophagy, an eating of a god, but it is no partaking of the Lord's Supper. It is communion that makes the Eucharist an occasion of joy, a means of grace, a sign of Immanuel. The people who come together in a church are the church, and the church is where the people of God assemble together before their God. But these people exist by their communion, and God is present to them in their communion. It is in communion that grace abounds, and so does joy, as God and his people, in Christ and the Spirit, eat and drink together. These people come together from their homes and work, from their political life in their city and world, bringing with them their sin and their hope, rejoicing and repentant, and approach Him who is their life and their Lord. So they eat and drink, and their eating and drinking becomes the sign of communion by which the Lord feeds them with his body and nourishes them with his blood, and they are satisfied. So they go their ways, for the communion of flesh in a common life in the world. And their God goes with them, to be their light and their strength in their life together. In short, the communion of saints is the proper setting for the Lord's Supper, and without it we have neither the Lord nor his Supper. However, here also is much to be thought through. It should be possible to clarify our ideas and to make them useful for the glory of God and the peace of his people, without pretending to have done away with the mystery that appears to be integral to our very existence.

3. THE CONTEXTS OF COMMUNION: PROBLEMS

a. The Physical World

There are doubtless other things that have to be worked out in a theology of communion. If orthodox theologies and their variants were deficient in their doctrines of the church, a theology of communion tends to be deficient in its doctrine of the created world. Communion is a human phenomenon, and it may be hard, and even questionable, to try to understand "stars and atoms" in terms of it. However, this kind of difficulty is not new in the history of theology, and the traditional ways of dealing with it have been less than impressive. As man's relation to nature is ambiguous, so also the relation of "the living God of his people" to God the Creator or "nature's God" is ambiguous. When we start with "natural theology," we are not able to proceed to " revealed theology," with its doctrines of sin and salvation. When we start with the doctrine of the triune God, we are not able to proceed to "monotheism" except by way of metaphors and mystification. The difficulty has been, and is, that man the fellowman is in nature but hardly of it. When he is seen as continuous with nature, his humanity is obscured. When he is seen discontinuous with it, his finitude is obscured. One may, of course, say that he is the locus of "finite freedom"; but this must not be allowed to cover up the mystery of his relation to the physical world. Communion, which is by way of the word, is not a physical process; at the same time, it occurs among organisms, and without them there is no communion as we have spoken or may speak of it. Perhaps in a theology of communion the best way to approach the question of man's place in nature is to acknowledge that the word that one man utters to another is the word of "flesh" or the creature; from this it may well follow that the God whom we know in communion is the God of the creature, or that God the Savior can be none other than God the Creator. However, it should be clear that the people of God may not speak of him as though they knew a God other than "the Lord of the covenant," or a God who is other than "God and Father of our Lord Jesus Christ." But this matter requires fresh investigation, especially in an "age of science."

b. The World of Artifacts

Considering the context of communion, the chief impediment to natural piety, and therefore to natural theology, is the modern city, which has become the proper environment of man. The business of man in "developed countries" today is with machines and industrial products rather than "nature," the things enumerated in the first chapter of Genesis as having been created in the beginning by God. It is needless to point out in detail that the performances, the ways, the forms, the powers, of our machines, pervade our total common life, and form as well as inform our lives in spirit as well as in body. We are absolutely dependent for health, peace, prosperity, power, upon our artifacts, no less than upon our natural resources. These artifacts are the things we transact with and the things by whose transactions with us we exist and have life as we, in fact, live it. In short, our communion one with another is inseparable from our transactions in our environment of artifacts.

The consequences of our existence in "the Power Age" are crucial for our being as well as complex in their many workings among us. The common failure of contemporary theology to explore the meaning of this age for the Christian life and therefore for the Christian faith is rather a scandalous failure in intelligence, which has no little to do with its unavailability for the edification of the church and the world alike. The people live in and by an environment of artifacts, which are thus integral to "human ecology." If this fact is uninteresting to theologians, then there should be no surprise in the fact that their theologies are uninteresting to the people.

A theology of communion demands disciplined and persistent

attention to human life as formed in a "technological society." The setting of communion is made up of the transactions of fellowmen in a world of machines and machine power. Like the physical world, the world of artifacts is the place where men do good and evil, are tempted and sin, and need the freedom that is in the church by Christ Jesus. Therefore, there is no doctrine of the church that can be properly "interpreted" without attention to communion in the artifactual world. Hence, a theology of communion needs to pay rigorous attention to the phenomenon of human existence in "the Atomic Age," and so to state the doctrines of creation, providence, sin, and salvation that the Christian faith may be the faith of the people in this age and not in another. To this end, the theologian needs to concern himself much more seriously with literature that will make him sensitive to the life of man in the city than has been his wont in the past. Theologians have, as it were unconsciously, by virtue of their being more or less "modern men," responded to the modern world in more or less fruitful ways. We need not begin *de novo*. However, it is most probable that disciplined analysis of communion in the context of our transactions in and with the artifactual environment will result in much illuminating theological activity.

c. Science, Theology, and Culture

The age of the machine is also the age of science. We are living in an age of "two cultures": the humanistic and the scientific. Through its powerful and all-pervasive influence upon society by way of massive technological developments, it is the scientific culture that dominates our common life. Yet most of our theologians, by tradition and training, are at home in the humanistic culture. The Bible is literature and not science. Augustine and Thomas, Calvin and Luther, Schleiermacher, Barth and the Niebuhrs—there has not been a practicing scientist among the lot. And there is the doctrine of the incarnation, according to which Jesus, a man, is the truth as well as the way and the life. All in all, theology belongs in the humanistic and not in the scientific culture, especially as formed by the recent revolutions in physics and biology.

There is, of course, very good defense for this situation. The God and Father of Jesus Christ is the living God of his people, and the faith and faithfulness of God's people, in the world of fellowmen, is what the prophets and teachers of the church have rightly been concerned about. The God of the theologian in the church is the Creator-Savior; and in sending his Son to save the world, he has declared himself, by his Word and Spirit, peculiarly as God over and among the race of fellowmen. Theology is a humanistic discipline.

On the other hand, theology that remains alien to the scientific revolution and culture and refuses to consider its significance for the human enterprise with all its mind and heart, refuses to face the human situation and may well condemn itself to futility. It will not do to take sides with idealism, humanism, existentialism, or any other ism proposed as a foil to "technical reason." It will not do to put science, either as method or as accomplishment, in its place, and to cultivate the humanistic field. It will not do to embrace piety, or morality, or some mysticism, in preference to the scientific enterprise. In short, theology cannot forthwith choose between faith and science, any more than the human community can choose between them. And the traditional ways of "reconciling science and religion" do not appear to be sufficient for the making of a concert between faith and science that will overcome the debilitating double-mindedness of our age.

The recognition that "the scientific culture" may, and perhaps must, become the occasion for authentic communion among fellowmen may open the door for the hoped-for concert. Since life together occurs in our common life, and our common life is formed by the artifacts that constitute our environment, and these artifacts are products of science and technics, faith and science belong together, "the depth of reason" and technical reason are inseparable one from the other, though distinct and not to be confused. But here also is much to be done.

In such a postscript we cannot take up the question of the relationship between theology and culture, that is, between theology and art or literature, theology and philosophy, theology and social psychology, etc. However, it is clear that a theological interpretation of the several elements of our culture presupposes theology as an intellectual discipline with its own *locus operandi*. It has been the thesis of this book, stated or implied throughout, that the *locus operandi* of theology is "the communion of saints," or life together in Christ's company, by the interdwelling of the Spirit of the living God. It is the business of the Christian thinker to consider in a disciplined way this life that is to be lived, with all the requisite "works of love," in our situation as illumined by our culture, humanistic and scientific alike. A theology of communion has to be a distinct intellectual discipline; however, its discipline has to be exercised with regard to a life that embraces the human enterprise in all its aspects. There is no communion outside of our culture or cultures. The word of the fellowman is spoken to fellowman in our common world and institutions. We are to live as fellowmen in our common life, and we have to live our common life as fellowmen; otherwise we neither commune nor transact as human beings, and human life is not in us. So it is that theology and culture belong together, inform each other, and together make for truth, mercy, and peace. But here also is much to be thought through. Only, we may not forget that thinking occurs among the living, and theology is a function of communion, which is life among men and, as such, the life of fellowmen.

Finally, it may well be that the distress of our world is due to a failure in the communion of fellowmen. It is as though some necessary condition of peace were lacking among us; and this condition may be the communion of flesh with flesh in the fear and love of the Lord. But here again much needs to be done to show that such is the case, which is a responsibility given to the church first, and to theology in the church secondly.

NOTES

INTRODUCTION. TOWARD A NEW "IMAGE" OF MAN

1. Paul Tillich, *Systematic Theology* (The University of Chicago Press, 1951), Vol. I, pp. 168 ff.

2. Johannes Pedersen, *Israel, Its Life and Culture* (London: Oxford University Press, 1926, 1940), Vols. I, II, pp. 46 f., 263 ff.

3. Bernard Meland, *The Realities of Faith* (Oxford University Press, Inc., 1962), Chs. IV, V.

4. John Dewey, *Human Nature and Conduct* (Henry Holt and Company, 1922), pp. 106 ff.; John Dewey and Arthur F. Bentley, *Knowing and the Known* (Beacon Press, Inc., 1949, 1960), Ch. V; H. R. Niebuhr, *The Responsible Self* (Harper & Row, Publishers, Inc., 1963), pp. 76 f.

5. Joseph Haroutunian, *Lust for Power* (Charles Scribner's Sons, 1949), Chs. I and II.

6. Ibid.; Arthur O. Lewis, Jr., ed., *Of Men and Machines* (E. P. Dutton & Company, Inc., 1963). Selections from writers old and new.

7. C. Wright Mills, "The Mass Society," in *Man Alone*, ed. by Eric and Mary Josephson (Dell Publishing Company, Inc., 1962), pp. 201 ff.

8. David Riesman, Nathan Glazer, and Reuel Denney, *The Lonely Crowd* (Doubleday Anchor Book, 1953), Ch. I.

9. Karen Horney, *The Neurotic Personality of Our Time* (W. W. Norton & Company, Inc., 1937), esp. Chs. I, III, VII, X, XV.

10. Sigmund Freud, *Group Psychology and the Analysis of the Ego* (Bantam Books, Inc., 1960).

11. Martin Buber, *Between Man and Man*, tr. by R. Gregor Smith (Beacon Press, Inc., 1955), Ch. I; Nicolas Berdyaev, *Slavery and Freedom* (Charles Scribner's Sons, 1944), pp. 130 ff.

12. C. Wright Mills and Hans Gerth, *Character and Social Structure* (Harcourt, Brace and World, Inc., 1953), Chs. II, IV, *passim.*

13. George Herbert Mead, *Mind, Self and Society*, ed. by Charles W. Morris (The University of Chicago Press, 1934), pp. 144 ff.

14. Ibid., pp. 164ff.; H. R. Niebuhr, op. cit., pp. 76ff.

15. Reinhold Niebuhr, *The Nature and Destiny of Man* (Charles Scribner's Sons, 1941, 1943), Vol. I, Ch. VII; Emil Brunner, *Man in Revolt*, tr. by Olive Wyon (The Westminster Press, 1947), Ch. III.

16. See above, notes 11, 13, 14. See also Henry Nelson Wieman, *Man's Ultimate Commitment* (Southern Illinois University Press, 1958), Chs. I, VIII, *passim*; Karl Barth *Church Dogmatics*, Vol. III, Part 2, ed. by G. W. Bromiley and T. F. Torrance (Edinburgh: T. & T. Clark, 1960), pp. 243 ff.

CHAPTER 1

REFLECTIONS ON THE DOCTRINE OF THE CHURCH

1. *Vom Abendmahl Christi*. Bekenntnis, 1528. Quoted in *La Confession d'Augsburg* (Paris-Strasbourg, 1949), p. 46.

2. Quoted from *Institution de la Religion Chrestienne*, 1541, ed. by Jacques Pannier (Paris: Société des Belles Lettres, 1937), Vol. II, p. 121.

3. Ibid., p. 123.

4. John Calvin, *Institutes of the Christian Religion*, ed. by John T. McNeill, tr. by Ford Lewis Battles (The Library of Christian Classics, Vols. XX, XXI; The Westminster Press, 1960). Heading for Book IV, Vol. II, p. 1011. All references made to the *Institutes* hereafter are from this edition.

5. Ibid., IV. i.1.

6. Ibid., IV. iii.1.

7. Ibid., IV. iii.1, 2.

8. Ibid., note on p. 1016. From Calvin's commentary on Eph. 4:13.

9. Stuart M. Brown, Jr., "The Theology of Reinhold Niebuhr," *Review of Religion*, March, 1948, pp. 262 ff.; John Herman Randall, Jr., "The Ontology of Paul Tillich," in *The Theology of Paul Tillich*, ed. by Charles W. Kegley and Robert W. Bretall (The Macmillan Company, 1956), pp. 132 ff.

10. Alexis de Tocqueville, *Democracy in America* (Vintage Books, Inc., 1954), Vol. I, pp. 310ff.

11. Emil Brunner, *The Misunderstanding of the Church* (The Westminster Press, 1952); Barth, op. cit., Vol. IV, Part 1, E.T., pp. 643ff.; Dietrich Bonhoeffer, *Life Together* (Harper & Row, Publishers, Inc., 1956); H. Richard Niebuhr, *The Purpose of the Church and Its Ministry* (Harper & Row, Publishers, Inc, 1956); J. E. Lesslie Newbigin, *The Household of God* (London: SCM Press, Ltd., 1953); Paul S. Minear, *Images of the Church in the New Testament* (The Westminster Press, 1960).

12. This is eminently true of Barth's *Church Dogmatics*. It is true also of Rudolf Bultmann, H. Richard Niebuhr, Henry N. Wieman, Paul Lehmann, and others.

13. John Calvin, Preface to Olivétan's New Testament (1534), in *Calvin: Commentaries*, ed. by Joseph Haroutunian and Louise Pettibone Smith (The Library of Christian Classics, Vol. XXIII; The Westminster Press, 1958), pp. 58 f.

14. Josiah Royce, *The Problem of Christianity* (The Macmillan Company, 1914), Vol. I, Lecture 4.

CHAPTER 2. THE SPIRIT OF THE LIVING GOD

1. Gregory of Nyssa, An Answer to Ablabius: That We Should Not Think of Saying There Are Three Gods in *Nicene and Post-Nicene Fathers* (The Christian Literature Company, 1893), 2d Series, Vol. V, pp. 331 f.

2. Henry P. Van Dusen, *Spirit, Son, Father* (Charles Scribner's Sons, 1958), pp. 25 f.; Barth, op. cit., Vol. IV, Part 2, E. T., pp. 323 f.

3. Calvin, *Institutes*, III. i.1.

4. The Nicaeo-Constantinopolitan Creed.

5. Cyril Richardson, *The Doctrine of the Trinity* (Abingdon Press, 1958), pp. 62 f., 133 f.

6. John Oman, *Grace and Personality* (The Macmillan Company, 1925), pp. 44f., 160ff.

7. Augustine, "On the Spirit and the Letter," Chs. 26-36, in *The Works of Aurelius Augustine*, ed. by Marcus Dods (Edinburgh: T. & T. Clark, 1872), Vol. IV; Barth, op. cit., Vol. IV, Part 2, E. T., pp. 304 f., 330 f.

8. George S. Hendry, *The Holy Spirit in Christian Theology* (The Westminster Press, 1956), Ch. I.

9. Calvin, *Institutes*, II.v.15 f.; Karl Barth, *The Epistle to the Romans*, tr. by E. C. Hoskyns (Oxford University Press, Inc., 1933), Ch. 8.

10. George Ernest Wright, "The Faith of Israel," in *The In-terpreter's Bible* (Abingdon Press, 1952), Vol. I, pp. 365 f.

11. Gerardus van der Leeuw, *Religion in Essence and Manifestation*, tr. by J. E. Turner (London: George Allen & Unwin, Ltd., 1938), pp. 23f.; Zech. 4:6; I Cor. 2:4.

12. Ernest DeWitt Burton, *The Epistle to the Galatians* (Edinburgh: T. & T. Clark, 1921), pp. 487 f.

13. Van der Leeuw, op. cit., Chs. 1, 74, 75.

14. Compare, e.g., I Sam. 11:6 with Isa. 44:3, or Acts 1:8 with I Cor. 12:13.

15. Barth, *Church Dogmatics*, Vol. I, Part 1, E. T., p. 537.

16. Tillich, op. cit., pp. 111 f.

CHAPTER 3. THE KNOWLEDGE OF GOD IN THE CHURCH

1. Calvin, *Institutes*, I.iii.3.

2. John Hick, *Classical and Contemporary Readings in the Philosophy of Religion* (Prentice-Hall, Inc., 1964).

3. Heinrich Heppe, *Reformed Dogmatics*, tr. by G. T. Thomp- son (London: George Allen & Unwin, Ltd., 1950). The church appears in Ch. 27, after the Christian life and the Sacraments.

4. Ibid., Chs. 1-3.

5. E.g., Tillich, op. cit., Vol. I, pp. 75 f.

6. Cf. Barth, *Church Dogmatics*, Vol. I, Part 1, E.T., pp. 243 ff.

7. Gerhard Ebeling, *Word and Faith* (Fortress Press, 1963), pp. 196f.

8. Augustine, "Grace and Free Will," Chapters 17-20; "On the Spirit and the Letter," Chapters 28-29, 36, 41, 59. See especially, Martin Luther, "Treatise on Good Works" and "Treatise on Christian Liberty," *The Works of Martin Luther* (A. J. Holman Company, 1915, 1916), Vols. I, II.

9. Calvin, *Institutes*, II.viii.51-52; III.xix.45.

10. See Chapters 7 and 8 of this book.

11. Tillich, op. cit., Vol. III, pp. 138 f.

12. Reinhold Niebuhr, op. cit., Vol. I, pp. 167f.; Tillich, op. cit., pp. 186-210.

13. Augustine, *City of God*, XI.28; XIII .10-15; *Confessions*, I.i. 1.

14. H. Richard Niebuhr, op. cit., pp. 32-33.

15. Cf. Dorothy L. Sayers, *The Mind of the Maker* (Meridian Books, Inc., 1956), Chapters 2, 4.

16. Barth, *Church Dogmatics*, Vol. III, Part 1, E. T., pp. 181 ff.

17. Ibid., Vol. I, Part 1, E. T., pp. 474 f.

18. Ibid., Vol. IV, Part 1, E. T., pp. 200 ff.

19. William Pepperel Montagu, *Belief Unbound* (Yale University Press, 1930), pp. 68 f.; Walter Lippmann, *Preface to Morals* (The Macmillan Company, 1929), pp. 213 f.; Albert Camus, *The Myth of Sisyphus and Other Essays* (Vintage Books, Inc., 1955).

20. See Chapter 7.

21. Calvin, *Institutes*, II.ii.11.

22. Ibid., III.i.1.

23. Erich Frank, *Philosophical Understanding and Religious Truth* (Oxford University Press, 1945), Ch. 4; Richard Kroner, *The Religious Function of the Imagination* (Yale University Press, 1941); Paul Tillich, *Theology of Culture* (Oxford University Press, Inc., 1959), Chapter 5.

24. William Ralph Inge, *Christian Mysticism* (Charles Scribner's Sons, 1899; Meridian Books, Inc., 1956), Lectures 3 and 4.

CHAPTER 4. THREE DIMENSIONS OF WILL AND WILLING

1. Aristotle, *Ethica Nichomachea*, III. 1-3 (11091^b-1113^a).

2. Arthur Cushman McGiffert, *A History of Christian Thought* (Charles Scribner's Sons, 1932), Vol. I, pp. 197, 225, 317-318.

3. Augustine, *Confessions*, XIII. 10; *City of God*, XI. 28.

4. Calvin, *Institutes*, Ixv 6f., Martin Luther, "The Magnificat," *The Works of Martin Luther* (A. J. Holman Company, 1930), Vol. III, pp. 131 f.

5. Descartes, *Meditations on the First Philosophy* (Everyman's Library, E. P. Dutton & Company, Inc., 1927), pp. 114f.

6. Locke, *Concerning Human Understanding*, Book II, Ch. 21.

7. Ibid., paragraph 8.

8. "Fundamental Principles of the Metaphysics of Morality," in *Readings in Ethics*, ed. by G. H. Clark and T. V. Smith (F. S. Crofts & Co., 1931), pp. 227f.

9. Thomas Aquinas, *Summa Theologica*, First Part of the Second Part, Q. 50, Arts. 3,5; Dewey, *Human Nature and Conduct*, Part I, Secs. 1-3, 5.

10. John Dewey, *The Quest for Certainty* (Minton, Balch & Company, 1929), Chapter X.

11. Aristotle, op. cit., VIII. 1-8 (1155^a-1160^a).

12. Dewey and Bentley, op cit., pp. 84, 136, 306; Anselm Strauss, ed., *The Social Psychology of George Herbert Mead* (The University of Chicago Press, 1956), pp. 128 f., *passim*.

13. Étienne Gilson, *The Spirit of Medieval Philosophy*, tr. by A. H. C. Downes (Charles Scribner's Sons, 1936), p. 204.

CHAPTER 5. GRACE AND FREEDOM RECONSIDERED

1. William Newton Clarke, *Outline of Christian Theology* (London: T. & T. Clark, 1900), pp. 150-151.

2. Barth, *Church Dogmatics*, Vol. II, Part 2, E. T., pp. 13-14.

3. Ibid., Vol. II Part 1, p. 440.

4. Ibid., Vol. II, Part 2, p. 315.

5. Ibid., p. 321.

6. Ibid., pp. 181, 184-185.

7. Augustine, "Treatise on Rebuke and Grace." See Paul Lehmann, "The Anti-Pelagian Writings" in *A Companion to The Study of St. Augustine*, ed. by Roy Battenhouse (Oxford University Press, Inc., 1955), Chapter VII.

8. Barth, *Church Dogmatics*, Vol. III, Part 1, E. T., pp. 186 f.; Part 2, pp. 228 f., 243 f.; Part 4, pp. 163 f.

9. Martin Luther, "On the Councils and the Churches "; Calvin, *Institutes*, IV.i; Thomas Müntzer, "Sermon Before the Princes," and Dietrich Philips, "The Church of God," in *Spiritual and Anabaptist Writers*, ed. by George H. Williams and Angel M. Mergal (The Library of Christian Classics, Vol. XXV; The Westminster Press, 1957); Friedrich Schleiermacher, *The Christian Faith*, ed. by H. R. Mackintosh and J. S. Stewart (Edinburgh: T. & T. Clark, 1928), pp. 525-585.

10. Royce, op. cit., Lectures I-IV; Mead, op. cit., pp. 135-226.

11. *Nature, Man and God* is the title of William Temple's Gifford Lectures for 1932-1934 (London: The Macmillan Company, 1934). See esp. Lecture XV.

12. See note 10 above. See also John Dewey, *Experience and Nature* (The Open Court Publishing Company, 1925), Chs. VI-VIII.

13. Augustine, *Confessions*, XIII. 9-10; *City of God*, XI. 25, 28; *An Augustine Synthesis*, arranged by Erich Przywara (Harper Torchbook, 1958), pp. 345-356.

14. See Mead, op. cit., in note 10 above; Søren Kierkegaard, *Sickness Unto Death*, tr. by Walter Lowrie (Princeton University Press, 1941), Ch. I.

15. Reinhold Niebuhr, op. cit., Vol. I, Chs. 7, 8.

16. Bronislaw Malinowski, *Magic, Science and Religion and Other Essays*, ed. by Robert Redfield (Doubleday Anchor Book, 1954), "Magic, Science and Religion," Secs. 1-3; "Myth in Primitive Psychology," Sec. 3; Baloma: The Spirits of the Dead in the Trobriand Islands"; Haroutunian, op. cit., Chs. III, VI; Camus, op. cit.

CHAPTER 6. ON HEARING THE GOSPEL

1. Brunner, *Man in Revolt*, pp. 129 f.; Mary Frances Thelen, *Man as Sinner in Contemporary American Theology* (King's Crown Press, 1946), pp. 97 f., 120 f., 153 f., 168 f.

2. Nicolas Berdyaev, *Christianity and Class War*, tr. by Donald Attwater (Sheed & Ward, Inc., 1933), Ch. I; Pitrim A. Sorokin, *The Crisis of Our Age* (E. P. Dutton & Company, Inc, 1942), Chs. 1-3, *passim.*

3. H. R. Niebuhr, *The Purpose of the Church and Its Ministry*(Harper & Row, Publishers, Inc., 1956), pp. 26 f.; Barth, *Church Dogmatics* Vol. IV, Part 2, E. T., pp. 727-751.

4. Calvin, *Institutes*, III.xxiii.13; III.xxiv.13; Augustine, "Treatise on Rebuke and Grace," Chs. 2-9, *passim.*

5. Claude Welch, *The Reality of the Church* (Charles Scribner's Sons, 1958), pp. 42 f. See Chapter 2.

6. Søren Kierkegaard, "Joyful Notes in the Strife of Suffering," in

Christian Discourses, tr. by Walter Lowrie (Oxford University Press, Inc., 1939), Ch. II, *passim*.

7. Søren Kierkegaard, *Works of Love*, tr. by David Swenson (Princeton University Press, 1946), pp. 199 f., 243 f.

8. F. H. Heinemann, *Existentialism and the Modern Predicament* (Harper Torchbook, 1958), Chs. VI, X; Albert Camus, *The Rebel*, tr. by Anthony Bower (Vintage Books, Inc., 1956), Chs. III, V.

9. Deut. 30:11-14; Calvin, *Institutes*, II.viii.1,3.

10. Haroutunian, op. cit., Ch. IV.

11. John 1:14; II Cor. 5:19; Calvin, *Institutes*, II.xii.4; xvi.2.

12. Jonathan Edwards, "God Glorified in Man's Dependence" in *The Works of President Edwards* (Leavitt, Trow & Co., 1849), Vol. IV, pp. 169 f.

13. See Chapter 7.

CHAPTER 7. THE PROBLEM OF LOVE

1. George F. Thomas, ed., *The Vitality of the Christian Tradi~ tion* (Harper & Row, Publishers, Inc., 1944), p. 352.

2. Ibid., pp. 304305; Henry Pitney Van Dusen, ed., *The Christian Answer* (Charles Scribner's Sons, 1945), pp. 143 f.

3. Ibid., p. 333.

4. Anders Nygren, *Agape and Eros*, tr. by Philip S. Watson (The Westminster Press, 1953), pp. 75 f.

5. Barth, *Church Dogmatics*, Vol. II, Part 2, E. T., pp. 10 f.

6. Emil Brunner, *Justice and the Social Order*, tr. by Mary Hottinger (Harper & Row, Publishers, Inc., 1945), pp. 125-126.

7. Ibid., p. 126, note.

8. Nels F. S. Ferré, *Christ and the Christian* (Harper & Row, Publishers, Inc., 1958), pp. 63-64.

9. Paul Ramsey, *Basic Christian Ethics* (Charles Scribner's Sons, 1950), p. 162.

10. Ibid., p. 148.

11. Reinhold Niebuhr, op. cit., Vol. II, p. 24.

12. Ibid., p.72.

13. Ibid., pp. 68, 69.

14. Compare Calvin, *Institutes*, III.vii.6; Barth, *Church Dogmatics*, Vol. I, Part 2, E. T., pp. 412 f.

15. D. M. Baillie, *God Was in Christ* (Charles Scribner's Sons, 1948), pp. 88 f.; George S. Hendry, *The Gospel of the Incarnation* (The Westminster Press, 1958), Ch. VI, *passim*.

16. See note 14; also, Mark 5:21f.; Luke 7:1f., 36 f.; 15:1f.; 19:1 f.;

Hendry, *The Gospel of the Incarnation*, Ch. VII.

17. Compare Augustine, "On Christian Doctrine," Bk. I, Chs. 35-37.

18. Compare Brunner, *Justice and the Social Order*, Ch. XV.

19. Tillich, *Systematic Theology*, Vol. I, pp. 189 f.; Paul Tillich, *Love, Power, and Justice* (Oxford University Press, Inc., 1954), Ch. II.

20. Calvin, *Institutes*, I.xv; II.i.4.

21. Jonathan Edwards, "Dissertation Concerning the End for Which God Created the World," Ch. I, Sec. 3-4; Ch. II, sec. 7.

22. Nygren, op. cit., pp. 127 f.

23. Barth, *Church Dogmatics*, Vol. II, Part 2, E. T., pp. 509 ff.

24. Jonathan Edwards, *Dissertation on the Nature of True Virtue* (Leavitt, Trow & Co., 1849), Vol. II, pp. 261 f.

25. Nicolas Berdyaev, *The Destiny of Man* (Charles Scribner's Sons, 1937), p. 96.

26. See note 24 above.

27. Bernard of Clairvaux, *On The Love of God*, Chs. 8-10. Epistle, XI. 8. See Kenneth Kirk, *The Vision of God* (Longmans, Green & Co., Inc., 1932), pp. 242 f.

28. Heppe, op. cit., Ch. XV.

CHAPTER 8. THE PROSPECT OF LOVE

1. Emil Brunner, *The Mediator*, tr. by Olive Wyon (The Westminster Press, 1947), pp. 267f., 318f.; Barth, *Church Dogmatics*, Vol. I, Part 2, E. T., pp. 147 f.

2. Jonathan Edwards, "On Efficacious Grace," *Works*, Vol. II, p. 580: "But God does all, and we do all"; also, pp. 547 f.

3. Calvin, *Institutes*, II.vii.10.

4. Barth, *Church Dogmatics*, Vol. I, Part 2, E. T., p. 38.

5. Calvin, *Institutes*, IV.xii.

6. Welch, op. cit., Ch. V.

7. Edwards, "Dissertation Concerning the End for Which God Created the World," Ch. I, *passim*.

8. John Baillie, *Our Knowledge of God* (Charles Scribner's Sons, 1939), Sec. 16, pp. 178 f.

9. Barth, *Church Dogmatics*, Vol. IV, Part 2, E. T., pp. 809 f.

CHAPTER 9. FREEDOM AND LIBERTY

1. Thomas Aquinas, *Summa Theologica*, I-II, Q. 90, Art. l; Calvin, *Institutes*, III.ix.15; IV.x.3; xx.16.

2. Aquinas, ibid., Q. 91, Art. 2; Q. 84, Arts. 1, 3; Calvin, ibid., II.ii.26.

3. John Dewey, "The Unity of the Human Being," in *Intelligence in the Modern World* (Random House, Inc., 1939).

4. Calvin, *Institutes*, II.xvi.5.

5. Haroutunian, op. cit., Ch. III; Jacques Choron, *Death and Western Thought* (Collier Books, 1963).

6. Reinhold Niebuhr, *Moral Man and Immoral Society* (Charles Scribner's Sons, 1932), Chs. I, II, *passim*.

7. Tillich, *Systematic Theology*, pp. 186 f. See above, note 6.

8. Augustine, *City of God*, V. 16, 18, 24-25; XI. 25; XIV. 28; XV. 18; XIX. 4,17, 20, 26; Calvin, *Institutes*, III.ix-x.

9. Jacques Maritain, *Scholasticism and Politics* (The Macmillan Company, 1941), Ch. V; Dorothy Fosdick, *What Is Liberty?* (Harper & Row, Publishers, Inc., 1939), Ch. I, *passim*.

10. Reinhold Niebuhr, *An Interpretation of Christian Ethics* (Harper & Row, Publishers, Inc., 1935), pp. 105 f.; *The Nature and Destiny of Man*, Vol. II, pp. 81 f.

11. Sidney Hook, "The Justifications of Democracy," in *The American Pragmatists*, ed. by M. R. Konivitz and Gail Kennedy (Meridian Books, Inc., 1960), pp. 379 f.

12. See note 7 above.

13. Matt. 5:43 f.; Calvin, *Institutes*, II.viii.56.

14. See Chapter 2.

INDEX

Agape, chs. 7 and 8

Alienation, 109, 161-2

Anselm, 204

Anxiety, 24, 191-2

Aristotle, 7, 81, 91, 147, 227n.

Athanasius, 209

Augustine of Hippo, Augustinianism, 8, 45, 65, 67, 75, 81-2, 99-101, 104-6, 118, 122, 154, 179, 213, 219, 228n., 230n., 231n.

Baillie, D. M., 229n.

Baillie, John, 230n.

Baptism, 38-40

Barth, Karl, 33, 44, 103-5, 146, 206, 219, 224n., 225n., 226n.,228n.,229n., 230n.,

Bentham, Jeremy, 88

Bentley, Arthur F., 1, 223n., 227n.

Berdyaev, Nikolai, 13-4, 228n., 230n.

Bergson, Henri, 8

Bernard of Clairvaux, 230n.

Boethius, 7, 90

Bonhoeffer, Dietrich, 33

Brown, Stuart M., Jr., 224n.

Brunner, Emil, 33, 145-7, 166, 224n., 228n., 230n.

Buber, Martin, 14

Bultmann, Rudolf, 206, 224n.

Burton, Ernest Dewitt, 225n.

Butler, Samuel, 13

Calvin, John, 8, 27-9, 44-5, 75, 83, 118, 219, 225n., 226n., 228n., 229n., 230n, 231n.

Camus, Albert, 226n., 228n., 229n.

Choron, Jacques, 231n.

Church: chs. 1 and 3 *passim*; and authority, 59-60; and communion of fellowmen, 23-4; and faith, 36-7, 75; and forgiveness, 116-7, 174-7; as institution, 23, 27-8, 61-2,; and the means of grace, 36; as the people of God, 23, 27, 32-5, 62-3; and the Sacraments, 38-40; and the Spirit, 51-8; and the state, 30-2. *See also* Communion of the saints

City, the, 12, 14, 218-9

Clark, William Newton, 227n.

Clement of Alexandria, 81

Common life, 15, 17-8, 19-20, 141-2, 220-1

Communication, 133-4, 208

Communion: and the common
life, 20, 141-2; and creation,
72; discontinuous with
organic life, 1, 90, 217-8;
and faith, 36-7; and for-
giveness, 118-20; the heart
of the church, 23-4; and the
knowledge of creatureliness
69-70; and the knowledge of
God; 67-73, 79-80; and the
love of Jesus, 67-73; and
the means of grace, 36; as
mutual presence, 20; and
politics, 215; resistence to,
133-4; and salvation, 213-4;
and scientific culture, 219-
20; Theology of, Conclu-
sion, *passim*
Communion of the Saints: and
the Sacraments, 39-40, 215-
7; and the Spirit, 52-3, 56-
8; and the Trinity, 72-3
Covenant, 35, 56
Creation, 64
Creature: as fellowman, 69-70,
135, 150-1, 157; as object of
God's love,154-5

Darwin, Darwinism, 11, 187
Death, 112, 136, 189-90, 213-4
Descartes, 8, 83
Dewey, John, 1, 86-90, 91,
223n., 227n., 228n., 231n.
Dignity of man, 20-1
Dualism, 21
Duns Scotus, 82

Ebeling, Gerhard, 226n.

Ecumenical movement, 23-5,
32, 62-3
Edwards, Jonathan, 229n.,
230n.
Election, 103-4
Epicurus, 88
Ethics, 9, 33-4, 214-5; of self-
interest, 21, 130-1; and the-
ology, 62-3
Existence, 106-7

Faith: as hearing and communion, 37; and the
knowledge of God, 60-1,
73-80; in man and in God,
178-9
Faithfulness, 62-3, 76-8; of
fellowmen, 159; of Jesus,
76-7; the work of God, 56
Fellowman, fellowmanhood:
and the church, 34-5; created in God's love, 72-3, 107;
and forgiveness, 67-70, 72,
115-6, 172-3; and hearing
the Word, 137-9; and the
hope of love, 180; and intelligence, 17, 22; knowledge of God, 77-80, 208;
and the knowledge of man
as, 16, 68-9, 89-92, 106-7;
and the love of Jesus, 68-9,
168; and the modern
world, 12, 15-7
Ferre, Nels, 147
Forgiveness: basis of the
church, 174-7; and com-
munion, 72; difference between God's and man's, 115-

Forgiveness cont'd
6; faith as acknowledgement of, 74-75; as faithfulness, 173-4; and grace, 112-3; and the knowledge of God, 71; as miracle, 112-3; among sinners, 113, 115-6, 175-6

Fosdick, Dorothy, 231n.

Frank, Erich, 226n.

Freedom: to forgive, 116; and grace, 24-5, ch. 5 *passim*, 204-5; and liberty, ch. 9 *passim*, 197-8. *See also* Will, willing

Freud, Sigmund, 13, 223n.

Gerth, Hans, 223n.

Gibson, Etienne,227n.

God: action of, 56-7; and communion, 71-2; and the covenant, 56; creator, 153-4; depends on the church, 59-60, 207; and faith, 73-4; forgiveness, 75-6; as free, 138-9; knowledge of, ch. 3 *passim*, 207-8; revealed and hidden, 75, 77-8, sovereign, 138-9, traditional approach to, 63-7

Grace of God: cooperating, 120-2; and faith, 36-7; and forgiveness, 112-3, 118-9, and freedom, ch. 5 *passim*, 122-3, 204-5; habitual, 118; means of, 27-9, 36, 98, 116, 180, 204-5; prevenient, 120-1; and the Sacraments, 39-40; supernaturalism and individualism, 100-1, 203-40; and the world of the creature, 155

Gregory of Nyssa, 225n.

Habit, 86-7

Haroutunian, Joseph, 223n., 228n., 229n., 231n.

Heidegger, Martin, 13

Heinemann, F. H., 229n.

Hendry, George, 225, 229n.

Heppe, Heinrich, 226, 230n.

Hick, John, 226n.

Holy Spirit, ch. 2 *passim;* and the communion of saints, 51-8, 192-3, 199; and experience, 48-50; as person, 54-6; as Power, 205

Hook, Sidney, 231n.

Hope 137-8, 139-40, 177-8

Horney, Karen, 223n.

Human Nature, 9-10, 17, 86, 104-5, 186-7

Humility, 118-9

Idealism, 21-2

Immortality, 7-8

Individualism: and the doctrine of the Spirit, 52-3; in history, 6-9; and institutionalism, 100; and the problem of grace and freedom, 104-5

Inge, William, 226n.

Institution: the church as, 29-30, 64, 98-9, 172, 175-6; as context of behavior, 9; and forgiveness, 175-7; modern dependence on, 12-3; and willing, 85

Jesus Christ: and the church, 34-5, 37-8, 170-1; in the

Jesus Christ cont'd.
communion of fellowmen, 2, 67-8, 73, 76-7, 95, 113-4, 137; and forgiveness, 73-4, 118-9, 172-3; and the law of God, 188-9, 198-9; love for, 69-70, 114-5, 147-8, 165-6; mutuality of, 147-8; obedience and death of, 56, 166-70, 189; Person of, 71, 167, 208-10; and the Spirit, 43, 56, 58, 77

Justice, 169-70, 182-4, 196-8

Kant, Immanuel, 8, 84
Kierkegaard, Soren, 13, 228n., 229n.
Kirk, Kenneth, 230n
Kroner, Richard, 226n.

Laity, 40-1
Law: and freedom, 93-4, 191, 197-8; God's, 187-93; and institutions, 185-7; natural, 185-7, 188-9
Lehmann, Paul, 224n.
Lewis, Arthur, 223n.
Liberal theology, 101-3, 145-6, 178-9
Liberty,193-201
Lippmann, Walter, 226n.
Locke, John, 8, 83-4
Lord's Supper, 38-40, 215-7
Love, chs. 7 and 8 *passim*; and *agape*, 146-9; as faithfulness, 111-2, 159, 162-3; and free will, 108-9; as gift, 109-

10; of God the Creator and of fellowmen, 153-6; and justice, 161-2; mutual, 148-53; and sacrifice, 152-3; and self-love, 157-8; among sinners, 114-5
Luther, Martin, 27, 83, 219,

Malinowski, Bronislaw, 228n.
Maritain, Jacques, 231n.
Marx, Karl, 13
Mead, George Herbert, 105, 223n.
Meland, Bernard, 223n.
Mills, C. Wright, 23n.
Minear, Paul, 33
Miracle, 74-5, 112-3, 174
Montagu, William Pepperel, 226n.
Muntzer, Thomas, 228n.

Natural theology, 60, 111, 207-8, 217-8
Naturalism, 186
Neoorthodoxy, 145, 206
Newbigin, J. E. Lesslie, 33, 224n
Niebuhr, H. Richard, 33, 219, 223n., 224n., 226n., 228n.,
Niebuhr, Reinhold, 31, 147-9, 219, 224n., 226n., 228n., 229n., 231n.
Nietzsche, Friedrich, 13
Nygren, Anders, 146-7, 166, 230n.

Obedience, 57, 101, 168-9, 189, 191
Oman, John 101-2, 225n.

Origen, 81
Organism: man as, 11-2, 17, 91, 185-6

Pederson, Johannes, 223n.
Pelagius, 105 *See also* Augustine of Hippo
Philips, Dietrich, 228n
Plato, 7
Politics, 199-201, 214-5
Power: of God and man, 100-1, 116, 167; in society, 15; supernatural, 56-7, 100, 205
Preaching, 125, 130-2, 139-42
Protestantism, 27-31, 36

Ramsey, Paul, 147
Randall, John Herman, Jr., 224n.
Rationalism, 185-6
Reason: and faith, 59-63, 208; and natural law, 185-7; in not hearing the Word, 128-30; and will, 81-5, 91
Religion in America, 31, 97-8, 129-30
Religious language, 78-9
Responsibility and response, 62-3, 107-11
Richardson, Cyril, 225n.
Riesman, David, 223n.
Royce, Josiah 105, 225n.

Sacraments, 38-41, 177-8
Sacrifice, 152-3
Salvation, 212-15
Sayers, Dorothy, 226n.
Schleiermacher, Friedrich, 66-7, 105, 219

Science, 219-20
Scripture, 32-3, 125-7
Self-interest, 6-7, 11-2, 20-1, 130-2
Self-love, 88-90, 151, 157-8, 160, 196, 198
Sin, sinners: and anxiety for life, 191-2; and the church, 34-5; as failure of communion, 133-4, 210-1; forgiveness among sinners, 190; and knowledge of man as creature,69-71; as resistance to the Word, 131-2; and temptation, 210-2
Socrates, 7
Sola fide, 37-8, 67, 99, 207
Sorokin, Pitrim, 228n.
Supernaturalism, 100-1, 206

Technology, 11-2, 218-9
Temple, William, 228n.
Temptation, 108-9, 128, 184, 210-2
Thelen, Mary Frances, 228n.
Theology, 1, 33-4, 59-60
Thomas Aquinas, 8, 82, 86, 90, 219, 231n.
Thomas, George, 229n.
Tillich, Paul, 31, 70, 223n., 225n., 226n., 230n., 231n.
Tocqueville, Alexis de, 224n.
Tradition of theology, 63-7, 203-6
Transaction, 1, 9-10, 19-20, 211-2
Transpersonal, 1-2
Trinity, the, 43-4, 72-3, 95, 207-8

van der Leeuw, Gerardus,
   225n.
Van Dusen, Henry Pitney 44,
   229n.

Welch, Claude, 228n., 230n.
Wieman, Henry, 224n.,
Will, willing: in the common
   life, 85-6; and freedom,
   91-2; and habit, 86-7; in
   life together, 88-9, 108-9,
   119; and love, 109-10; and
   reason, 87-8
Witness, 31-2
Word of God, ch. 6. *passim*;
   difficulty in hearing the,
   125-8; and preaching, 139-
   42; and the word of man,
   135-6
World Council of Churches,
   23
Wright, George Ernest, 225n.

APPENDIX ONE

The Worship of God

In this address I wish to deal with three questions having to do with the worship of God: first, the question of the worship of *God*; secondly, the question of the *worship* of God; in the third place, the question of the place of worship in "faith and life."

I

Whether we like it or not, the question has arisen and is unavoidable as to the God we worship. As the Apostle Paul has said, "Indeed there are many gods and many lords." This is true not only of the many gods "in heaven or on earth" that have been worshipped by the nations, but also of the many gods worshipped in Christian churches. There are many gods worshipped by us in the sense that our symbols for God vary greatly among ourselves. We say "God," but have very different thoughts, almost always vague and wandering. We think of God as "the infinite, eternal, unchangeable"; as transcendent and ultimate Being; as the First Cause, and Creativity; as ideal Being, personal Being, ineffable Being; as God up there, God out there, God in there, God under there. We may think of the God of Nature, or the God of Goodness, or the God of "religious experience." The very variety of the ways we think about God, or in a sense the very multiplicity of our gods, so bewilders us that we hardly know whom in truth we worship. We find our thoughts about God shifting, unclear, and open to doubt. We may comfort ourselves in our intellectual confusion by saying that the fluidity of our thoughts about God is inevitable because he is incomprehensible Being. We may also conclude that it is not how we think about God but our experience of him that matters. Thus our attention may shift from God whom we worship to "the experience of worship." We may worship *worship* rather than worship our God, or our worship may become our God in the sense of "our ultimate concern."

It is true that since worship is an experience, without the experience of worship there is no worship of God. Nevertheless, since worship is the worship of God, it is logically necessary that *God* be worshipped. To worship is, to say the least, to ascribe worth; and we can ascribe worth only when we ascribe it to somebody. To worship without an object of worship is absurd. It is also in bad taste. It is in bad taste to make worship rather than God our main concern. It is blasphemous to suppose that God would stand for our worship knowing that we are more impressed with our worship than with the person and worth of our God. When the act of worship comes as it were between its Object and the worshipper, and even obscures the presence of the Person worshipped, it perpetuates an impertinence and becomes not worship but impudence. When we enjoy our worship rather than the God we worship, he may say to us, in the manner [of] the prophet Amos, "This pleases you, not me, O Israel" (4:5).

The God we worship is indeed transcendent, mysterious, and ineffable. He is not a man that we should locate him, or a thing that we should picture him. But the mystery of God does not give us the right to set our minds and hearts upon idols, and upon ourselves and our pleasure. If we cannot point to him, saying, "Lo here" and "Lo there," we may not wave our arms aimlessly or let our minds wander to this and that thing, in our worship of him. Although God is not a thing among things, he is contradistinguished from all things as the God we worship; as God whom alone we worship.

This last statement has the sound of a paradox. We say that God is not a thing among things (*Deus non est in genere*); and yet we say that he is contradistinguished from all things as the God we worship. If he is contradistinguished from all things, as not one of them, then he must be another thing, himself and not something else. If he is himself and not something else, then he is a thing among things. But we also say that he is not a thing among things.

If we are not to let this paradox plunge us immediately into difficult and confusing speculation, we must remind ourselves that the God we worship is, to use a standard biblical expression, "God and Father of our Lord Jesus Christ." In spite of all protests from Jews, Muslims and others who acknowledge the absolute supremacy of God the Creator, the Christians have insisted upon the confession that God is Father, Son, and Holy Spirit; and that we worship the Father in the Son and through the Spirit. This confession means, for our present purpose, that God, Jesus of Nazareth, and his people, are mutually so present that God as the object of worship is inseparable from Jesus who is a historical figure and our fellowmen who are flesh with us. If the living God is his Word, and his Word is Christ, and Christ is the Head of the Church, as the Christians confess, then it is improper to worship a holy haze on the ground that God is not "objective" to us. On the contrary, as God who in Christ reconciled us to himself, he is clearly and firmly over-against us. No Christian may confuse Jesus Christ by whose call he exists with himself who is called and saved from the law of sin and death. Jesus of Nazareth who died for our sins and rose again for our life, enjoys, with regard to us who worship God, an objectivity and individuality which we can confuse only by unreason and deny only by our infidelity. In so far as we have, as Christians, the presence of mind to worship God who is the Father of the Lord Jesus, that is, God whom we know by the mission of Christ for us, we are made free, both in logic and piety, from the farce of worshiping either idols or vanities; and we worship the living God.

In our worship, we have to be careful of two things: of identifying the Father with the Son, in which case we are without God; and of separating the Father from the Son, which plunges us into superstition. We may not identify the Father with the Son, who is Jesus of Nazareth. This man Jesus is not God simply as a member of the human species. In our worship of him, we do not indirectly worship ourselves. Our worship of Jesus as the Son of God is idolatrous unless it is by the confession that he and his cross are the revelation of the wisdom and power of God. When we worship the Son with the Father, we do so in our confession that our adoption as children of God is the work of both God and Jesus of Nazareth. Our life as Christians is a gift from the Father and the Son; and the Son is Jesus who by the Spirit of God makes us free from "the law of sin and death." It is the work of Jesus, not in human need and weakness, but in the power and sufficiency of God. In short, we may not identify with God a Jesus whom we conceive as we do ourselves. Our salvation does not presuppose our deity. On the contrary, it opposes God who saves us to ourselves who are saved. The Sonship of Jesus may not obscure this distinction between God and man.

On the other hand, we may not separate the God we worship from Jesus of Nazareth. We do not worship God properly—as Creator and Providence, as all gracious and all mighty, or in any of his perfections—unless we worship him as God the Savior. To us who are Jesus' people, there is no God except he who "was in Christ reconciling the world to himself." We know no saving act of God which is not by the faithfulness of Jesus of Nazareth. In God's grace and wisdom, he has saved us by the love and obedience of Jesus, which are qualities of Jesus' humanity and exercised in the freedom of this man Jesus. We do not know the wisdom and power of God without the strange wisdom and power of this man's mission. We do not know the Word of God apart from the word and deed, the person, of this man. We know God as God manifest in this man. When we speak of God we cannot but refer to this historical Jesus and to the things recorded of him in Scripture: to the things he said and did in Palestine twenty centuries ago. In short, as we might say, the empirical signs of the presence and perfections of the living God are works and work of this man Jesus.

When we worship God we are to be mindful of "the things which have been accomplished among us" (Luke 1:1), and of him by whom they were accomplished. This is why we, in our worship, read the Scriptures: the Old Testament as promise and the New as fulfilment. This is why we turn to the ten thousand things recorded in Scripture and to the inexhaustible riches of the words of men as vehicles of the Word of God. Thus it is that we are constrained to attend not to our worship and our own sensibilities, but to the living God and his Christ as presented to us by the prophets and apostles in the Israel of God. Our worship is the worship of the living God; and the living God is the God of the people of the Bible, under the Law of God and the Gospel of God, with all the things that happened to them and were heard by them, according to the Word of God.

It must here be added that the salvation of God we celebrate in the worship of God is by the Word of God *in the Church*. As the worship of God is by the confession that Jesus Christ is the Son and Lord, so it is also by the confession that the same Jesus Christ is the Head of the Church. It is as the church or as God's people called to a life of faithfulness that we worship God. The church it is that worships God because we worship God as his people bound to him and one to another under the covenant of God which is in Christ Jesus our Lord. We have no life with God without our life together. We have no communion with God without our communion one with another. We may not worship God except as those in communion one with another: as those who hear one another, and care one for another. We know no God without the Son, and no Son without his people. The Son we know as the Head of the Body; and without the Body, we do not know the Head. But the Body is made up of its members, so that without the members we know no Body. Moreover, we know ourselves as members of the Body in that the Head presents himself to us in our communication one with another; in which communication each member is the sign to another of the presence of the Head of the Body, being Christ's representative and servant. It is in this way that the worship of God is by the presence and working of Christ in the church as the communion of the faithful. If Christ is the sign of the objectivity or presence to us of God, Christ's people are the signs of the objectivity or presence to us of Christ, who sits at the right hand of God the Father as the Son of the Father and the Head of the church. By these signs, we worship God.

II

Now we turn to the *worship* of God. Our first and last word about the worship of God must be silence. Before the Father, the Son, and Holy Spirit, it is logical that we should be silent as those who have come not to speak but to hear. It is quite improper, and even in bad taste, to present ourselves before Christ with our mouths open and our ears closed. If it is his presence we seek after, and if we seek after him because he speaks to us the words of life and good, or rather because he himself in his word to us is life and good, it is only right that we should come before him in the silence of acknowledgment and hope. We should not speak before we are spoken to, and we should speak after him. Neither our praise nor our petition, neither our intercession nor our offering, should precede his Word with which he presents himself to us as our Savior and Lord. There is a silence in worship which corresponds to the Word of him whom we worship, and this silence is the first act of worship. Without this silence there is no worship of God and

Father of our Lord Jesus Christ.

However, silence is first of all neither for self collection nor for meditation. It is not for entering into a worshipful mood or for stimulating ourselves for a repetition of a "worship experience." In worship we are to turn to God, and to remain turned to God. We may not divide our time between God and ourselves. We may not think of God a little, and a little about other things that may concern us. In the presence of God, and his Christ, we are to collect ourselves in order that, as we might say, we may not be present in body and absent in spirit. If it is dishonorable, when we meet our fellows, to let our minds wander from their words and our hearts from their presence, it is no less dishonorable to do so when we meet God. In short, the silence of worship is the silence of attending to God and hearing his Word.

We have to be clear that it is to God we attend. There is here a temptation which must be acknowledged and, by God's grace, avoided. We do not know God except by his Word; but, by his Word, it is God that we know. We may not so attend to the Word of God that we attend to his Word rather than to himself. We may not so listen to his word of favor and hope, with the good news of our well-being and peace, that we ignore him who himself is our blessing. We are, in our worship of God, at all times tempted to confuse God with his favor and gifts. We are tempted to rejoice in the gifts rather than in the Giver. We are tempted to celebrate our good fortune in having a beneficent Father, rather than to rejoice in him and his presence with us as our original Good without whom all good is empty and vain.

The thing to remember and hold on to is that the presence of Christ with his people is our absolute good. The man Jesus, the Son of God, without whom we have no God, himself is our good. His love of us and his gifts to us are no substitute for his presence with us. Even while it is true that he is not present to us without his love and gifts, he must be contradistinguished from his love and gifts absolutely as the Object of worship and praise. Even while we may, or rather must, love him for his love of us, our love of him logically is prior to our gratitude for his gifts, because in his gifts he presents himself to us as our Lord and Brother, whose existence as our fellowman is our primal good.

The existence of Jesus, his presence to his people, is, as it were, the ontological ground of their being; and therefore, he himself is the object of their joy in worship. He is the object of worship not as the source of their being first, but as himself in his existence toward them.

He is not worshipped truly unless he is so distinguished from his gifts, even the gift of his people's existence, that he is loved and celebrated for his presence as such. It is true that if we did not enjoy his gift of life and good, we should not know his presence. But unless we enjoy him as present to us, we enjoy neither life nor any good. There is an ontological love, a love of the being of Jesus as such, that we owe him by reason of his existence as our fellowman. Since he is our fellowman, and it is as fellowman that he is all else to us, we owe him the fidelity of fellowmen in acknowledging his person and presence as the Good as such. And since he is the Son of the Father, in the love of his person, we love the Person of the Father. Such is the first principle of theocentricity of Christian worship. We have no other way of resisting the temptation to love God's gifts rather than himself, except by the love of the presence of Jesus as our fellowman.

Christian worship is the celebration of God's presence among his people. The people of God have no solid good to celebrate in his absence. It is God himself we are to celebrate, and our celebration needs to be congruous with his presence. It is one thing to celebrate the things we enjoy, and quite another to rejoice in God the Father, Son, and Holy Ghost. It is one thing to celebrate the presence of Jesus and his people, and quite another to celebrate the things we buy and consume. There is a pleasure in eating and drinking, and there is a joy in the communion of God's people. These two, although not separate, are distinct. The joy in worship is the joy of meeting; of hearing and speaking; of expressions and gestures which signify the mutual acknowledgement of "living souls"; of deed and desisting from doing which give our hearing and speaking their substance and value. Joy may be quiet or noisy. It may be in the midst of working together or eating together. It may accompany ease or hardship. In whatever time or place, as the joy of the presence of God, it is, as the joy of being itself, solid, constant, and good absolutely. It fills our lives as the blessing in all blessings, the substance of all happiness, and source of all good hope among us. It depends on nothing except the presence of God; everything good depends on it. Nothing but God increases it; it increases everything. It nullifies every evil, fills every good, and suffuses the world with the glory of God. It does all this because it is the joy of being which is by the communion of fellowmen in the presence of the living God. In short, worship is joy before God and his people; rather, this joy is presumed in worship.

But we may not stop here. God is as he does. Even while he himself and in himself is the Object of worship, we meet him not as a quiescent Being but as the living God. We meet him in his grace; in his creating, redeeming, and preserving; in his goodness, wisdom, and power which are qualities of his action, and as such are perfections of his being. We meet him as the God who delivered his people "out of the land of Egypt, out of the house of bondage." We meet him as the God who so loved the world as to give his only Son for its life and blessing. We meet him in his Spirit who works reconciliation, sanctification, and peace among his people. Even while we rejoice in his presence as such, we rejoice in his works of grace and righteousness toward us. We know our God as gracious; if we do not meet his grace, we do not meet him. God and his grace, though distinct (so that we are not to celebrate his grace in his stead), are inseparable, because God is known to us by his grace. For this reason,there is no worshipping God without celebrating his grace, in his gift and gifts, which are first Jesus and his people, and secondly, with them, all the things we enjoy as flesh and bones.

We worship God in this sense because he is worthy of praise, and thanksgiving, and honor, and blessing, and awe, and obedience, and love, with all our heart, soul, and strength. God is worthy, and shows his worth by his grace and all his gifts, beginning with life and ending with the peace of his Kingdom. It would be dumb and deadly in gratitude if we ignored the goodness of God in the land of the living; if we failed to respond in joy to his ineffable gifts of life and good, among his people and in his world. It would be stupid and insensitive and unfaithful if we, pretending to love and worship him for himself, became indifferent to the works of his hands for our life and joy. In this way, we would be despising the works of God, and we would be violating his Person. We would be violating Jesus, and his people, and even our own souls.

The worship of God suffers from nothing so much as the contempt of men who are the bearers of his grace among his people. The worship of God fails when men fail to meet one another with joy; and so do the love and honor due to Jesus fail. The chief among God's gifts are Jesus and his people, who are One to the other as the head to the body. When our worship of God excludes our joy one in another, it is no longer the worship of the living God, but of a fiction of our imagination. The worship of God and the communion of his people in the presence of Jesus the Son of God are inseparable one from the other, so that where communion is not, worship is silly, however solemn and heartfelt. If we do not praise God, and thank him, and cleave to him, for the existence of our fellowman, by whom and through whom we live and move and have our being, we neither worship him nor give him his due in any way, no matter what we say or do before him. In short, the God we worship is the living and gracious God, who has bound us with our fellowmen in the covenant of life and truth. We worship him truly by our faithfulness to his covenant, which in turn we do in our grateful joy in the presence of his Son and his people, who are the means of all grace, with life and good, toward us. In the worship of God, the love of God and the praise of God belong together. The love of God is directed toward his person, and the praise of God is for his grace, of which the chief gift is the communion of fellowmen by the grace of Jesus. If we cannot praise God without loving him, we also cannot love him without praising him. But we praise him for his people, and with them for all his works.

Everybody knows, as it were, that worship of God is, almost in the first place, grateful joy before him. But it should also be known and clearly known that gratitude among us has a tendency to become corrupt by turning our attention from God to ourselves and from the glory of God to our own pleasure. There is no escape from such corruption of gratitude except by recognizing that our chief reason for giving thanks to the living God is the presence to us of our fellowmen, in the presence of Jesus Christ. When we learn and hold that God's primary gift to us is the people of God whom we are bound, by the covenant of human life, *to love as ourselves*, we have the proper logic for worship which is the worship of God and not of idols. Our brothers are indeed the gift of God to us. But they exist for communion and not for our use and consumption. They are the first gift of God to us, but they neither belong to us nor are they at our disposal. In their communion with us, in their speaking and hearing, in their responding which is free and as such faithful, they exist over against us and remain over against us, objective to us as our fellowmen whose objectivity is the ground of our existence and being.

When, in the worship of God, the logical priority of Jesus and his people to all the other gifts of God is acknowledged in word and deed, then we are bound to love and praise God for all the good things of this life which satisfy us and give us pleasure. We may now, rather we logically must, celebrate the sun and the seasons, the air we breathe, the water we drink, the fruits of the earth and the beauties everywhere around us, and all the unending occasions of delight to our souls. It is a distressing failure as well as ingratitude to exclude a lively sense of the wonders of the physical world from the worship of God. Not to experience, to feel and think, light and darkness, land and water, food and drink and raiment and shelter, and the dispositions and proportions of things living and not living, is an ignoring which is nothing less than contempt of God and life alike. The worship of God and the celebration of the good things of life, with an abhorrence of things evil and ugly, so belong together that the one cannot be without the other. For this reason, worship is celebration, and it is an act of happiness. Both reason and Scripture leave no place for doubt in this matter.

But here we have a problem. Today, we may be disturbed not by an excess but by a want of natural piety in the worship of God. We seem to have become incapable of the kind and degree of celebration of nature which belongs at the heart of religion, both biblical and "natural"; perhaps more biblical than natural. Nature has become distant to us, and we are apparently alienated from it. The praise of God for the things enumerated in the first chapter of Genesis, and remembered in the Psalms and many other places in the Bible, has become hollow and sentimental. We may repeat the words of such praise, but we hardy feel them; or if we feel them, we do so as spectators rather than as fellow creatures with bird, beast, or flower. And this is a serious failure. Our God is the Creator of heaven and earth, and we do not worship him properly unless we worship him as his creation of "the sixth day."

Our problem arises from the fact that in civilized life our dependence upon nature as "living souls" is obscured by the massive interposition of the world of artifacts which gives our way of life as people of "the Power Age" its peculiar values and enjoyments. Most of the things in our environment which we want and use are not natural objects. They are the products of human intervention and construction. The materials out of which our houses and their contents are made are of course extracted from the earth. But the things themselves as we buy and possess them are products of human industry and not produce of the land. We owe them not to nature but to society, not to organisms but to organization, not to Providence but to human intelligence and ingenuity. Absolute dependence upon nature, which is integral to natural piety, has been replaced with absolute dependence upon political process. Such piety is, therefore, not readily exercised by the civilized man. Usually it has become a poorly remembered and felt enjoyment which lacks both the seriousness and the joy of non-civilized experience. For this reason, our worship, as an expression of our piety, is at once conventional and lacking in "reality."

There is no easy solution of this problem. Better esthetics in our worship will help. But they cannot evoke authentic piety. What is not natural cannot be made natural by artifice. The fact is that we do not live by the Power or Powers of the physical world, and have little "sense of the holy" in the presence of natural objects. Since for our life and good we depend upon a socially created world of artifacts, our piety must emerge in our transactions with our fellowmen with whom we are bound, in a new way, for life and death. For worship and piety today, what is needed is an intelligence, or a sensibility, which constrains us to approach our fellowmen as "living souls" with whom we exist under a covenant of fidelity and justice. Our access to nature today has to be by way of our acknowledging one another as fellow-creatures, as "flesh and bones" who live not only by bread but also by their communion one with another. The proper occasions for the exercise of natural piety today are the meetings of human beings in which they see and hear one another as physical beings, with the wants and passions and hopes of "organisms" who are nonetheless "rational animals." Our piety towards nature depends upon our existence as "flesh," and our existence as flesh is the existence of fellowmen. We are fellowmen who are physical beings, and it is as physical beings that we live in a physical world and exercise "natural piety" toward living and nonliving things. As in Scripture piety toward nature is subsumed under a piety of faithfulness, so also it must be among us who live in a "city culture." Our worship of God the Creator (for we have no God who is not the Creator) and the natural piety which goes with it, presuppose our existence as fellowmen who are fellow-creatures and fellow-flesh. In short, a piety of gratitude by which we worship God requires a piety of faithfulness toward all things, in which our knowledge of one another as flesh logically comes first. As his "intelligent creation," we worship God, and as such we worship him for all his works as our fellow-creation. So it is that we are able with the Psalmist to sing:

> Bless the Lord, all his hosts,
> his ministers that do his will!

> Bless the Lord, all his works,
> in all places of his dominion.
> Bless the Lord, O my soul!
>   (Ps. 103. 21-22, RSV)

III

The new predominance of city culture in human life requires that our worship and our life together mutually inspire and inform one the other. It is as people working and living together that we come to the presence of God to worship him. Biblical worship, as the worship of God by a people bound together with a common memory, common covenant, common destiny and hope, has a new significance for us who must, under the conditions of existence today, find both life and good by our communion in our transactions in a socially created world. When we come to the presence of God, we come not as self-subsistent individuals but as fellowmen who exist by speech and hearing. We bring to God's presence ourselves as we are bound one with another in our going in and coming out, in our rising up and sitting down, all our days and in all our ways. We who worship God are his people who remember our words and deeds together; who have sought and found one another, only to lose one another by the mystery of turning away one from another; who have suffered injustice at one another's hand, and need to repent in order that we may have peace and hope together. These things we have done outside the house of God, and with these things we enter into it. Hence we worship God in "the hope of righteousness"; for righteousness' sake outside the house of God, in the world where we live and seek peace. We worship God in the hope of the communion of fellowmen in our caring one for another and giving one another joy as occasions follow one another. So it is that we hope in God, remember his salvation in Jesus Christ, and rejoice and celebrate before him. It is true that the grace of joy before God is the gift of God by the minis-try of his Word. But it is also true that we receive the same grace by our mutual communications as we seek good and suffer evil in our life together. The grace that is in worship and the grace in our daily transactions one with another are the two aspects of the one grace of God which we celebrate in our worship of him. The grace of the forgiveness of God and the grace of our repentance so occur together that we cannot praise God for the one without praising him for the other. But the grace of repentance and the grace of forgiveness belong in the communion of God's people in their pursuit together of the good things of this life. In short, we worship God as those who, being his "intelligent creation", everyday and everywhere seek good and avoid evil together.

It is for this reason that our caring one for another as a matter of justice as well as mercy, and our doing daily of those things which increase the prosperity and peace of our fellowmen, are integral to the worship of God. We all know, even though we all forget, that the worship of God in his sanctuary and the obediences of faith and justice, in all things great and small for the joy of our fellowman, belong together in the Israel of God. God's people exist and have joy in his presence when each man loves his neighbor as himself, that is, when he hears his brother and speaks to him in justice, mercy, and peace. This pleases God; and so it is that, when we enter his house, we worship him so as to please him, which we logically should be happy to do most.

It is naturally our hope that, for many years to come, generations and multitudes of people who shall share in the life and work of this seminary, shall find joy in the worship of God in this chapel. We have in this convocation address sought to remind you of the following conditions of such joy: first, that you and they remember to worship God, and not his favors and gifts toward us; secondly, that you and they remember to *worship* him, by gratitude and thanksgiving for all his various mercies, beginning with Jesus Christ and his people; in the third place, that you and they remember to come to this house of God as his covenanted people, with your life and work together, with your hope of righteousness in your communications together. The Lord who has bound you to himself, has also bound you together with all men, for life and every good. Know this, so that you may please him in doing his will; and so, in Christ Jesus and in the Church, you will worship him in truth, to give him joy by the joy you give one another and all men; to the glory of the living God who is worthy, in all his works, of honor and dominion, of thanksgiving and praise and blessing, all our days. Amen.

I think you should make a habit, the season permitting, of arriving together at the door of this chapel in a few minutes before the time of worship, to greet one another with words of mutual recognition. Then you should enter the chapel together for the worship of God, and remain together in spirit as well as body in doing it. You should also, I think, at the end, in the house of God greet one another, and go out together, to remain together as God's faithful people, to show forth his praise, in building one another up in every way you are called upon to do, for the joy of God, and your joy among yourselves who are his and belong one to another.

EDUCATION
AND HUMANITY

To explore the bearings of Christian theology upon education we must begin by recognizing that both theology and education, or even Christian theology and American education, are large subjects, and that there is no unanimity as to what is meant by them.

Theology is disciplined thinking of the Christian faith. There is no universal agreement upon the Christian faith. But this need not embarrass us too much at this time. To think as Christians we need not so much an extensive common creed as a common history, a common life and a common mentality that go with the name we bear. To think as a Christian is to consider the question of Jesus, "Who do men say that I am?" It is to consider the meaning of this question for the nature and destiny of man, for our way of life, for our habits of thought and conduct, for our institutions, one of which is the school. The problem of this discussion in a sense is, What does Jesus Christ mean for American education?

Education is the process through which we prepare especially the young to participate, both effectively and creatively, in "our way of life and the institutions which support it." A country such as ours is a complex civilization, with special and highly developed habits of sensibility, thought, and action. It is necessary that our ways of feeling, thinking, and doing things, in our several institutions, be taught to our citizens, so that we may exist and prosper as this particular people. Our education is to a large extent the process by which we guide our young toward rich and fruitful lives in our society. Therefore, we are concerned with growth and adaptation, skill and competence, cooperation and contribution. We expect our young to maintain our way of life and to improve it; and we believe this is done best through a process in which discipline and freedom increase hand in hand. It is expected that both discipline and freedom will be exercised in the context of our several institutions, that those who are educated will play certain roles in our society, and play them well, at once for their happiness and for the continuation and progress of our way of life.

Now as a Christian thinker I do not feel called upon to "challenge" American education. It is not my business either to approve of or to condemn our education. I merely wish to examine it as a Christian. I wish to raise certain questions, hoping that you, as educators, will think them over and keep them in mind.

I think it is a disservice to the young that the one aim of education should be to enable them to function effectively in the institutions which constitute our way of life. An institution, whether economic or political, whether military or ecclesiastical, exists for the satisfaction of public and common needs. It represent habits and mores which enable people to share in a certain way of life. It requires that men behave as good family men or business men, as good voting men or church men. An institution is concerned with the roles people play, and identifies them with these roles. So, a person may be a father, a dentist, a Democrat, Giant fan, Presbyterian. Beyond these he is, we say, an animal; he is an animal who has been taught to play certain institutional roles. What makes him a human being is the sum of the roles he plays. He is recognized and acknowledged as this man by the particular conjunction of functions he fulfills in the institutions which make up our Society. He is recognized as this teacher, this voter, this buyer, this veteran, this church man. And he goes by the name of Harry Jones. Thus it is that he is acknowledged as a person and a self, as a human being. His humanity consists in the contributions he makes to the common good and in his participation in it; so that when another man meets him, he sees the organism, the salesman, the voter, the soldier, and nothing else— nothing that falls outside of his biological and institutional characteristics.

Now I think people are angered and frustrated by such an understanding of them and by the behavior that goes with it. Even though we are content to be frequently treated as teachers, buyers, voters, and so on, we are disturbed—I think it is not too strong to say infuriated—if we are not acknowledged as human beings. Our humanity does not consist in the roles we play. We do play roles, and we cannot have a common human life without them; without our habits and our public morality. But it does not follow that our humanity consists in the parts we play in our institutions and our way of life. This is a simple logical point. A human being plays a social role; but his humanity does not consist in his playing a social role. When a husband or a wife is recognized as a husband or a wife, he or she is not therewith recognized as a human being. When a teacher is recognized as a teacher, he is not recognized therewith as a human being. When a benefactor is acknowledged as a benefactor, he is not therewith acknowledged as a human being. When he does good to another man, he does not therewith see this other man as a human being. In short, there is no institutionalized relationship among people which constitutes the bond of humanity, and no conjunction of functions in a way of life which constitutes a human being. Education in favor of our way of life and the institutions which support it is not in itself education for humanity; rather, it makes for the suspension of humanity and for its annihilation.

I should now say more about humanity. When I look at a man as I look at my dog, I do him an injustice. He is an animal who eats and drinks, walks and sees as an animal. But this kind of thing which I share with him, which is important for him and me alike, is not what makes him a man. If I treat him as I treat my dog, he does not like it. He resents it as a violation of him, and I acknowledge that he is right and I am guilty.

If I see this man as a teacher or salesman, if I act as if he were real only as a teacher or salesman, if I see in him nothing but a man who "knows his field" or is about to sell me a suit of clothes, we do not enter into a human relationship one with the other. Our meeting may require that he act only as a teacher or only as a salesman; we may not resent this limited character of our concern one with the other; we may deal with each other with courtesy and success. But neither of us is deceived. He recognizes and I recognize that even though we have played our two roles properly, and have spoken and acted effectively in the institutions which support our common life, we have not met satisfactorily as human beings. Even if we have conversed, as we might have, about the weather, or scholarship, or business, or politics, or religion, the bare fact, as it were, of such conversation has not made our meeting human. Such things are occasions for the exercise of humanity, but are not in themselves such an exercise.

The intercourse engaged in by bearers of social roles who are recognized as nothing but animals performing institutional functions is empty of that humanity which makes a man a man. We often do meet people and transact some business, and go away without having felt, thought, or acted as human beings; but such meeting is empty of the joy and fulfillment which an authentic encounter of man with man engenders. In short, a man is not a role or any complex of roles. Every man plays roles, but unless he is recognized and acknowledged as a man who is playing his roles, he is misunderstood and treated ill. I admit that we do not meet a man except in our playing of a role; but in my opinion unless we meet a man in a role, we do not meet a man. A man is not known in abstraction from his institutional functioning;but the institutional activities of a man abstracted from his humanity do not present us with a human being.

Who and what is, then, this man who is not satisfied when I look at him as a beast and a role? What does he want and expect me to see in him? How must I see him and act so that I may be truthful and faithful toward him? What is there in his mind and on his heart besides his biological and institutional being that leads him to stand there before me hoping that I will understand and feel with him? There is no question that he demands some gesture, some intimation, perhaps some word, from me which will express the truth about him, even though he himself may not know what it is that he must have if I am to recognize him as my fellow man.

What my neighbor expects and demands of me is that I acknowledge him as this living being who is anxious for his life, this individual of flesh and blood who lives toward death and knows himself as living toward death. He is an animal who knows he is an animal, whose knowledge of himself is also knowledge of his fate—his fate being that he shall sometime cease to be, to enjoy, and to act. He not only knows his fate but also feels it; it is integral to his sensibility, to his feeling for himself and his world, to his encounter with his fellow men, to his playing his several roles, and to the future conduct of his life. While he stands there before me as a colleague, or a member of the family, or a salesman—in whatever institutional relation he is to me—he is and he feels as this "soul," this living person whose prospective nonexistence is a present qualification of his being and behavior as a whole and in parts. In every meeting where he acts and is acted upon so that he is aware of himself as over against another, he is aware of himself as a human being, as this creature and contingent being who is not in truth the lord of his life and is in no position to dispose of himself as he will. Even while he speaks to me of some business on hand and pursues a purpose in our common world, he is looking for a neighbor, a fellow man, a human being who will give a sign of recognition and evoke in him the joy that goes with recognition. The meeting may of course be too fleeting and too perfunctory. One or both of those who meet may be too preoccupied with the immediate reason for meeting to meet as human beings. Nevertheless, without the hope of mutual recognition as flesh and blood, there is neither human living nor the fulfillment and joy that go with it.

When a human being is treated as though he were identified as a member of a species and a complex of roles, he is violated. But what else is he? He is a being related not only to his species but also to himself. In a strange way he interprets this living and dying self of his as unique and unrepeatable. Since he lives and dies, and knows that he lives and dies, he alone is he. He is he; he *is* as this living being; and all his thinking, willing, feeling, doing is that of this person and not that of another. As the thinker, he knows himself by the contrast between his thoughts and the thoughts of others. As a will, he knows himself in his responsibility to others. So also he knows himself in his feeling and doing in relation to others. But in all this. he knows himself as this anxious and guilty being who violates himself and others in his rejection of others and of himself as creatures; which is sin. This sin is against God; against a grace which is prior to himself and his neighbor—the grace whereby he exists and is this human being. His God is his Creator, the origin of his and his neighbor's being. who has created them in his freedom as God, having no reason for his creative act other than his own "good pleasure." It is the creature's knowledge of this God, of his grace and faithfulness in the existence of his creation, that constrains the creature to acknowledge the sin of rejection as sin against God and the sign of his own and his neighbor's humanity. In this respect, and concretely, the recognition of humanity is inseparable from the knowledge of God, who is violated through the creature's refusal to be creature and his refusal to acknowledge his neighbor as his fellow creature

But such knowledge and acknowledgment come to the Christian thinker in Jesus Christ in the company of his fellow Christians. Jesus Christ is the source of his self-knowledge as a human being. Love of Jesus which restored "sinners" to their dignity as people and opened them to their Creator, to themselves, and to their neighbors is the sign and the power of humanity. The teaching of Jesus is the very way of humanity: the statement of what it means to live as a human being. The death of Jesus, with its victory over his own anxiety and the temptation put before him to deny God and his neighbor, with its faithfulness to God, who had circumscribed his life by the death on the cross and uncovered the misery of man by the very inhumanity of the crucifixion—the death of Jesus is the Christian's promise and hope which not only vindicates humanity but also creates it through the working of God in the society of his fellow man. In short, for the Christian thinker, humanity is known and hoped for in Jesus of Nazareth, in that love which moves us to see our neighbor as God's "intelligent creation."

There are two aspects to our social life. The one is our common existence through participation in our several institutions. Here we form certain habits of thought and behavior, engage in certain deliberations and exercise certain skills which enable us to cooperate with others in the interests of our security and prosperity. Here intelligence finds ways and means of uniting self-love with altruism, and we each benefit from a common success. Even while we pursue our own good, we keep mindful of others who pursue their own. Insofar as we are prudent, we seek our own good in the context of a common good provided for in our institutions, and we find our pleasures in the company of others. But it is incongruous with the nature of institutional occupations that we should be concerned with the good of others as we are with our own, or that we should love others as we love ourselves.

Where there are conflicting interests, we do, despite certain demurrings of reason and conscience, prefer, by the nature of our institutional life, our good to that of others. And there are frequent if not constant complaints that we use, more or less considerately, our neighbors for our own increase. It thus becomes an axiom of prudence not to place ourselves under the power of others, and so far as possible to place them under ours. We think not only for solving common problems for a common good but also for achieving superior power among our neighbors. And the pursuit of power for restraining others generates an enmity whose natural tendency is to turn each man against his neighbor, and to leave each man alone with his anxiety for life, which eats away at his joy in being. My opinion is that intelligence, competence, skill, exercised in the context of our institutions which provide for the fulfillment of needs related to security and prosperity, by people whose reality consists in the roles they play in these institutions, tend to become instruments of power for the domination of man by man.

There is a permanent conflict between social life as formed and informed by our institutions, and social life as evoked by mutual recognition of men as human beings, as creatures in their circumscribed existence, who have their fruition, not in the goods made available by the pursuit of enlightened self-interest, but in that love which is an absolute good because it is the good of the very practice of humanity. This second aspect of our social life, which is realized in obedience to the commandment, "Thou shalt love thy neighbor as thyself," is utterly incommensurate with institutionalized habits, acquired competences and skills, and "the pursuit of happiness." When a man loves his neighbor as himself, he loves not a conjunction of roles in an animal, but a fellow man, for whom his love or recognition is life itself and joy. Here instead of habits, we have decisions, free acts of love; instead of competences and skills, we have sensibility and diffidence; instead of "the pursuit of happiness" and the operation of enlightened self-interest, we have the joy of two "intelligent creations" and the workings of the creature's compassion as a creature. Instead of intelligence engaged in seeking ends and devising means according to a tried and dependable method, we have intelligence attending to the signs of a fellow man's sensibility as a creature, and responding to them with that love which one "soul" owes to another that is bound with him in the bundle of life. Here the function of intelligence is not to number our power but, as the Psalmist says, "so to number our days, that we may apply our hearts to wisdom": to that wisdom which enables us to live in the joy of the living and the sobriety of the dying, one with another. The struggle and cooperation for existence, and human fulfillment in love—these two aspects of our lives are indispensable for happiness and peace among us. It is the radical failure of our age and culture, of our philosophy and education, that intelligence has been separated from that wisdom which is the creature's thinking and acting as creature with his neighbor.

It is evident that we can be taught, trained, and educated to play our several roles in our institutions with more or less success. We can be taught languages and mathematics, our several physical and social sciences, our ethics, our world views and our arts toward an effective pursuit of enlightened self-interest. This is the kind of success our education is for. But, it is not evident that we can be taught, trained and educated, as we are for our role-playing, for loving our neighbor as ourselves. When it comes to love, we are, as it were, up against it. Loving is not primarily a matter of finding ways and means, of competence in the pursuit of an acknowledged end. It raises, every time I meet my neighbor, the question of my own being rather than of my competence.

The problem is not how I shall love my neighbor but whether I am a neighbor or a man who will love my neighbor as myself. When I take my responsibility to love to heart, when I consider my failure in this respect, I understand that I myself am the problem, and that loving requires a change in *me*; rather, that I myself change; that I who live for security and prosperity in my physical and social environment, live above all as a human being, by the love of my neighbor and in loving him: which demands that I who am not a neighbor become a neighbor.

When I consider the openness, the trust and hope, the self-limitation and renunciation of mastery that love involves, I recognize that if I am to love or act as a human being with my neighbor, I must become a different sort of person, with a new mind and heart. My present mind and heart, trained and quickened in the institutions which support my way of life, are in no position to lead me, or even to permit me, to recognize my neighbor; to acquiesce in, much less rejoice in, my neighbor who is the bearer of the sign of my circumscribed and contingent existence as well as my indispensable partner in the pursuit of my self-interest. I see in my neighbor my own limitedness both in being and in destiny, because his presence quickens in me that anxiety for life which turns me against both being and destiny. I see in him my enemy as well as my neighbor, and I protect myself against him by keeping him at arm's length, by closing myself to him and shutting him off from myself. Thus I deny effectively that he is my neighbor. I deny that he is a human being, and is to be treated as one. Since he depends upon me, upon my love, for his life and living as a human being, I, by denying his existence as a living soul, consign him to perdition. My repudiation and my indifference are to him signs of his death. Without my love his life is meaningless, or empty, a kind of dreaming without substance and without joy—the joy of a human being by love. I am judged by him a liar and a murderer: a liar because I deny him by my unfaithfulness, and a murderer because I deny him the love which is his life. He pronounces me a sinner and guilty; and this sin and guilt I cannot deny, either as truth or as power. Willing or not, I live as a violator of humanity and under condemnation. This is the wrongdoing and misery which ooze out the poison in all our wrongdoings and miseries, and turn our common life into an occupation with mutual defacement. In it we know ourselves as people.

Such confounding of our common life is so devastating that neither I nor my neighbor will assume responsibility for it. We will deny our misery; and if we cannot do that, we each will accuse the other as the lying murderer. But since this is too painful, we will agree to live by our enlightened self-interest, and try to be as pleasant and comfortable as possible. We will be considerate and try to outdo one another in doing good. We will benefit one the other in our institutions and congratulate ourselves concerning our way of life. All the while we will keep a safe distance between us, and continue to diminish one another by withholding the love which is the neighbor's access to a meaningful and joyful existence. So, we neither forgive one another nor hope to be forgiven. The one condition of life, the acknowledgment one of the other, is left unfulfilled, and we live, rather die, without hope. Each man's possibility of life is in the neighbor's love; but for liars and murderers there is no love, either given or received, except in forgiveness; and forgiveness of liars and murderers is contrary to the nature of things. Therefore, we continue to justify ourselves by our "good works," and condemn ourselves to a life of hypocrisy and violation, whose end is a living death.

Education serves a double purpose. It informs and trains the young for effective participation in our way of life. This function of education is well known as well as indispensable. But this is not the issue here. I am concerned rather with education as it serves what I should call "justification by works." A member of society who contributes to the common well-being of his fellow men by playing properly his several roles in our institutions is justified by his works. He acquires a sense of dignity and claims certain rights in the community by virtue of doing his part for the life and prosperity of others. A teacher, a worker, a business man, an artist contribute in definite and palpable ways to the common life of their fellow citizens, and in so doing acquire merit, and rightly expect to be rewarded not only with a living but also with security, status, power, and recognition as each a substantial being. They establish their right to "life, liberty and the pursuit of happiness" by the exercise of their own powers and competences, and are deemed "righteous" as long as they continue their contributions to society. If they are considerate and kindly toward others, so much the better. The more they attend to other people's interests, the more they deserve from others in return. They may be trained to be in emotional harmony with others, and thus enjoy their good will as well as those advantages which society offers its benefactors. Thus even their love and justice serve their enlightened self-interests, and establish their rights in the community.

Education which trains the young for such a life of usefulness and self-respect works against the creature's self-knowledge as creature and against the love of the neighbor as oneself. The enlightened pursuit of self-interest in our society is not only incongruous with the awareness of flesh and blood or the living soul; it is also a confusing and confounding substitute for humanity. The man who lives by his competences and the rights which his competences give him in his intercourse with others is in no mood to live by the forgiveness and love of his neighbor. He is irresistibly tempted to live and increase not as a creature bound to his neighbor, but as a god-man who binds others to himself through his own power over their destinies. The anxiety of a man for his life and his recognition of his neighbor as a concrete and effective symbol of his own contingent and circumscribed existence are sufficient inducements to substitute mastery for love as the condition of a happy life. Therefore, education which trains the young for competent participation in a common pursuit of security and prosperity in our institutions tends indirectly but powerfully toward the alienation of man from himself and his neighbor. This is why inhumanity among highly educated people is neither infrequent nor surprising. We give our young "the best education available," and they grow up to live lives without meaning and without joy.

Anyone who takes the problem of love as seen in this discussion seriously, can hardly help wondering if love is a matter of training and growth. Neither plants which grow nor animals we train give us an adequate analogy for the process through which we come to love our neighbor as ourselves, or to offer the respect we owe to God's "intelligent creation." It is one thing to be trained, another to grow. It is one thing to grow, another to be changed so that this lovelessness may put on love. This is why, according to Jeremiah, the Lord says, "I will put my law in their inward parts, and in their heart will I write it . . ." (31:33); and according to Ezekiel He says, "A new heart also will I give you, and a new spirit will I put within you; and I will take away the stony heart out of your flesh, and I will give you a heart of flesh."(36:26) For this same reason, the man able to love is spoken of in the New Testament as a new creation, a new man. It is recognized in the Bible that loving is a matter of conversion, or to put it in stronger terms, of being born again, and that the Author of this conversion and new birth is God. The man who learns what love is from Jesus Christ, and by a strange grace acknowledges his responsibility to love as crucial for his humanity—such a man knows that the love which is his despair as well as his hope is in truth a gift and remains a gift, a gift through his neighbor, from God.

Let a man set out to act in the integrity of a human being, to love his neighbor and enemy, and to hope for the love of the same neighbor and enemy, and he will confess, in spite of the profound disinclination of his mind and heart, that when it comes to the humanity which works by love, God alone is the Teacher; and that the Teacher is the Creator and Savior. In education for humanity there can be no question of training and growth without the replacement of the "old" man by the "new" man; and man is a creation, a work of God. Loving and being loved, the very existence of human beings, is a miracle. One who loves his neighbor as himself, one who is so loved, knows that "with man it is impossible; and he calls Him by whom it is possible "the living God."

One might say, "Well then, if it is God alone who enables a man to love his neighbor, let Him do it. This is no business for teachers, and has nothing to do with what we call education." It can be argued that if neither the creation of man nor his restoration to humanity is within human competence, we might as well disavow all responsibility in the matter and bend our efforts toward the training of the youth for usefulness in our public life. The difficulty is that when we thus set aside the problem of humanity we do more than neglect it. Education which ignores this matter of life and death for human beings, in effect works against it. When we train our young to identify themselves with the roles they are to play in our way of life, and to identify others in the same way, we provide them with a selfhood which is a substitute for a human being; thus we train them for non-humanity, which turns in practice into inhumanity and its consequences in cruelty and misery.

The educator cannot remain neutral in this matter. He who is not for man is against man. Indifference to humanity is the violation of it. When the goal of education is not love, then the end of it is enmity and death. Even though the educators cannot create love any more than they can create man, it is irresponsible and pernicious that they should set it aside as irrelevant to their task. The recognition of love as the proper exercise of humanity cannot but act as a factor in a proper fulfillment of their function as educators. When the young are educated grade after grade, class after class, by people who acknowledge the hope and promise of love in human life, this very acknowledgment cannot but give a new meaning to their work. To realize that neither language nor mathematics, neither science nor art, neither history nor sociology, as taught by us and learned by the pupils, can produce human beings or make human life meaningful without the reunion of man with man in love—to realize this and to teach with it in mind is indispensable in any education which does not end in the misuse of competence for the frustration of humanity.

I believe that an elusive but potent element of personal influence comes into play in this connection. Teachers of mathematics and language who know the problem of love envisaged in this discussion will, while they teach their subjects, while they mind their own business, act as midwives in the birth of the new man. As human beings who live in the hope of love, in the hope of forgiveness given and received, under the promise and faithfulness of God in the love of Jesus Christ, they will teach what they are competent to teach, hoping in God, who is competent to convert them and their pupils to a living humanity.

It is the peculiarity of God's way with us that He does not emerge among us as a gigantic and supernatural power, making a spectacle of Himself before our startled eyes, while we ourselves lean against a wall doing nothing. It has always been His way, since Abraham, to elect servants and to call them to fulfill His purpose of rehumanization among His people. God exercises a peculiar omnipotence which operates by the authentically human response of His people, so that while they act as creatures, He acts as Creator; while they follow their vocations, one man teaching, another farming or building, in the hope of faithfulness and love, God Himself, being faithful to His creation, converts sinners and fills our lives with the joy of humanity restored. Jesus Christ came eating and drinking like a man; he lived and spoke and died like a man. And God declared him His Son, and by him brought life and joy into the world; so that we call him our Savior as we do our God. It is offhand surprising that this Jesus should have been the wisdom and the power of God. But that he *was*, because we know both the wisdom and the power of God by what God did through the humanity of this man Jesus. So, also, it is offhand incredible that the creating

and saving work of God should be done by us who groan with the hope
of our own creation, our own loving and being loved. It is a strange
thing that while we, who hope in God, mind our business teaching this
or that, training minds and hands, helping the young to grow, God Himself should convert teacher and pupil, pupil and pupil to that openness
to Him, ourselves, and others which is the proper exercise of our humanity in love. But among us, this is how God acts and reveals Himself
in His proper divinity as God. When teacher and pupil, in their dignity
and equality as human beings, confront one another hoping for forgiveness given and received, for love offered and expected, under the promise of God in their history, even while they occupy themselves with the
academic business on hand, there occurs an education which is a new
birth of humanity and the making of a joyful existence in man's coming
to his own. Thus it is that in our schools, our young will become at
once good citizens and truly human beings.

Good citizenship in our country requires the practice of democracy. Democracy has its economic, political, and social aspects. It
means common opportunity, government by the people's consent and
participation, mutual respect among people of different states and conditions. It involves an awareness of humanity common to people of different race, color, religion, and class. Even while democracy has its institutional aspects in terms of public behavior, its vitality comes from
the repeated decisions of the people to recognize one another as human
beings, and to act accordingly. Democracy remains authentic and alive
insofar as the people are able to overcome their anxiety for life; insofar
as there is an antidote to their enmity and a way of reconciliation
among them. Democracy without forgiveness and love given and received among creatures lacks its own very substance, and becomes first
denatured and then moribund. The struggle for democracy must go on
not only on the political level but also in the minds and spirits of the
people. The people must acknowledge their responsibility to love their
neighbors as themselves. They must acknowledge their failure in this
respect, and live in hope. They must see the social life as an opportunity and a promise toward that justice which human beings owe one to
another. The people's integrity and seriousness in this matter is the very
life blood of democracy.

Education can and clearly does train people to participate in
democratic institutions. Our children are brought up to believe in opportunity for all in a representative government. They are taught fair

play, cooperation, reasonableness, altruism, and the like, which are democratic mores. But education cannot convert them to humanity. To look for methods and techniques of training which shall turn roles into persons, professionals into people, is absurd. Educators, human beings who are educators, alone can be and act as the "means of grace" for the making of forgiveness and love among us. Love is evoked only by love, freedom by freedom, and humanity by humanity. And since no man, educator or otherwise, can claim to be in possession of love, or freedom, or humanity, confession of incompetence in this matter, and the sensibility and humility that go with such confession, are indispensable in a good educator. The teacher and the pupil need to look to God for the grace which shall reconcile them one with the other, and in this common looking they are educated for humanity, and for democracy, by God, who alone is the Teacher in this respect.

Therefore, I am not sure that I wish at this time to "challenge American education." In fact, I do not wish to challenge. I only wish to remind you of the need in our time for a recovery of humanity. I wish to suggest that education for maintaining our way of life and the institutions which support it is not *as such* conducive to such a recovery, and does, as I argued, confuse the issue. Unless our educators recognize the distinction between human beings associated as "intelligent creation" and organisms playing several institutional roles, and permit this distinction to be effective in the school, the supreme need of our generation for the love of man for man will be unfulfilled, and we shall remain at the brink of disaster. Our situation is perilous; not only our way of life but our very existence as mankind is at stake. Therefore, I invite you to examine the argument I have presented. If it is not valid, you may forget it. If it is valid, I hope you will act on it.

I think I should make it clear before I finish that it is the business of education in our society to produce citizens who will operate effectively in our several institutions. It is obvious to me, as it is to many of you, that our institutions and organizations are indispensable for a common, American way of life. I love and respect this way of life, with all its defects, and consider it my duty as a teacher to contribute to its maintenance and improvement. But I am also aware that unless as an educator I am concerned with the problem and hope of loving my neighbor as myself and my pupils' recognition of their neighbors as human beings or "God's intelligent creation," I do a dreadful disservice to our way of life; because without love, enlightened self-interest operates in fact as a violation of man by man. Participation in public life through institutions is civilized living itself. But such participation without the love of creature by creature is inimical to human culture, and a way of death for human beings. Therefore, even while we educate our young to contribute to our way of life, we must do our work, as educators, with the hope that in our give and take with the students, God Himself will teach them to live as human beings one with another.

One final word. The synagogues and churches of our land are supposed to be sources of the kind of awareness which underlies my thesis. If they are weak, let us make them strong. Whether they be weak or strong, I think we should do our share in making them authentic associations of human beings, so that in our vocation as teachers we may behave as people.

DATE DUE

AP 15 '94			